SALT ON YOUR TONGUE

Charlotte Runcie is the *Daily Telegraph*'s radio columnist and arts writer. For several years she lived and worked in Edinburgh, where she ran a folk music choir, and she now lives in the Scottish Borders. She has a secret past as a poet, having been a Foyle Young Poet of the Year with a pamphlet published by tall-lighthouse. *Salt On Your Tongue* is her first book.

@charlotteruncie | charlotteruncie.com

'Just like [Runcie's] favourite kind of blustery beach,
it's strewn with pocketable treasures'
Observer

'A very beautiful book about myth and motherhood . . .
Salt On Your Tongue has a rare magic to it'
Sophie Mackintosh, author of *The Water Cure*

'Runcie has combined an exploration of Scotland's seascape
with the story of her pregnancy and the birth of her daughter . . .
Breathless, intimate . . . Very much in the vein of bestsellers *The Outrun*
by Amy Liptrot and *H is for Hawk* by Helen Macdonald'
Mail on Sunday

'Runcie has a beachcomber's mind and a poet's turn of phrase'
Daily Telegraph

'A wise and wonderful book, charting intensely personal moments
against the constant yet ever-changing sea. A story of birth, loss,
memory and motherhood, spliced with vivid observations of the
natural world and collected myth, lore and legend, Charlotte Runcie's
voice is by turns practical and poetic, objective and beguiling.
An utterly immersive read'
Jess Kidd, author of *Himself*

SALT ON YOUR TONGUE

Women and the Sea

Charlotte Runcie

CANONGATE

This paperback edition published in 2020 by Canongate Books

First published in Great Britain, the USA and Canada in 2019
by Canongate Books Ltd, 14 High Street, Edinburgh EH1 1TE

Distributed in the USA by Publishers Group West
and in Canada by Publishers Group Canada

canongate.co.uk

2

British Library Cataloguing-in-Publication Data
A catalogue record for this book is available on
request from the British Library

ISBN 978 1 78689 121 1

Typeset in Bembo by Biblichor Ltd, Edinburgh

Printed and bound in Great Britain by Clays Ltd, Elcograf S.p.A.

For B.

Thy way is in the sea, and thy path in the great waters, and thy footsteps are not known.

– Psalm 77:19

CONTENTS

III KELAINO

IV MAIA

V MEROPE

VI ELEKTRE

VII ASTEROPE

ATLAS AND PLEIONE

I

ALKYONE

Alkyone throws herself into the sea and drowns. She is the daughter of Aeolus, god of the winds. Alkyone and her husband, Ceyx, have angered the gods with their love, and so Zeus casts a great storm to drown Ceyx. After a distraught Alkyone has killed herself, Zeus regrets what he's done, so he transforms Alkyone and Ceyx into kingfishers. For two weeks every January, Aeolus calms the winds and seas so that Alkyone can make her nest on the smooth water. These are called halcyon days.

THE NORTHERN STAR

T<small>HE SEA BEGINS WITH THE</small> stars. I put my bare feet in a
rockpool near Elgol beach on the Isle of Skye to look more
closely at a starfish. The jagged black triangles of the Cuillin
mountains rise in the distance, together with a horseshoe of
islands making a natural amphitheatre of the stormy bay. We are on
holiday here, the furthest north I've ever been, after visiting my
mother's family in Fife. The sea is exotic to me, a girl usually to be
found growing up in the hills of landlocked Hertfordshire, far from
the shore. It's new.

The water is cold and my toes white. The ground is broken
shells, drawing beads of blood from the soles of my feet. My
parents are a little way away. All around limpets are stuck fast to
the rocks and birds are circling. The breeze is hard, the clouds low.
The sea around stretches into infinite mist. I feel completely alone.

While I've been looking to see where my parents have gone,
the starfish has inched its way into a clump of shadows and out of
sight. I remember reading in my Collins book of the seashore that
starfish can have babies in different ways: either by mating with

other starfish, or by having one of their arms removed. A disembodied starfish arm can sprout its own new arms, and then grow into a whole new star. The original starfish will then grow its lost arm back, too, so there would be two new and whole creatures grown from something mutilated and broken. Does this starfish have any babies – other versions of itself crawling across another rockpool floor?

Nearby there is a piece of driftwood shining under the surface, dark and slick with seawater, alive-seeming, like a little beached monster. When it's time for us to go, I drag the chunk of wood back to the cottage with me. (The water that comes from the taps in the cottage is brown with peat. Why can't we bathe and cook in the sparkling clear salt water from the bay below? I am a sulky child, and refuse to help with the washing up.)

On the way back up the steep road to the house, the blackened water from the piece of wood soaks into my clothes, into my favourite T-shirt, the one that I'd wear every day if I could, green and black striped like how I imagine a pirate's shirt to be, and full of holes from too much wear and clambering. I am a tall and loud child with a temper. I bite my nails and never brush my hair. I devour books, especially books about horses and seaside boarding schools, though I have experience of neither. I never feel, really, like a little girl, or know what that is meant to feel like.

My grandmother has tried to remedy the situation by giving me a series of flouncy ruffled dresses and telling me to brush my hair – which is naturally curly and full of tangles – with one hundred strokes of the brush every night to make it soft. This practice hurts so much it makes my eyes water, and tests my patience to its limit, so I avoid it. It didn't seem to improve my hair much when I did it, anyway, only succeeding in turning it into a static-buoyed bundle of reddish-brown hay. The dresses are itchy and too tight and so I take any opportunity to opt out. Always I want to get my feet good and cold and salty in the sea as much as possible.

On the windowsill in my grandmother's bathroom, with its avocado suite and cupboard full of painkillers and cancer medication for my grandfather, there has been, for as long as I can remember, a display of shells. These are shells my grandmother has collected from cruise holidays and trips around the world, some of them picked up from beaches, but most of them from gift shops, large and exotic and shining. There is an enormous conch that I have picked up and held to my ear in the bath so many times that it has a thin slick layer of old soap over the delicate curve of its pink opening, near to where the white ridges of the furled operculum twist round and up to the back of the shell. A particularly big scallop shell is perched on the edge of the bath, and used to keep soap in.

That afternoon I make a project of the dried-out driftwood. Somehow it has lost its slick magic back in the safety of the cottage, cracking and fading in the warmth. Using my art set and a thick brush, I paint it all over with the brightest red poster paint I have. I think I am trying to recapture its wet wildness, and the beguiling horror of when I first found it in the rockpool, shimmering and fat and soaked with brine. But no paint can make it again as bright and fierce as it was when I found it, when it glowed like moonlight among the starfish, as bright and fierce as I felt with my feet in the sea.

For years after that holiday, I collect glittering shells and sea glass from trips to beaches and take them home. I watch the magic fade from them as the water evaporates and their shining surfaces dry to nothing, and wonder what it would take to be able to keep a real piece of the sea with me, to keep its mystery alive.

•

Whenever it's late autumn and I'm by the sea, and the night is cold and the stars are stretching up into the dark, I go to stand on the edge of the shore, with the darkness so deep, and the sea so loud, that I can imagine I'm standing on the prow of a ship. If I'm far enough away from a city, the sky will be overwhelmed by stars, so many that the darkness seems to dip from their weight. Galaxies, planets and nebulae reveal themselves.

People have always projected poetry on to the light-shot night. Alnilam, we call the belt of the constellation of Orion. The string of pearls. Capella, little she-goat. Piscis Austrini, the mouth of the southern fish. Carinae, the prow of a ship. Eridani, the end of the river.

Sailors have used the positions of the stars to navigate for as long as there have been boats. The best way to determine where in the world you are, and how to get to the place you want to be, is by feeling everything around you. The wind, the seasons, the stars.

The Pleiades are the sailing stars. The word Pleiades, the name for the Seven Sisters constellation that, once you have identified it, will point you towards the Northern Star, and so to north, and so to your destination, comes from the Ancient Greek *plein*, meaning 'to sail'. Their heliacal rising begins in autumn in the Northern Hemisphere and, for the Greeks, it marked the start of the

Mediterranean navigational season. It is the star cluster that's easiest to see with the naked eye.

Journeys that follow the stars across the sea have inspired stories, songs, poems, paintings, myths, schools of religious thought and scientific breakthroughs. They've led to destruction and ruin. Say the stars of the Pleiades aloud and they sound like a spell: Alkyone, Elektre, Maia, Merope. Taygete, Kelaino, Asterope. And then there are their parents, the two extra stars that make up the visible cluster of nine: Atlas, Pleione.

The names of the Pleiades predate the Greek myths about the sisters that went by their names, their relationships, children and supernatural adventures. The stories the Greeks told about these sisters were first inspired by people seeing them in the night sky, and hearing the names given to them by men who navigated the seas, as the water moves all around, and the moon pulls the tides across the earth.

I'm not a maritime historian, and this isn't a history of tall ships. It's a story of women and water and love, with a birth and a death, songs and tall tales, and the wind blowing high on the waves.

OUTWARD BOUND

Y OU SMELL IT BEFORE YOU see it. That's mostly how you
know you're near the sea in Scotland. The first of January,
and we walk on the beach at Portobello, Sean and the dog and
I. It's so cold that ice fringes the waves as they lessen on the
sand, and there is a crunch to the air. The seaside promenade is
full of people, mostly down from central Edinburgh for the day,
breathing in the freshness of a whole new year. The dog crashes
in and out of the water, too scared to go in deep enough to
swim, and instead leaping and sneezing in the shallows as the
water nips her heels, chasing balls and losing them as they slip
beneath the foam and their scent dips out of reach of her nose.
It's early afternoon and already the sun is sinking down and
turning the light an eerie orange, bouncing off a clump of dark
purple snow clouds.

We tramp along the sand, watching hardy children building
freezing sandcastles, and still-tipsy students stripping down to their
underwear to risk the chill of a New Year's paddle. The dog shoots
into the distance and bounds happily back, her fat tongue lolling

out of the side of her mouth and a coating of sand all down her chest and paws. I absent-mindedly look for what I can forage on the beach floor. Bits of bladderwrack are disembodied fingers covered in blisters. There are some that look like tangles of hair, except for the barnacles knotting them together. And shells: the night-blue crescents of mussels with a gradient that fades to pure white, and perfect round cockles with their closely furled ridges on the outside, like little crimped pastries. Once, after a storm, thousands of starfish washed up on this beach and drowned in the open air. The mouth of the River Forth is parting its lips. The sea is somewhere further, somewhere beyond.

Everything I am reading, favourite stories from childhood revisited and new books discovered, is about water. I carry a copy of the *Odyssey* around in my bag like a talisman, and on steamy-windowed morning bus journeys to work on magazine shifts I open it up and am again pulled deep into all its sea-like currents of story and digression, moving always like waves against the hull of a ship. I discover Stevenson's *Kidnapped*, with its ill-fated sea voyage that becomes an overland adventure, and vast anthologies of sea shanties collected by a mysterious old sailor and storyteller called Stan Hugill, and I read Boswell's *Journal of a Tour to the Hebrides with Samuel Johnson*. I come across a quotation from Johnson in Boswell's biography that stays with me: 'Every man thinks meanly of himself for not having been a soldier, or not having been to sea.'

I have not been to sea. I am in my mid-twenties now, a time that should be spent finding out who you are, travelling, and going on adventures. One friend has moved to Australia; another to Canada. Facebook shows me university acquaintances who are now running marathons and securing dream jobs. I am doing none of these things. I don't have any fully-formed dreams to work towards. In late-night panics I research possible careers that would require a completely different set of skills. Would law, or medicine, or teaching be able to take me somewhere worthwhile? Initially excited by the idea of becoming someone new, each time I pull away. So I just read, and write, and work, and these don't feel like the sort of things you do when you're preparing to embark on something.

It seems as though it should be possible to live forever in a state of extended childhood, playing at life until adulthood gradually forms without me noticing. At what point does childhood end, or could it go on forever?

In the *Odyssey*, Athena sends Odysseus's son Telemachus on a sea voyage to Menelaus to find out what has happened to his father, a trip that she later explains is a gift. It will be an adventure that will define him and bring him into adulthood. Odysseus himself spends twenty years away, at war and then at sea. In *Kidnapped*, David Balfour's sea voyage and subsequent trek across the Highlands are what turn him from boy to man.

Is Johnson right? Is going to sea the ultimate challenge, the big and dangerous test, the coming-of-age experience that all men must face, or forever regret not facing? Going to sea is like going to war: something temporary, something overpoweringly physical, and a test that, if you survive it, changes you forever.

It's an experience that you know is going to be terrible, but you are shocked by it nonetheless when it actually happens. And then, afterwards, you look other people in the eye who have been through it too and, though they might be a complete stranger to you, already you share something with them. You look at them deeply and you know them. They know what you know, and can never explain. The pain and helplessness of it. The giving over of yourself to something greater. The danger. The beauty, and the poetry.

It sounds so thrilling and essential, this sea. Does art need to go to sea, too? If you don't go to sea or to war, the writers of the past seem to be saying, what kind of man are you anyway?

Or what kind of woman? What about Penelope, left behind in Ithaca with a newborn child, to spend twenty years fending off angry men who want to marry her and steal her lost husband's treasure? Penelope is trapped on shore, weaving at her loom and weeping, and wondering what adventures or dangers her husband is facing at sea.

The sea surges over my brain through the winter. I've come back to live in Scotland, to be in Edinburgh near to my family, to be close to the sea after working in the heat and noise of a busy London newsroom and a long commute. I need more sea, I'd said to people, and wider sky. I'm looking for something new, and I am looking for home, and I have no idea what I'm looking for at all.

I step down from the promenade at Portobello, with its iron railings painted the happy light green colour of pistachio ice cream, down to the level of the sea, to look it dead in the eye. Today the sea is a mirror. It stretches smoothly away. In the distance, I think I can glimpse seals, distant grey pebble-ish curves bobbing up out of the water to feel their backs against the sky. Looking out at the point where the river becomes the sea lets the mind flatten, and you can lay yourself out in its vastness, feeling as if you might, just for a moment, really be at the start of something. And you can pick up a cockle shell, and put it in your pocket.

•

As well as reading about the sea with a new appetite, I've been writing about it too, making diaries of tide times and shells I've found, and the names of boats spotted in harbours. And always I come back to thinking about my grandmother. She loved being on the sea, on boats and on cruises, though she never romanticised it. Once she had been away with my grandfather on a cruise in the Caribbean, and sent me a postcard. Their postcards usually followed a formula: on the printed side of the card, there would be a collage of images of shimmering tropical beaches, jewel blues and clean white hotel resorts – impossibly glamorous all – and on the other, two sets of scrawling handwriting, both different, both strangely like my own. Grandpa would write the top half of the card, and then leave the bottom for Granny to fill in with her own message. This particular postcard said:

Thinking of you as we sail across the most beautiful blue ocean, under clear and sunny skies. Lots of love from Grandpa.

I banged my eye on the luggage rack and have a bruise. Granny.

I don't think it was meant to be funny. That was actually her most important news from the trip. I wondered what she had seen when she'd looked out to sea with her bruised eye, Cyclopsified.

•

We haven't yet seen snow this winter, twenty years on from the rockpool in Elgol. Edinburgh has been sleeping through the season in a dim and grim torpor, without any sparkling snowflakes to cheer away the cold. So when another cold January day finds me bundled under the duvet in hibernation, with the dark days clouded around me and dampening all my senses, I need the freshness of the sea proper. I want to run away to it, to defy the cold and blankness of a month-long hangover from Christmas feasting. That feeling of wanting to run away is familiar. It means there's something to run from, even if I don't immediately know what it is. My thoughts have begun to nestle uncomfortably on top of an idea, a possibility at the back of my mind, always aware of its presence as they try to ignore it. I am like the princess detecting a pea under all her mattresses, and I can't sleep. Something is about to change.

I want to see sea, and Sean wants to see snow. Both of us are craving real, sharp coldness, and the tingle it brings to the senses. And an open expanse wider than the Forth, something that goes infinitely onwards around islands and away into nothing. On a whim one Saturday we get in the car, pack the dog and drive west, following a Google Maps-defined route towards Oban, a town

I've wanted to see for a long time. Some friends have been to visit, and told me it's beautiful. From the harbour, they said, you can stare across the 500-yard stretch of sea towards Kerrera, home to the tiny medieval Gylen Castle, sketched several times by Turner on his Scottish travels.

It's a popular tourist destination in the high season of summer but is unlikely to have much going on in the bleak midwinter. The three-hour drive takes us through the snowy Trossachs to skirt the long edge of Loch Lomond, with the white peaks of Ben Lomond and Ben Vorlich visible from the car window. We leave in the early morning and stop the car as soon as we get far enough north to hit snow, letting the dog out for a gleeful bound in the drifts that come up to her chin. Loch Lomond is still and slumbering on my shoulder during this, the scenic part of the drive.

•

When we reach Oban, it's more of an industrial townscape than the pretty harbour that I had imagined, with large-hulled boats moored in the ferry terminal and vans navigating a busy central roundabout, and the whole town clustered around the blackish shingle of a dark beach lightly strewn with plastic bottles and cans. The dog poses on the jetty and sticks her nose into the wind. The town is mostly shut up for the winter, and the most warm and welcoming places seem to be the outdoor equipment shops. At lunchtime we stop in at a pub that allows dogs and serves fish and chips, and together we shelter from the cold. Afterwards, we wander the streets and into one of the outdoorsy shops. I buy a pair of very thick woollen socks in their January sale as a memento of the trip. We spend some more time on the dark beach, looking over at Kerrera as a weak sun makes a brief appearance. The land you can see from the beach looks as reachable and tangible as all the islands Odysseus washes up on, hopping from one glorious disaster to the next.

Around twilight, we head home, a little underwhelmed. On the way back through the Trossachs, the mountains are looming in cut-out paper shapes. Though I know Loch Lomond is beside us, keeping us company on the way home, I feel its presence more than I see it, a blank expanse on the left-hand side of the car. The route is completely exposed to the sky, with the mountains in the distance, the loch beside, and the sea behind. The journey hasn't been the epic, distracting adventure I'd half-hoped it would be, though I know that would have been impossible – I'd romanticised it too much in advance – and anyway I am grateful for the socks and hot lunch. When we reach Edinburgh again there is a full moon and the snow has beaten us there, palm-sized flakes settling on the car roof as we park outside our tenement. It's already beginning to freeze the windscreen over as we walk away.

It isn't until a week later that I take the test. When I turn over the plastic stick on the bathroom windowsill, the word engraved on the little digital screen flows through me like electric current and I recognise the shiver across my shoulders as fear. A different kind of voyage to navigate, after all. A jolting shift into adulthood. A new kind of creature to understand.

Odysseus was blown off course on his way home from Troy. He wanted to get home.

I wanted to have an adventure. But I'm going to have a baby.

LIBATIONS

MY GRANDMOTHER LIKED A DRINK. Once, eating lunch out in a restaurant with us on holiday, she ordered a bottle of wine with her meal. It was soon finished. 'Gracious,' said a woman at the next table, wide-eyed and disapproving. 'I've never seen anyone drink a bottle of wine as fast as that.'

'Well, you can see it again,' said my grandmother. And she ordered another.

I didn't grow up in Scotland but in Hertfordshire, with a Scottish mother and an English father, and all the arty jobs I aimed for after university seemed to be in London. So, London was where I headed straight after graduating. And yet, in London in the dawn years of my twenties, just as I had done as a child, I read books about the sea and waited all year for a holiday by a crunchy beach, when I could spend all day collecting seashells and painting pictures and washing my paintbrush in the shallows. And best of all in those childhood seaside summers, on days that weren't Arctic-cold, there had been swimming, dipping my shoulders at the point where the sharp shingle underfoot dropped away, and letting go, letting the waves move my body. And then sinking my head into the ice of it, opening my eyes underwater to the salt sting and the murk and looking out for the silvered flash of fishes, and all the while fighting the nervous thrill of getting swept out too far.

I had always thought I was drawn to the sea because I was British, and being British comes with a catalogue of sea-themed clichés: fish and chips on the beach, or in the car while the rain pelts down; 'Rule Britannia' at the BBC Proms; the shipping forecast playing out over and over every night, a warning for sailors, a lullaby for those of us safe in our beds and never at sea.

If I had grown up in a landlocked country, I wondered, would I still feel this saline connection, or would I feel drawn instead to a romance of the prairie or the mountain? Maybe it would only be a different way of feeling the same desire. Longing for the sea is the longing for adventure and the longing for home, all at once. The sea is delicate and powerful, shaping the planet, forming the weather, the place we evolve from, providing everything the planet needs for life. Even if we live hundreds of miles from saltwater, it's inside us. That's what I've always felt. A sense that, no matter how far I get from the sea, it will still be calling me back. I just didn't know why, or what I'd find if I went to sea, or if I should even go at all.

I kept reading and writing about the sea in the hope that I would understand why I felt so unable to escape from it. If I had nothing to do with the sea, why did it always seem to want to have something to do with me?

All through the *Iliad* and the *Odyssey*, Homer refers to the Aegean as οἶνοψ πόντος, most often translated as 'the wine-dark sea'. *Oinops* is a combination of the word *oin*, for wine, and *ops*, for eye or face. Translated closely it means something more like wine-eyed, wine-faced, or wine-looking.

It's an epithet used again and again in the *Odyssey*, balanced by the similarly frequent rosy-fingered dawn which rises on new adventures each morning. Homer's epithets are a persistent drum beat to the stories. They become anchor-point moments where the journey comes back to its structure and home, before launching again into the unfolding unknown.

Scholars can't agree on the most likely meaning of οἶνοψ, or *oinops*. Sea doesn't really ever look like wine. It isn't red, for one thing, though the former prime minister and critic William Gladstone did bravely argue that Greeks were somehow less highly evolved than modern humans, and could perceive fewer colours. That seems both very unlikely and too easy. Scientists have tried to find natural weather phenomena that could have turned the sea a wine-like red in Ancient Greece: maybe a particularly vibrant type of sunset, or vivid crimson algae blooms underwater, or high levels of dust in the atmosphere changing the quality of the light.

That all sounds too literal, though. There are things, other than colour, that sea and wine share. The sea isn't red, but then it isn't blue, either. It's green, and brown, and grey, and pink, and black and white. Sea is nothing like wine, and it's everything like wine. There's the quality of depth, the combination of opaqueness and clarity that means you can see through it for just a moment at the surface, before it quickly deepens into unknowable darkness. Wine has that same glassy translucence and sparkled surface just at sipping depth, giving way to an opaque underlying richness of hues and shades deeper down. The colour of the liquid moves with the light, changing its character depending on whether the sun is shining overhead or a candle is burning nearby.

And then there's the way that it pulls on your senses. People were shocked by the sight of my grandmother drinking wine. Wine is beautiful, and powerful, and has driven people to ruin. It's seduction and romance, addiction and destruction, disintegrating the brain and body. It's the sea. To the Greeks, wine was used in religious ritual in libations poured on to the earth, in mourning and at the beginning of new things. The sea is ritual, too. And it gets you drunk.

MOUTH

I LOVED EDINBURGH AGAIN AS SOON as I saw it with fresh adult eyes. It was the place my sister and parents had lived before, though I'd only visited for holidays, and heard about it wistfully in stories, until my parents finally decided to move back when I turned eighteen. Then, when I carelessly betrayed it by studying in England, it became my refuge during university holidays.

In Edinburgh I fell in love with the heat that builds encouragingly in your calves when you find yourself walking breathlessly up the hills and over the bridges in the Old Town, late to meet a friend. My lungs love the sensation of Edinburgh's atmosphere, the biting freshness of it, never still but always thrilled with a shock of salted air, and sometimes the yeasty smell from the brewery on thick evenings. And the way the city is always almost entirely at the mercy of the spooky mystique of the haar, the rolling sea fog that comes on quick with its smoky white haze on a chilly evening and blinds you, if you don't see it coming first, as it rounds the corner and somersaults its way towards you through the Cowgate.

On a clear day, I love that you can see right the way over the bright blue water towards the green and mauve hills of Fife. You can see the islands nestling there. Inchcolm, with its twelfth-century monastery. Inchkeith, where in 1493, King James IV is said to have performed a strange and entirely unethical language experiment, leaving two babies on the island to be looked after by a deaf and mute nurse in order to determine which language they eventually learned to speak, and which he could therefore conclude was the natural language of mankind as given by God. According to sixteenth-century historian Robert Lindsay of Pitscottie's *The Historie and Cronicles of Scotland*, 'Some say they could speak Hebrew, but for my part I know not.' Walter Scott was unconvinced (in *The History of Scotland*): 'It is more likely they would scream like their dumb nurse, or bleat like the goats and sheep on the island.' Maybe, of course, it never happened at all, and is just a legend attributed to a king who was known to be a polyglot, an eager amateur scientist, and an oddball.

Then Fidra, another nature reserve with its own automated lighthouse, and the Isle of May, a boat trip away from Anstruther in the East Neuk on a boat called the *May Princess*, and St Baldred's Boat, the rock formation off Seacliff Beach in East Lothian, where the medieval monk and hermit St Baldred is said to have retreated for contemplation. Go up high enough and look past the islands and over to the right of the three broad, spiked bridges that bind Fife to the Lothians, the Forth Rail Bridge, the old Forth Road Bridge and the new Queensferry Crossing, one red, one silver, one white, with the water stretching across towards the little white dots of the coastal towns, winking in the sun as they bend right around towards the East Neuk. The three bridges, each constructed in a different century, binding the land and the sea. The estuary is the only place we can do that, with the sea at its narrowest point that we can still just about build across, the last point at which it's not yet so inscrutably large.

•

There is no easily exact difference between the river and the sea; no invisible line where the freshwater ends and saltwater begins. The sea is a gradual process of becoming, of widening and ageing and growing into more. There's a human scale to an estuary. Settlements cluster around them, growing into industrial heartlands over the centuries because they're so useful for transport and trade and connection to the world. Even before industry, though, people were drawn to them to build their homes. They are poised on the edge, but still connected to home, to land, and to life-giving fresh drinking water as it turns to the salt of the sea.

In salmon you see the difference that a saltwater environment makes to living creatures. Salmon are small mud-brown creatures when young and just-hatched in the freshwater. By the time they have made the journey from the river into the sea as adults they are transformed: big, shimmering rainbow-streaked blue dashes of light, ready to return home to their origins upstream to lay their eggs and begin the process of life over again. The river is where they begin, but the sea is where they become brightest and strongest.

Estuaries are where we can control the tide a little. At the Thames Barrier at Woolwich, London is kept safe from flood, the sea a little tamer because of a human presence. At Cramond, the village on the beach to the west of Edinburgh, there is a causeway path out to the tidal Cramond Island, the concrete on the route cracked into rockpools by thousands of days of tide washing in and out. In Cramond itself – where the River Almond drains into the Firth – there's a decent pub (which means that dogs are allowed in the bar, with biscuits provided for them), a café with a good line in Cullen skink and hot chocolate, and generally an ice cream van parked out beside the small harbour, hard by the sign warning about tide times and instructing walkers to make sure to time their journeys out to the island so as not to get cut off.

If the tide is far enough out to be safe, two hours either side of its lowest point, you can walk right out along the causeway towards the little grassy islet with a few stony ruins on the top. As you walk, you're flanked always to your right by a line of tall, imposing, triangular anti-boat pylons, put there during the Second World War. Once you get to the island you can look at the Firth from its middle, the water all around you and Edinburgh settled and finite before you, with Arthur's Seat and the southern hills in the far distance. You are standing in the middle of the estuary, the river behind you, and the wide sea beyond, out into the myth and unknown. As you hurry back to the mainland – which you will want to do, for the cold of the coast winds will have by this time stirred within you a violent appetite for soup from the café or a pint of beer in the warmth of the decent pub with the dogs – if you've timed your trip right, the water will only just be beginning to fill in either side of the causeway, lapping around the bases of the anti-boat pylons, bringing more seaweed and fish to leave in the rockpools it cracked open on its last visit. If you feel the sea anywhere close to your feet, walk faster, because soon it will be several feet above your head, and you'll be left to swim with the seals, and the legends of others caught out by the tides before you.

THE MAID ON THE SHORE

M Y GRANDMOTHER WAS A WOMAN of piano keys and
seashells, and distant sparkling cruise ships, and ambition
and defiance. When I think about the women who appear in folk
songs of the sea, I think about my grandmother. Many of these
women you meet in folk song are wily and fun, enjoying tricks
and mischief and winning in the end. She was like that too.

There's a repertoire of folk music of the sea that's uplifting, a
joyous accompaniment to a warm day by the seaside, and it's to
these songs I turned when I decided to make my way back north
for good. There are songs of wistfulness – the distance that the sea
forces you to think about makes it hard for songwriters to resist a
good dose of wistfulness, apparently – though there are also songs
of love. As I started to listen addictively to music about the sea, it
was the songs about love that kept grabbing me, kept making me
feel as though northwards, with my feet on the eroding east coast,
was where I had to be.

'Braw Sailin'' was one of them. It's a Scottish song and included
in *Ord's Bothy Songs and Ballads*, a book by John Ord and Alexander

Fenton first published in 1930, recording folk songs known by people living in farms and bothies in north-east Scotland. The chorus is one of those rousing sea-song choruses that praises a life on the waves, and makes you smell the sea air and feel the joy and freedom of standing on deck with the waves crashing around you, almost intoxicating enough to make up for the pain of those left behind. The sense of pure optimism is undercut with a story of two lovers in the verses.

> *And it's braw sailin' on the sea*
> *When wind and weather's fair*
> *It's better to be in my love's airms*
> *O gin that I were there*

It's a short story of a boy and a girl. A girl wakes up in the morning and receives a letter saying that a ship is due to set sail in the morning. Soon she is visited by a boy who offers her a ring from his pocket, which cost him guineas three, saying, *Tak ye that my bonnie lass, and aye think weel o' me*. She takes a ring from her own pocket, a ring which cost her shillings nine, and gives it to the boy, saying, 'Tak ye that my bonnie lad, for I hae changed my mind.' It shows the sea as a place of freedom and sadness, and the coast as a location for parting and meeting again, for embarking on love and loss and adventures that change you. The sea is as much about who is left behind as it's about the adventures on the voyage.

•

My grandmother had trained classically at music college, and maintained her career as a performer and teacher even in a time and a society when married women weren't really expected to do such things.

She tried to teach me the piano as a child, but it never quite worked out. We were too close, I think, too similar in temperament – impatient, with a competitive streak, and quick to get over-excited about things – and maybe too fond of one another. Though I got the hang of a few simple tunes and scales, I was easily distracted and too stubborn to listen to her properly. She taught me other things instead: how to hold a knife and fork properly. How to do a crossword and feed the fish in the garden pond. How to bake chocolate cake and vanilla biscuits (she always made hundreds of these for church events, stacking tinfuls in high towers on her kitchen counters), and the best mince pies at Christmas. The secret, she said, was to roll the pastry out *thin thin thin*, much thinner than you think. And add a splash of extra brandy for the mincemeat, right at the end before you put the star-shaped pastry lids on each individual pie.

You could glimpse her bloody-mindedness in her two personal mottos: 'Nobody likes a moaner', and 'No surrender'. She would rarely complain about anything in her life, and met each day with stout-hearted determination. Life was one long To Do list that she could tick off with satisfaction as she went. If she could save money doing it, all the better, and family lore relates that she once won the local newspaper's 'Economical Housewife of the Week' award. She loved a cruise holiday, which I always suspected was less to do with her affection for the freedom of the sea and more a matter of economy for the sheer number of sights you could pack into one short-ish trip.

She cheated flamboyantly at board games, especially when playing with her grandchildren. The younger we were, the more determined she was to beat us, crying, 'I win!' and raking massive heaps of Monopoly money away from a pair of bewildered under-fives. She once told me about when she had been evacuated to Canada as a small girl during the war, and had slid down a banister and broken an expensive vase belonging to her host family. The memory still made her laugh sixty years later.

She did a crossword every day. Her house was full of solver books and electronic devices to help you cheat your way towards the answers. Sometimes she would ring us up if she was stuck on a clue. When I was eight, I picked up the ringing phone in our house one afternoon to hear the cheery trill of her voice.

'Charlotte! Bread is a filling lunch in itself.'

'Er . . . Can I have a think about it?'

An hour later I phoned her back. 'Granny! Wholemeal?'

'That's it! Pass me to your dad.'

She worked all her life and never retired. I don't know if this was a consciously feminist act or merely because she liked it. I never got to ask if she would have described herself as a feminist, and I don't know what she would have said if I had. I knew her as an independent-minded and uncompromising woman through-out her life, including many decades when that was not considered a seemly thing to be. Her home was the smell of marmalade toast, and sweet treats baking, and the sound of the piano playing as her hands stretched their way through Bach and Handel and

Mendelssohn. I think of her when I hear Ravel's 'Une barque sur l'océan', from his *Miroirs*, a fluttering and difficult piece, with arpeggiated sequences that trill from high to low and mix in and out of one another. It sounds just like waves, all eddying together with no beginning or end. I loved her. And I held her hand as she was dying.

•

It's five years after her death when I am sitting in the back room of a cramped, cosy little pub in Edinburgh's Old Town in winter, in a place near the castle that does a good beer called Trade Winds, and everyone is at least two pints down. It's the kind of pub that has a folky open mic night once a week, but where almost any day of the week a group of you could start up singing and nobody would mind, and someone friendly with some good stories to tell would probably wander over and join in.

Lots of the company are musicians and a few have guitars. Someone had a gig the night before and is laughing about forgetting the words to one of his songs, and someone else starts off the singing with a take on the many-versioned folk song, 'The Maid on the Shore'. Friends who know the song well join in with low harmonies, while men sing the high ones, improvising counter-melodies that trip and swap over one another, up and down, musical waves. More voices join in, more female than male, until the sound becomes dense and complicated.

The incarnation of the song they're singing is similar to one sung by Eliza Carthy when she performs, with a few added ornamentations and harmonies, just slightly too complicated for anyone who had never heard it before to join in, yet swinging with the same-again rhythm of a rocking boat. So I listen.

> *There was a young maiden who lived all alone,*
> *she lived all alone on the shore-o.*
> *There was nought she could find that would comfort her mind*
> *but to roam all alone on the shore, shore, shore,*
> *but to roam all alone on the shore.*

The story is, at its most basic, a common one found across lots of folk songs and tales: a young maiden is captured by a man wanting to take her virginity, but she escapes while he is asleep. It's where the song embellishes that old story that it becomes more interesting. The young captain of a ship sees the maiden and commands his crew to bring her to him, promising to divide his wealth of silver and gold with them if they do. The crew manages to capture her and bring her on board, but in the still calm night under the watchful moon, the maiden reveals her power. *She sang charming and sweet, she sang neat and complete, she sang sailors and captain to sleep, sleep, sleep.*

After she sings, and the men have fallen unconscious, she robs them of the captain's silver and gold and makes off in a rowing boat back to the shore, where she roams once again in peace.

The beauty of the song is in the power of the maid. She is a creature of the shore, brought on board a boat by men of the sea who suspect they can overpower her, but she finally has the upper hand. Like all good folk songs, infinite versions of it exist and its origins are murky. It has some resemblance to the 43rd Child ballad, 'The Broomfield Hill', also about a maiden fleeing a sleeping man with her virginity intact. In Child 43, however, she flees through the woods, and is an altogether more simpering figure, and the man who seeks to take her is shown as being cheated out of something he feels he deserved.

The maiden in 'The Maid on the Shore', on the other hand, is our hero. We meet her in the first verse, before we meet the sea-captain. By the time he arrives and makes his intentions known we want her to escape, to cheat them out of what they want and to roam once again on the shore by herself, even though her reasons for living a life like this are never explored. We don't need to know her reasons. We only know that she deserves to be there, if that's what she wants, and with all the gold she has robbed from the sailors to help her. The song of the sailors has no power compared to the mystical song of the maid from the shore, in harmony with the wind and rain: *Let the wind blow high or blow low-o*, the song goes.

The shore is the place where women are. It's important for the song that the sailors find the maid there. The shoreline is a place where two states meet, earth and water.

Shorelines are evocative places. The tides come in and out on the beach, guided by the moon. Women and coasts are constantly changing and physically redrawing themselves in cycles. Boundaries are blurred and washed away, and anything is possible at the line between this life and another. Shorelines are where the known world drops away into unseen depths. You can feel the change happening as you wet your toes on the beach and wade deeper down a slope of wave-covered sand. Already I am starting to be aware of motherhood making itself known as a brink.

SHANTY

ODYSSEUS SURVIVED THE DECADE-LONG HORRORS of the Trojan War. And then he endured ten more years at sea, including shipwreck, being kept as the slave of Kalypso, the loss of all his crew to various grisly ends, and complete separation from his wife and son. His adventures were hard to endure, but that made for better stories, and that's the point. The gods allowed the devastation of the Trojan War to happen for a reason, Alcinous says in the *Odyssey*. It was to give us all something to sing about. 'The gods did it – spun the thread of the ruin of men – so that for those yet to come there would be a song.' And the *Odyssey*, after all, was composed to be sung.

As well as reading about the sea, I am singing about it. Inspired by the pub singing, I've got some people together to start a folk music choir, and we meet weekly in the evenings, sometimes in pubs, sometimes in a rented room in a quiet office building, singing together with no accompaniment. The repertoire of songs that are intended to be sung without accompaniment is wide, from sacred music to modern clap-along versions of pop songs. Quickly, though, we have been drawn to sea shanties, work songs of hardship and struggle and longing for women left behind on shore. Their rough-and-readiness suits our rough-and-ready sort of choir: an eclectic group of people, none of whom have auditioned, and most of whom like the choir best for its habit of having a few pints after rehearsals. The choir consists of more women than men, and still we like singing these old, masculine sea songs about seagoing terms we had never known before, squaring a yard and heaving in the anchor. We are getting ready to perform a gig of sea songs, shanties and old folk songs and new ones, against the backdrop of the sea.

It's while researching songs for the gig that I look again at my copy of Stan Hugill's book *Shanties from the Seven Seas*, a collection of maritime work songs from the age of sail gathered from around the world by a man who called himself 'the last known shantyman'. Hugill had been employed full-time to lead the unaccompanied singing of sea shanties aboard ships in the golden age of sail, an era that stretched from the nineteenth into the early twentieth century until the rise of the mechanised navy. He seems to have sailed his way across the globe having adventures, some of them much more believable than others, some of them dark and dangerous, and all the while singing. He sounds a bit like Odysseus.

The book was published in 1961. The more I find out about Hugill, the more his life seems like a swashbuckling Boy's Own story. He was shipwrecked many times and learned to speak Maori after being wrecked on one particular island, only being rescued when he talked his way aboard a ship carrying manure. He was a

POW in the Second World War, where he kept spirits up for himself and his fellow captives by painting boat pictures on bed sheets. During this time he also learned fluent Japanese. Or so he would like us to believe, and so he relates in wild explanatory notes to his books about sea shanties.

He became a folk music sensation in the 1960s, when his days at sea were behind him, though he still – if only to preserve his image as an authentic relic of the days of sail – carried a full-sized harpoon in his hand luggage on international flights. His performances of sea shanties attracted big crowds in America and Europe during the folk music revival.

If Hugill were sitting in the back bar of the pub nursing a pint and listening to us as we rehearse, he'd probably think it a strange sound, a choir of mostly women singing these old sea songs. Sea shanties, the great work songs that kept sailors in time as they hauled ships across oceans, were always sung by groups of men without any accompaniment. Their voices had to be loud and in time and in tune with one another, a musical machine as efficient as the ship itself, to keep the ship moving. The music was a by-product of men's physical relationship with the water. These songs bound men together with each other and with the sea, kept their bodies working, a musical force using human bodies alone.

Nearly every verse of every hauling shanty begins with a yell, an 'O!' or an 'Ey-yo!', and most of the choruses in capstan shanties contain them too, readying the men of the crew to begin each next hard pull. The 1950s German sea shanty collection *Knurrhahn* takes the German word for the shantyman's shout as its title, and translates it as something that sounds like either 'a cockerel with a sore throat' or 'a fish that grunts'. These shouts are something like Walt Whitman's 'barbaric yawp', sounded over waves instead of rooftops. They are pain and joy and effort. The sound is desperate, unimaginable, guttural, and – when taken out of context – ridiculous.

That risk of ridicule was one reason why Hugill wrote that shanties shouldn't be performed on land at all. They needed the accompaniment of the sea to make sense, and if you're kept on land, you're excluded from understanding them properly. Singing shanties when not actually at sea is something Hugill felt was taboo for him and his fellow sailors (or so he claimed, though this view didn't seem to stop him performing them in folk clubs in later life), saying that shanties without the natural harmonic accompaniments of blowing gales and cursing sailors were no shanties at all. Shanties were work songs, and they only truly existed when sung at work. Shanties performed with smooth choral harmony, or crooned into microphones by professional musicians, were an entirely different discipline.

On Hugill's ships they called the yells 'hitches'. To sound a hitch, the men's voices broke over the tones once or more as they called out at the beginning of a shanty verse with the note rasping against the wind, or else flicked out a high yelp from the throat at the end of a sung line before turning to the next.

The yells are the most ancient parts of the shanty, sounds that 'have always been part and parcel of a sailor's life when working ship, from dim, remote times', Hugill says. The earliest roots of the shanty began with these yells. Before sailors sang shanties, they performed 'sing-outs', proto-shanties, embryonic forms of sea-singing whose tunes are lost to us but that slowly emerged from the primordial soup of rhythmic voiced cries, always called out to aid in keeping time during work aboard ships.

Hugill notes that the monk Felix Fabri travelled to Palestine by sea in 1493, and recorded 'there are mariners who sing when work is going on, because work at sea is very heavy'. There are mentions in Ancient Greek texts of rowers singing to keep time with one another, but the sea shanty is music built to accompany heaving and hauling work, Hugill believes. And that requires yelling, when the work is exhausting and actual words become impossibly strenuous.

In the anonymous 1549 *Complaynt of Scotlande*, a propaganda tract published during the Rough Wooing conflict between Scotland and England, a Scottish 'anchor song' is recorded with identifiable yells:

> *Vayra, veyra, vayra, veyra*
> *Gentil gallantis veynde*
> *I see him, veynde, I see him*
> *Porbossa, porbossa*

We don't know what the tune sounded like. But the definition-less 'vayra' words chime with the yell-sounds peppered through Hugill's shanty collections. When Hugill first went to sea, it was the wordless sounds that first reverberated around his head. They were the first way he could join in with the centuries-old musical traditions that now surrounded him, long before he learned the words.

A hundred years since Hugill first worked at sea, I stand in my living room and try to recreate the sound. Even so, shouting 'veyra', or 'O', or 'Hey, yo, ho, ru' and trying to make your voice sound as ugly, salty and physically aggressive as possible is freeing. You have to jerk your navel and diaphragm quickly inwards, forcing all of the air out of your lungs the way wind is loosed from a sail by the haulers. A hitch de-pretties a song if you throw it in at the end of a line or halfway through a chorus. Wordless voicing permeates all kinds of sung music, but the roughness and physicality of the sea shanty hitches feels like the truest throwback to their physical, work song origins, a conversation had directly with the rough sea.

Women are at a disadvantage. Women are expected to sound sweet and pretty when we sing. Sounding like a sailor three bottles of rum down is not always desirable for a professional singer, or an amateur choir member. It's less frowned on in folk clubs, particularly for men, but even in these sacred halls of traditional music, women can find it hard to let loose their musical aggression without feeling somehow out of place. Sea shanties were not written for women. A female presence at sea was always more likely to be in the form of a ship named after a woman – and ships are always referred to as 'she' – than in any real-life human on board.

•

At the pub in Portobello that opens out its doors directly towards the shore, our fledgling choir assembles in front of a big bay window overlooking the water on the night of the gig. I am on door duty, and not actually singing, and so for the first time since we started rehearsing together I have the chance to listen to the sea songs we had been practising for weeks. My breathing has deepened during the year that we've been singing together, and my voice has strengthened. I feel taller.

The lights dim. Someone has lit some candles and placed them on the pub's mantelpiece. Through the window, the waves are moving gently on the horizon, over the heads of the choir as they start to sing. *Away, lads, away, away for Rio! And fare you well, my bonny young girl, and we're bound for the Rio Grande.* There are harmonies and dynamics and women's voices reaching up high. Hugill would hardly recognise it as a true shanty – though, in the quieter moments, you can just make out the sound of the sea as it draws up outside beyond the pub's front wall. It's our version of a sea shanty, a shorebound telling of the hardships of sea, the only version we are capable of making.

Evening falls calm and mild as the light on the water fades to indigo. If you were standing outside the pub that night, all you would hear would be songs and the splash of the waves.

WORM'S HEAD

S PRING IS HATCHING AND I have been thinking about myth and pilgrimage, of the *Canterbury Tales* pilgrims who set off in April, and taking myself on long walks and finding writers and historical figures who had made the same journeys. It's as if my small everyday decisions, the minutiae of life, need a sense of the epic to give them meaning. I'm trying, I suppose, to find the sea in the land.

Years ago, in the sacred silence of the college library, I had read 'The Seafarer', the anonymous tenth-century Old English poem from the *Exeter Book*. It's a poem about isolation and exile, and there's something strange about that: given the way that poetry was shared and performed in the time 'The Seafarer' was composed, it's most likely to have been sung aloud with accompanying harp music at lively community gatherings and feasts. It's a song of loneliness, which probably would have been sung among friends. The person who speaks in the poem is in exile, but he finds company in listening to the screeching of sea birds. He hears the calls of curlews, singing gulls, icy-feathered terns, a dewy-feathered eagle. He imagines their sounds are the laughter of his friends, but *þær ic ne gehyrde / butan hlimman sæ / iscaldne wæg* – 'I heard nothing but the roaring sea and the ice-cold waves'.

On days when I was missing home and felt a grim and over-dramatic kinship with the isolated, banished Seafarer, I would walk right out of my medieval college in the bright mid-afternoon with a textbook in my bag, and keep going in one direction for as long as I could. Usually it took until night fell to feel a clearing in my head, and then I would turn back and grudgingly walk the miles in reverse towards my desk, bats swooping around my head.

The land between Cambridge and Ely, some eighteen miles of river towpath, was once underwater. Ely itself was an island on a flooded marsh. I walked the whole way one summer day, all along the River Cam, vastly underestimating the distance in advance and so forgetting to eat breakfast or take any food or water with me, and therefore inadvertently imitating the fasting pilgrims who would have taken the same journey hundreds of years before.

As I walked the path along the river, the occasional punt or coxless pair swished gently past me on the water. I spent most of the way feeling faint and grumbling to nobody in particular about a blister forming on my heel. To distract myself from the irritation of it, I imagined how it would have been along this path when the whole landscape was submerged. I pictured the fens as not just marsh, but a giant sea. The fields of cows and beds of reeds just sand and rock, constantly washed clean by the waves. And the cathedral rising above it all in defiance, a miracle, its bells ringing.

Would this lost stretch of water, long ebbed away, really have looked like a sea, the way the pilgrims had known it? Or would the peaty Cambridgeshire mud on the bottom colour it darker, a sea in cola-brown, more a lake than an ocean? What wildlife was there – long-legged curlews and godwits picking their way across the marshy edges? Gulls? Slippery fish darting at the height that my shoulders were now? In the midday light the surface of the long summer grass rippled in the wind.

The distance felt as though it would have been less if the way had been over water instead of paths, as if the pilgrims had been skimming magically and easily over the surface, like flying fish. Did they take boats for the final stretch?

By the time I arrived at Ely that day I was dizzy and sick. I had intended to revisit the impressive octagonal tower of Ely Cathedral, an abbey founded in 672 AD by another Anglo-Saxon, St Æthelthryth. I had been once before – on the train – and admired the way the coloured light dappled lavishly in from the stained glass. But I was much too hungry when I arrived, and by the time I'd eaten, the cathedral had closed. In any case I'm not sure that the original pilgrims to Ely would have wolfed down an entire large pizza and two starters at Pizza Express when they finally arrived, even if I was so ravenous that I might, if pushed, classify that meal as a religious experience.

The sea had left traces on this landscape but it wasn't there any more. Maybe it had been a mistake to go hunting for the sea's footprints instead of the beast itself. Magical sea adventures don't happen on dry land. Do they?

•

In the early spring of the following year I went to visit a friend who lived in Swansea. Izzy had recently acquired a puppy, a little cross-breed fluffball that looked almost exactly like a teddy bear, and wanted to introduce me. There was a beach, she said, not too far away, and we could go together and take some sandwiches and a flask of tea and stretch the dog's tiny legs. Afterwards we could visit the Dylan Thomas Centre in Swansea itself, and see the statue of the great man, and get some coffee at Hoffi Coffi (the café named after the rhyming Welsh sentence *Dw i'n hoffi coffi*, which in English is 'I like coffee'). I hadn't ever been to Wales before.

Her parents drove us to the beach and we packed the tea and sandwiches, and Izzy walked fast and strong ahead while I struggled to keep up with her. Izzy was a runner, and ran seriously in races, and her legs were lean and muscular. At the time, I had the legs of an introverted bookworm, which are not much use on bracing country walks. There was something about this walk, though, that made me realise in new detail that walking beside the sea was just the very thing to exercise the mind. Walking could be the route to something better, somewhere I have never travelled, gladly beyond, like in the e e cummings poem, where there is power in the fragility of the new, and everyone's a pilgrim.

This was a walk along the beach long before I knew how much I loved walks along the beach, with a sandy-pawed dog darting ahead and the weather blowsy and bright and our hair full of it. There were white horses on the waves, and spindrift blowing, and the yellow sand packed hard under our booted feet. I had been indoors too long, spent too much time on books and computers and the fusty feeling of days that slip away from you without anything experienced or achieved.

•

One of the most distinctive features of Rhossili Bay is the Worm's Head, the rock formation that stretches out in a causeway from the grassy patches of the mainland, a mile long. The name comes from the old Anglo-Saxon and Norse word *wurme*, which didn't mean worm but dragon, or serpent. This part of Wales is where the Welsh dragon lives, written in rock. The most westerly point of the Gower peninsula, it sticks out of the water for all the world like the head and neck of a dragon lying down in the sea. It's another walk that can be taken in the five-hour window of low tide, though we don't know this when we visit, and don't attempt it. Like the walk at Cramond, unwary visitors can be caught out by the tide.

Dylan Thomas was one such hapless tourist. He wrote about the Worm's Head in his short story, 'Who Do You Wish Was With Us?', and gave more detail of his own visits to Rhossili in his letters, seeming equally captivated and appalled by the place, describing the bay in a letter as 'the wildest, bleakest and barrenest I know – four or five miles of yellow coldness going away into the distance of the sea'. He called the Worm's Head 'the very promontory of depression'. He once got trapped out there between the tides. He was scared of the incoming sea and wrote:

I stayed on that Worm from dusk till midnight, sitting on the top grass, frightened to go further in because of the rats and because of the things I am ashamed to be frightened of. Then the tips of the reef began to poke out of the water, &, perilously, I climbed along them on to the shore, with an 18 mile walk in front of me. It was a dark, entirely silent, empty road. I saw everything on that walk – from snails, lizards, glow worms & hares to diaphanous young ladies in white who vanished as I approached them.

On going back into Swansea city centre after our trip, we visited the Dylan Thomas statue, and amused ourselves by taking photographs sitting on his bronze lap and gazing longingly into his eyes. Back in Cambridge I kept thinking about Thomas and the beach and looking out to sea. I went out and bought a copy of his *Selected Poems*, and read 'Fern Hill' as I walked from my college across to the English faculty along the Backs one daffodil-lit morning. The poem, about youth and memory and being young and easy in the lamb white days, lifted me up by the hair, the way that the salt winds had done at Rhossili: *Time held me green and dying, / Though I sang in my chains like the sea.*

•

In Edinburgh the sea always seems to be singing, and eternally percussive in a planet-wide heartbeat. My grandmother and my mother had both taught me to listen out for the sea in a conch held up to the ear. A shell to your ear will let you hear the sea, even if the nearest coast is thousands of miles away. Like all the best tales, it's both true and not true: the swirling sound that you hear inside shells is an echo of the swirling of blood inside your own head. The sound of the sea is really just the sound of the water and salt that moves inside us, and when we listen to the echoes of our own bodies in shells, the song we hear is brine.

II

TAYGETE

After she is seduced by Zeus, Taygete gives birth to Lacedæmon, founder of Sparta, and becomes a goddess there. She is afraid of Zeus after this, and so in an act of friendship the goddess Artemis transforms Taygete into a doe. Now Taygete can hide from Zeus's everlasting hunt for all eternity.

DIVE

THE EARLIEST WEEKS OF PREGNANCY are chimerical. Now you are more than one creature. You are changing and nobody knows but you. You look the same, and all the while the chemical composition of your body is busy altering itself. The liquid of your body is the first and biggest part to change as it spreads through your veins and your cells, the truth readable only in blood and urine by those trained to detect it. Doctors and chemistry sets now, soothsayers once upon a time. It's a state of half-being, and it's both new to me and completely familiar. I both am and am not. The woman in the mirror looks the same as she did a month ago. The post-war philosopher and civil servant Oliver Franks said that a secret was something that you 'may tell . . . to only one person at a time'. This is that sort of secret, for now, but it's the sort of secret that gathers momentum, like a storm, until the truth is loud and obvious.

Every month of adulthood I have felt possibility in my body. That's the gift and burden of being a woman, and it's what scares the people who don't understand it. We have the potential for the most extraordinary creativity, to make new people and ensure the survival of the species through enormous physical change and sacrifice. And it is sacrifice: plans are put on hold and responsibility replaces them. When you're young and single and wondering how to pay next month's rent, pregnancy looms like a disaster. We try to ignore the worry for the most part, take the pills and act like we're not bothered, and still it's always there, a power and a threat.

Reproduction, the desire for it, the fear of it, the confidence that it will never happen, the fear that we're wrong, the horror of the very idea of it: I've felt all of those things at different times, and sometimes all at the same time. Pregnancy has sometimes seemed aggressive to me, an ugly biological reality with the instant ability to destroy the life for myself I've already made. Every month has held the possibility of my own life being dashed on the rocks. And what then – would I be lost? Reshaped by the currents into something new? Or would I sail for ever onwards, month after month, my own person forever? We have such a short time to decide if we want to have children, and then to see if our body is capable of making good on the threat-promise it gave us in adolescence. *Time held me green and dying, though I sang in my chains like the sea.* Whether we choose to have children or not, to some people we'll be defined by our choice for the rest of our lives. My body has seized the moment and snatched its prize.

•

The Bass Rock is the capital city of gannets. Planet Gannet, I call it in my head as I look out at the rock while picking my way along the beach at North Berwick in a pelting afternoon of storm, the kind of storm that has gathered darkly for hours in the morning and then broken all at once, the kind of storm I feel a kinship with, these days. I have the grey beach as entirely my own. The cold and horizontal water has driven everyone else inside, presumably to a sensible arrangement of warm stoves and dry socks. The wind has bite in it, the iron sky unyielding. Nobody is buying ice creams on the beach today, and the only walkers are those with dogs to be appeased, or a craving for the solitary, and here I am both, wandering through every possible future scenario in my head. Spring shows itself only in glimmers, in the seaweedy green of the leaves on the coastal trees, and in the sight of a growing spread of the gannets nesting on the Bass. I watch them from this side of the Forth, and picture my mother at her home over the water in Fife, looking at them from the other side through the small pair of binoculars she keeps on the living room windowsill. I try to imagine what it will be like to be a mother.

Just like the Bass at the dawn of the year, gannet chicks themselves don't start off white, but blue-black, and gradually grow whiter and fatter until the time comes for them to fledge. By the end of October, they've left for Africa to avoid the bitter Scottish autumn, returning just as the light returns again to wassail in the new year.

I watch them searching for sardines. They rise on the air with their eyes on the water underneath, taking full command of the airspace between the waves below and the international planes high above, making their own descent towards Edinburgh airport.

Gannets are part of how we see the sea from the land. In the *Beowulf* poem, the sea is described as a *ganotes baeth,* a 'gannet's bath'. The gannets circle in stacks thirty, sixty, ninety feet above the water, waiting to glimpse a shadow of prey. When the sighting comes, the reaction is blink-fast: their huge wings fold in behind their bodies to turn themselves into elegant, deadly razors, cutting through the air at sixty miles an hour. They shape themselves like space rockets. The speed of the dive and the force of the impact would kill other birds, but gannets were built for this. Underwater, they dive thirty feet deep. Their black-tipped wings help them to swim towards their prey in a scrambling underwater parody of flight. They can hold their breath for up to forty-five seconds.

•

The gannet's-eye view of the East Lothian coast has the sea stretching into the freezing Scandinavian distance. To the west there are hills, which hide the winding routes used once by smugglers – though it's hard to see now where they laid their trails, overlaid by dunes and long grasses brushed by coastal winds – all the way to Eyemouth, where the grand mid-eighteenth-century Gunsgreen House stands as testament to the profits gained. Two enterprising brothers there called themselves merchants, and stealthily imported tea, brandy, claret and Dutch gin, stowing it in caves and passages riddled like holes in cheese along this coastline. For the benefit of the tourist trade, Eyemouth's now as proud of its smuggling heritage as its fishing history: most summers since 1939, a 'Herring Queen' has been crowned at Gunsgreen, chosen from among the local Eyemouth girls and celebrated at a summer fair.

The sighting of gannets has traditionally been a good omen for sailors, and an indication of plentiful waters for fishing. The gannets have a good view of Eyemouth from their home on the Bass Rock. The Rock itself is a great hunk of an island sticking out of the water, the plug of a long-sleeping volcano that looks like a cannonball thrown into the sea by a giant. Its colour changes during the year. In winter it stands stark against white sky, slate black and sheened with rain. In his novel *Catriona*, Robert Louis Stevenson called the Bass 'an unco place by night, unco by day ... When the waves were any way great they roared about the rock like thunder and the drums of armies, dreadful, but merry to hear, and it was in the calm days when a man could daunt himself with listening; so many still, hollow noises haunted and reverberated in the porches of the rock.' Considered inhospitable and bleak, the Bass has in its past been a prison for high-profile convicts, from royals to Jacobite rebels, though a band of the latter did once manage to seize control of the island by overpowering guards and making off with a supply boat. Now it has a lighthouse and a seabird sanctuary.

The year's first gannets, *solans* as Stevenson calls them, arrive at the end of January. At first they are just freckles of white against dark stone, seen from the mainland. As the spring warms, the gannets increase in number, firmly establishing themselves at home by March. In May they're joined by 90,000 puffins, and plenty of other seabirds besides: kittiwakes, terns and razorbills, guillemots and cormorants – the birds said to embody the spirits of those lost at sea – and fulmars and more. This combination of sea birds is relatively unusual. The writer of 'The Seafarer' refers in the poem to a similar composition of seabirds, which suggests the possibility that it was written with the wildlife community of the isolated, evocative Bass Rock specifically in mind. Life on the rock is dominated, though, by a thick coating of the gannets outnumbering all others, 150,000 of Britain's largest seabird – excepting the occasional rare visit from an albatross – in all. It's the largest gannet colony on Earth.

In the haze of midsummer June, they feed their chicks. They make the rock entirely their own territory, covering it in their nests, using it as a base for fishing trips which they attend in groups of hundreds at a time, returning to stow their catch away on the rock and keep it safe. They were smuggling long before the smugglers and they keep the tradition alive.

•

At first I thought they were ugly things, gannets. They are known for greed, aggression and ungainliness, a reputation built on their violent and precise hunting style. With their physical construction of spiky angles, a needling beak and long, streamlined body, they've evolved to attack the split between water and air. Of course their biggest home on Earth is an aggressive, jagged place, their nests built into the steep drops of the Bass Rock in the midst of blasting winds. Other features help them in their life's purpose of diving: they have no external nostrils like other birds, and air sacs in their faces and chests cushion them from the water's impact.

The Ancient Greek sea goddess Leukothea, literally 'White Goddess', was, according to Homer, originally a nymph called Ino who became a goddess only because of the wrath of Hera. After being found caring for the newborn Dionysus, Ino was punished by Hera and sent insane, jumping into the Aegean. The other gods on Mount Olympus saved her from doom by transforming her into a goddess of the sea. In the *Odyssey*, Leukothea appears to the shipwrecked Odysseus as a gannet and presents him with a protective veil that saves his life during rough waters. There's a kinship between the gannet and the human.

They are not decorative birds. Like humans, gannets are creatures of the shoreline. They are a chimera of earth and water, above and below, hunting at speeds inches from death. Their every feature is ruthlessly practical and their all-over sharpness a perfection for rough seascapes. At their leanest, when they extend into the dive, they resemble long icy raindrops pulled down to the sea, drawn to the expanse of water where they belong. Their colours are created from their habitat: creamy white feathers for the foam on the waves, black tips on their six-foot wingspan for the dark of the depths, and a blush of yellow on the head, with a blue-rimmed eye, the sparkle of bright morning sun on the sea.

CREATURES OF THE DEEP

I TRY NOT TO LOOK AT pictures of what the baby is supposed to look like as it forms in the earliest weeks of pregnancy. I could say that it's because I don't want to get too attached to the hypothetical, to something which might vanish. It's more accurate to say that the artists' impressions of this tiny creature, too small to photograph, unnerve me. They look so unlike a baby, and so much more like an alien, or a misshapen root vegetable that has had to grow through stony ground: lumpen, malevolent, not at all recognisably human. I have to accept that it's there, though, this stranger a new constant, lurking in the dark watery depths of my body. It is contained in the perfect saltwater environment of my body. I am a mobile aquarium.

I project imaginative forms of the creature on to my mind's eye. It's a will o' the wisp, a speck of glitter, a tiny crab, an invented sea creature painted on to a map of a place I've never visited. And I am afraid of what I don't know.

The tradition of painting sea monsters on to nautical maps is an illustration of our fear of the unknown. In the Middle Ages, the sea was a gateway to the rest of the world and a source of food and prosperity. Though it was used daily and mundanely by medieval peoples in Europe, they never forgot that as well as being a lifeline, it was also a place of terrible danger. The weather was one reason. Wooden ships in coastal Europe were, by 1000 AD, well evolved after centuries of seafaring tradition, and most could cope reliably with storms, yet even so, the way across the sea was inevitably treacherous. Its dangers infected the imagination. The ornately designed and inked maps of the period show us how. They were used as instructions for travel as well as art in their own right, as illustrations of the world as people understood it and as warnings of the dangers in the depths.

.

Martinskirche, the small church of St Martin in the tiny village of Zillis in Switzerland, doesn't look remarkable from the outside. It is small, Romanesque, typical of the period and the area, built solidly to serve the limited local population and to withstand the cold and snowy winters of the mountains. Inside, the walls are whitewashed and decorated simply, with a relatively plain light wooden organ to one side and a matching pulpit to the other. The atmosphere is light, airy, and minimalist. And then you look up.

The church is known best for its extraordinary ceiling, on which is painted a heavily detailed and impeccably preserved Mappa Mundi dating from around 1100 AD. The church itself is much older; there are records that it existed in Roman times in the place where it has perched ever since, high in the Alps with its black spire shaped like a witch's hat. Positioned far inland, close to the Via Mala and San Bernardino passages through the Alps to Italy, it has always been a place visited by travellers. These days, people come from all over the world to see the rare art of the ceiling with its heavy detail.

It looks very different from modern maps of the world. It's also very different from other examples of contemporary medieval cartography. The map is laid out like a chequerboard of 153 painted wooden squares, each with its own patterned border, each depicting its own self-contained small scene, which, when taken with the others surrounding it, makes up a puzzle piece as part of a broader picture of the world. It was likely painted not by one single artist, but by a range of local craftsmen specialising in smaller-scale manuscript illumination, each one taking charge of painting their own wooden square which was then installed into a mosaic of square images on the ceiling as a tile along with the others.

The whole effect looks like an Advent calendar with all the doors opened. At the centre of the mosaic is a depiction of the life of Christ, with Jesus painted ministering to his followers, wearing the crown of thorns. Then, as your eye travels further out towards the edges of the ceiling, you find more Biblical scenes, as well as images of general medieval monastic day-to-day life and specific events from the life of St Martin of Tours, the local patron saint. In one, he shares his coat with a beggar suffering from the cold, an often-recounted episode in his life which is also depicted in the Zillis town flag. St Christopher, patron saint of travellers, is here on the ceiling too, with a range of Old Testament stories such as the flight to Egypt.

Surrounding all this busy Christian activity is the sea. A swirling ocean wave pattern borders the land and frames the story of Christ. And it is not empty.

The forty-eight panels comprising the outer border of the ceiling show mythical figures emerging from the water. In each of the four corners is an angel, and together the quartet represent all of the four winds. Between them swims a procession of creatures altogether less holy-looking, all evidently much more intimately familiar with life at sea. There are Sirens playing music on their own stringed tails, forming human-harp chimerae. There are more hybrid monsters fusing roosters with stags and elephants alongside them, and bulls with scales and twin mermaid flippers curving out behind them. There are looming oversized fish being ridden by naked humans holding weapons, or with hairy red faces and matching manes and moustaches. There are more creatures that are half-human, half-monster, sometimes surfing on the waves, sometimes feeding their fellow beasts from ornate jewelled bowls.

Are the creatures supposed to scare us, or to be marvellous? It's hard to tell, at so many centuries removed, whether the artists intended them to be hellish demons or symbols of the diversity of God's creation. Although they're monstrous and strange, they don't seem wholly malevolent. The artists have taken such care in the details of their facial expressions and manners, the turns of their head, the swish of their tails, to make them entirely characterful, and sometimes funny. They are creatures with lives and backstories.

The person who assembled the overall scene, though, has a clear message to get across. The creatures' position on the fringes of the picture, at a distance from the familiarity and holiness of Christ and daily monastic life at the centre of the church's ceiling, suggests that the sea that surrounded medieval life was a place of mystery, strangeness and the other, the *non plus ultra* yet to be conquered by Christian teaching. It was a concept integral to the work of evangelical missionaries, who believed in spreading Christ's influence out as far as possible from the *oikumene*, the Holy Land at the centre of the world. The Mappa Mundi, too, puts Jerusalem at the centre of the world.

The concept of the known Earth as flat land mass encircled by water is suggested in Genesis as well as in the Old Norse name for Earth as *Miðgarðr*, literally Middle-Earth, a name pinched by Tolkien. It's the name for one of the Nine Worlds of Norse mythology, the only realm visible to humans, entirely encircled by uncrossable ocean. This ocean is said to contain within it a colossal sea serpent known as Jörmungandr, surrounding and enclosing the Earth and of such length that it clutches its own tail in its mouth. The myth crops up again and again: in Ancient Greece, Okeanos was the Titan who personified the sea and encircled the world, crossed by Odysseus on his journey to the land of the dead, and the ouroboros serpent eats its own tail in an illustration in the Ancient Egyptian funerary text *The Enigmatic Book of the Netherworld* in the shrine of Tutankhamun.

•

The Martinskirche ceiling is a map of an imagined, impressionistic landscape, not based on the shape of a real place. The Gough Map of Britain, on the other hand, is the first map in history to give something approaching an accurate outline of the British coast-line – or most of it, at least; Scotland's shape doesn't bear too much resemblance to reality. Maybe the map-maker was a little over-whelmed by her complex outline of inlets, sea lochs, rivers and small islands, all of which swirl right the way through the image and poke so many holes into the island of Britain that they make it look ready to sink.

It's not known exactly when or how the Gough Map came into being. Believed to date from around 1360 AD, and inscribed on two pieces of sheepskin parchment sewn together vertically, the map also shows a number of British road routes in detail and with clear name labels. Instead of being orientated as we would arrange it today, with the north of the country at the top of the page, on this map England is positioned towards the top edge, with Wales underneath it and Scotland to the left hand side. The map points this way so that the country then looks as if it faces Jerusalem, Christ's territory at the centre of the earth.

Searching through the towns shown on the map for familiar places and modern names, detectable here and there as small castle vignettes alongside towns and villages, gives a few jolts of recogni-tion. What did the towns of Britain look like when this old map was made, and how metropolitan and influential were some compared to others? Scottish settlement names are written in brown ink, and the names of settlements south of Hadrian's Wall are written in thick black lines. London and York are the only two place names rendered grandly and lovingly in gold leaf. The vignette of houses representing London is the most ornamented settlement on the map, with long-since-tarnished silver leaf details edged on to the tiny portcullis of the city gates, and careful round windows drawn on to all the buildings. Major rivers are enlarged to show their importance, and attentively plotted, with their sources marked as green circles. The artwork of the original fourteenth-century inscriber has been overwritten in parts by a fifteenth-century scribe, who seemingly attempted to 'freshen up' the work by darkening some lines and text, but the ghosts of the original hand are still detectable in places around the edges of the rivers and coastline and towns, and the effect is of an idea of Britain and its waters being continually redrawn and refined.

And of course it's encircled by sea. In the top left-hand corner of the parchment, in the faded hand of the original scribe, you can still see the grandest residents of the map. Occupying the expanse of North Sea are spectral figures that the later reviser didn't bother to refresh: a detailed ship, accompanied by a trio of creatures lurking in the green ink-wash. The three animals are a whale, a swordfish, and a shark. They are intertwined, maybe locked in a battle with one another, or maybe embracing. They could represent England, Scotland and Wales, all tussling together, the people of the island of Britain defined as sea creatures.

Although we don't know much about the creation of the Gough Map, or for whom it was intended, it was around this period that people interested in marine navigation could begin to commission a cartographer to design a map to suit their needs. The cheapest and most perfunctory maps were the ones used by sailors, and simply showed ports and coastal settlements and basic shipping routes and directions as clearly as possible. If you were willing to pay a little more for your map, for example if you were on the wealthy side and wanted to display it proudly in your opulent personal library, you could ask the cartographer to add decorative flourishes of your choice. You could choose to add elaborately rendered cities, flourishes of silver and gold, family crests or intricate compass roses. And mythical embellishments were available, too, for the right price: why not adorn your seas with Sirens and sea monsters and dream-like fantasy aquatic versions of land animals, dogs and lions with flippers and fins? Even maps, records of the landscape, recognise the sea as a place of mystery, wonder and the unknown.

•

There are real sea monsters. They exist through deep sea gigantism, the phenomenon that makes creatures living deep down in the ocean depths much bigger than other life forms, and they are so far in the deep and dark of the ocean's depths that humans are unable to travel down to see them face to face, and so they emerge in legend as well as in reality. There's the twenty-foot-long ribbon-like giant oarfish, the living embodiment of the ouroboros, found in waters all around the world. The giant squid and the colossal squid, competitors for the title of the planet's largest invertebrate, reach somewhere between twenty and sixty feet in length, but these size estimates are extrapolated from only a few specimens that have ever been observed. The giant squid was only photographed alive for the first time in 2004, and first captured alive by Japanese zoological researchers in 2006. The giant squid's eyes alone have a diameter of ten inches each, the largest eyes of any known creature. The colossal squid, from rare observations, seems to have a larger beak and big claws on its tentacles. They live so impenetrably deep down that much of what we know about them comes only from studying dead ones that have washed up on beaches, and so our imagination is left to fill in the gaps. Science fiction is rife with stories of aggressive, angry giant squid wrapping their tentacles around troubled ships in storms, squeezing them to pieces and dragging them underwater.

Since the eighteenth century, stories of the Kraken – a huge and terrifying creature, shifting and undefined like all good horror villains but roughly resembling a squid or octopus, and residing in the sea somewhere between Norway and Greenland – have tantalised writers and artists. The myth of the Kraken may well have originated from glimpsed sightings of giant squid in the wild by sailors convinced the creature would spell their doom. Building on paintings of squid-like mermaid hybrids in the margins of medieval manuscripts, the legend of the Kraken has evolved over time. You see it in *Under the Seas*, the director Georges Méliès's spoof 1906 film of Jules Verne's *Twenty Thousand Leagues Under the Sea*, a dream narrative in which mermaids dance in water-grottoes that are also home to enormous shellfish, and a violent octopus-like Kraken. It was filmed using real sea creatures – but small ones, the ones you might find in British rockpools, swimming across miniature model sets to make them look big and scary.

Méliès's film is surreal and funny, but Alfred, Lord Tennyson's 1830 sonnet 'The Kraken' is a darker version of the myth. Tennyson combines the unknown of the sea and its unstudied creatures with visions of a future hellscape at Judgement Day. The poem isn't so far removed from the Martinskirche ceiling at Zillis, and the monster-infested waters of the fringes of medieval maps that point to the Holy Land.

> Below the thunders of the upper deep,
> Far, far beneath in the abysmal sea,
> His ancient, dreamless, uninvaded sleep
> The Kraken sleepeth: faintest sunlights flee
> About his shadowy sides; above him swell
> Huge sponges of millennial growth and height;
> And far away into the sickly light,
> From many a wondrous grot and secret cell
> Unnumbered and enormous polypi
> Winnow with giant arms the slumbering green.
> There hath he lain for ages, and will lie
> Battening upon huge sea worms in his sleep,
> Until the latter fire shall heat the deep;
> Then once by man and angels to be seen,
> In roaring he shall rise and on the surface die.

Even though Hell is so often depicted in cultures throughout the centuries as a place of fire and heat, when it comes to mapping out the world, the depths of the sea are the places you'll find the darkest horrors. Here are the places that even the all-pervading light of Christianity can't shine. The Kraken, the unfathomable sea monster that lurks at the back of our subconscious nightmare, will remain unknown and feared, *until the latter fire shall heat the deep.*

The Kraken is ageless, sexless, lurking half-seen in its horrors and all the more terrifying for being inspired by real-life sea giants that we don't know all that much about. Some of the most ferocious mythological sea creatures, though, are more specifically described. They do have a sex, and that sex is female.

In the *Beowulf* poem, the most horrifying creature that the hero fights isn't Grendel, the first monster he encounters, but Grendel's mother. Grendel's mother lives deep down in watery depths, and seeks vengeance after Beowulf attacks her child.

Beowulf is a sea-story. Before the shield-Dane warrior meets Grendel for the first time, he reaches the mead-hall Heorot in a condition described using the word *saemeþe*, sea-weary. His voyage over the water towards this adventure was treacherous, but he's no stranger to sea dangers, having faced them before in his youth.

When Beowulf arrives at Heorot he is full of bravado, ready to fight Grendel on behalf of the tormented local people. At the feast welcoming him, a man called Unferth speaks and is suspicious of Beowulf's claims of strength and fighting prowess. Unferth asks if he is the same Beowulf who, in his youth, once lost a week-long swimming competition *on deop wæter* with another lord named Breca. Beowulf replies that the stories are true, yet incomplete. Although he may have lost the race, that was only (he says) because of the horrifying sea monsters he encountered and had to fight off on the way.

Beowulf takes up the story. On day five of their intense swimming race, conditions were stormy and freezing with *wado weallende wedera cealdost*, 'water surging in the coldest of weathers'. To make matters worse, the sea-fishes became angry: *merefixa mod onhrered*. Amid the churning waters with the angry sea creatures all around, one such beast finally grabbed Beowulf and dragged him under to the bottom of the sea, holding him tightly in its grip. Beowulf claims he was forced to slay the mighty sea-beast, the *mihtig mere-deor*, as well as several of its monstrous friends for good measure, and eventually was able to make it safely ashore. Breca, he adds a little disdainfully, only made it home first because he was carried back to land on a favourable tide.

It's a fine excuse for coming second in a race, though barely believable even within a story that has dragons and mythical monsters attacking humans at almost every turn. The listening crowd at Heorot, so desperate for a warrior to save them from the attacks of the mysterious Grendel who has been picking them off one by one, takes the story as proof that Beowulf is experienced at slaying monsters. When Beowulf does duly go on to conquer Grendel, Unferth is contrite for suggesting there was any weakness in Beowulf's past, and even presents him with the loan of an heirloom sword by way of apology.

And yet there is still a water-beast more terrifying than this catalogue of sea monsters that Beowulf must face. When he must go on to confront Grendel's vengeful mother, he finds she too lives deep underwater, in a dark sea-cave. She is described as *se þe wæteregesan wunian scolde / cealde streamas*: 'she who had to inhabit the dreadful waters, the cold streams'. When Beowulf sets off to find the pool where she lives, he finds the water to be *dréorig ond gedréfed*, 'bloody and churned up', and filled with strange sea-dragons, *sellice saedracan*. The thing that is unknown and more terrifying than any of the creatures that Beowulf has already fought and beaten is a female sea-beast, and a mother.

The femininity of Grendel's mother has been drawn out by the inevitable film and TV adaptations of the story, with the 2007 animated movie starring Ray Winstone as Beowulf and taking enormous liberties with the content of the original poem, casting a hyper-sexualised Angelina Jolie as Grendel's mother. Jolie's character is a variant on a succubus, luring men to their doom with her sexual wiles rather than by raw violence. I think the Grendel's mother of the original poem is scarier, though. The original Grendel's mother isn't aggressively sexual; she is just aggressive. Modern fictional female villains do not tend to be ferocious or murderous without any kind of sexual element, but ancient myths are full of powerful and brutal women at sea. Grendel's mother is not unlike Scylla in the *Odyssey*, with her menacing teeth and penchant for swallowing men whole.

Like Grendel's mother, Scylla has been portrayed visually in subsequent paintings as beautiful, but her first appearance in the *Odyssey* is anything but attractive. She has enormous and hideous teeth: πλεῖοι μέλανος θανάτοιο, 'full of black death'. The word πλεῖοι, *pleion*, here describing Scylla's teeth, suggests a sense of fullness like the wind in ship's sails, because of its etymological links to Pleione and the sailing Pleiades. But it's also used elsewhere in Greek by Sophocles to signify a rag filled with infection. That doesn't sound very sexy. These malevolent sea-women in the ancient myths were nothing like the tempting seductresses that subsequent artists have tried to sanitise them into being. They were female, and they were mothers, and they were able to bring men to their doom through pure overpowering violence. These sea-women are the ultimate animals to be feared, and Beowulf and Odysseus only narrowly escape them.

A FISH IN THE SHAPE OF A MAN

ST BRENDAN THE NAVIGATOR WAS a sixth-century monk, and Ireland's answer to Odysseus. Of all of his saintly adventures and exploits, the best known are his extensive voyages in search of paradise on earth, an entrance to the Garden of Eden. It was a journey that took him seven years and saw him travel across the seas meeting with many strange and fantastical encounters. His story belongs to the collection of mythological Christian Irish folk tales of voyage, the *Immrama*, all concerning stories of adventurous speculative trips to the far west of Ireland in search of a land of promise and plenty, Christian fulfilment, a land of other gods and fairies, or, in some cases, eternal youth.

The story is told in different forms across many different medieval manuscripts, but the core details remain relatively consistent, and are contained most definitively in the ninth-century Latin text *Navigatio Sancti Brendani Abatis*. St Brendan selected a band of fourteen followers to join him on his holy quest. They fasted for forty days and nights, and then set forth in a boat made of animal hides tanned with oak bark and sealed with fat, and headed towards the setting sun.

In one event on his travels, St Brendan anchors his boat on an island, disembarks and celebrates Easter. He and his crew light a campfire, and it's only then they discover that the land on which they are standing is not in fact land at all, but the back of a colossal fish named Jasconius. Such a sea creature, mistaken for an island, is found in other medieval stories too, where it's more generally known as the aspidochelone. It's sometimes described as a fish, sometimes a whale or a turtle, and sometimes as having mountains, valleys and vegetation formed on its enormous back. It appears in Old English as the Fastitocalon, the subject of the poem fragment 'The Whale' found in the Old English poetic version of the Ancient Greek *Physiologus* text. The tenth-century Anglo-Saxon bestiary from the *Exeter Book* describes it, as well as a panther and a partridge, but the whale is the most other-worldly of the trio, and the one with mystical powers. Together the three creatures represent water, earth and air, and fish, beast and bird.

The whale in 'The Whale' is devilish. He schemes and tricks the travellers deliberately to make camp on his skin, so that he can drag them under the water and devour them. He is an allegory for Satan on the hunt for sinners. The same is true in the Irish story of St Brendan, who must, in the stories of his voyage, prove himself to be perfect and holy before he will be able to reach his destination. His journey is really a journey of the soul; he must resist and defeat the colossal whale, just as he must resist the temptations and machinations of the devil in order to reach paradise.

Whale-road, *hronrad*, is another of the many Old English names for the sea. It's the domain of the whale and the place of temptation, misery and the downfall of good men.

St Brendan isn't the only monk to meet a mythical water monster while in the midst of holy adventuring. St Columba is said to have encountered the Loch Ness Monster in the sixth century AD, around the same time that St Brendan was apparently sailing from island to island to the west. Columba Christianised much of Scotland as a missionary and founded the Iona monastery, and in 565 AD, there's a legend that one of the ways in which Columba won the respect of the pagan Picts in the Scottish Highlands was by overcoming a monster in Loch Ness, shortly after discovering a man that had been killed by the beast.

St Adomnán of Iona's *Life of Saint Columba*, written a century after Columba's death, records an event in which 'a certain water beast' was driven away by the power of Columba's prayers. He describes Columba on his travels coming to a point where he needed to cross the waters of the River Ness, when he came across some local people burying the body of a man who had been seized and savaged by a monster while swimming in the loch. Columba ordered one of his companions to swim into the loch and retrieve a boat moored there, but the presence of another swimmer aroused and angered the monster lurking on the bottom. The monster rose up, roared, and made for the man with its mouth gaping open, while Columba, his companions and the local Picts watched from the banks.

Columba, so Adomnán relates, chose that moment to let God intervene through him. He raised his hands and made the sign of the Cross in the air, saying, 'You will go no further. Do not touch the man; turn back speedily.' Immediately the beast recoiled in terror, turned away from the swimmer in the water, and fell back into the depths, never to harm another soul. This event was, apparently, significant enough to convince the local pagans that Christianity might have its advantages, including the power to vanquish monsters at will.

This is the first written record of there being a monster in the Ness waters, and has been taken by many believers in the monster across the centuries as proof of Nessie's existence. Why sightings of Nessie continue to persist into the twenty-first century, when Columba supposedly vanquished it so thoroughly back in the sixth, is a bit of a mystery.

In Richard Baker's 1670 *Chronicle of the Kings of England*, he records in passing another incident concerning a monk and a sea monster, during the reign of Henry II in 1180. In a passage entitled 'A Fish Taken in the Shape of a Man', immediately after recounting the effects of an earthquake that destroyed Chichester, Baker writes that:

This year also, near unto Orford in Suffolk, certain Fishers took on their Nets a Fish, having the shape of a man in all points, which Fish was kept by Bartholomew de Glandevile in the Castle of Orford six moneths and more; he spake not a word; all manner of meats he did gladly eat, but most greedily raw Fish, when he had pressed out the juyce; oftentimes he was brought to the Church, but never shewed any sign of adoration: at length, beeing not well looked to, he stole to the Sea, and never was seen after.

Baker moves quickly on to describing a fire in the town of Beverley eight years later, and then the discovery of the bones of King Arthur under an oak tree. As bad luck would have it, as soon as the finder touched the bones, they turned into powder and disappeared. Baker's attempts towards historical accuracy are not necessarily reliable.

But this episode shows us that monks in the middle of the first millennium AD and even into the second were interested in over-powering sea monsters as proof of their holy credentials. As Christianity was just beginning to spread through Britain and northern Europe, the maps and the legends of the missionary monks all tell the same story: that the sea was the fringe of the good, safe, ordered and dependable Christian world, and monsters lurked on the fringes. The sea was alive with creatures beyond human imagining, and God's unearthly power alone could send them back down to the deep. If you were scared of what was lurking in the unseen depths of the waters, faith was the answer.

A BITTER DRINK

Merveille est k'om la mer ne het
Qui si amer mal en mer set,
E qui l'anguisse est si amere!

It's a marvel that man doesn't hate the sea
When he knows such bitter evil is at sea,
And that its sorrow is so bitter!
Tristan de Thomas

AWAY FROM LAND, THE SMELL of salt thickens the silence of the ocean air. I once joined my friend Jack on a short fishing expedition. 'Isn't it strange,' I said, 'that when you're out at sea, the smell of salt gives you a real craving for fish and chips when you get back to land?'

'Yes, it's strange,' said Jack. 'If you spent a day in an abattoir, you wouldn't go home craving a burger.'

I suppose he was right that the sea is full of death. Life on the open sea can be bitter and dangerous, a place where evil might appear at any moment. For most of recorded history, certainly up until the Renaissance, it has been men who have gone to sea. Female sailors have become more common since the middle of the twentieth century, and in the days of whaleships the captain's wife was sometimes aboard for long voyages, but for hundreds of years life on the ocean was primarily a man's world. The further back into history you look, the more you encounter stories of men rowing and sailing towards the horizon in search of adventure and greater prosperity. Women of the sea were, instead, women of the shore, relying on husbands and fathers who fished and travelled for their incomes, with one storm having the ability to devastate a whole community.

One of the exceptions to the rule in ancient history is Hatshepsut, the most well-known female ruler of Egypt after Cleopatra, who came to power in 1478 BC. She oversaw a great deal of significant building projects that lasted long after her death and showed that her reign was a prosperous time. Around nine or ten years after she ascended the throne, she had possibly her greatest accomplishment as ruler, and in launching her own lavishly equipped expedition, she established a 1,000-mile sea trade route to the 'Land of Punt' (which is likely to be the coast of modern-day Somalia, Ethiopia and Eritrea). It took six months to reach it by water. More than her predecessors, Hatshepsut saw the benefits of expanding the world and finding new ways to trade ebony, gold, myrrh and precious animals.

Her temple at Deir el-Bahri has carved on its walls images of the five ships she took with her to Punt, one of the earliest pieces of wall art showing a nautical trip in the world. The engraving also describes the rich variety and luxury of the goods that Hatshepsut's mission brought to Egypt:

The loading of the ships very heavily with marvels of the country of Punt; all goodly fragrant woods of God's Land, heaps of myrrh-resin, with fresh myrrh trees, with ebony and pure ivory, with green gold of Emu, with cinnamon wood, Khesyt wood, with Ihmut-incense, sonter-incense, eye cosmetic, with apes, monkeys, dogs, and with skins of the southern panther. Never was brought the like of this for any king who has been since the beginning.

Hatshepsut's reign should have been one of Egypt's most glorious. And yet, for reasons largely unknown, details of her time in history and even her name were erased from Egyptian monuments after her death. It's possible that a female pharaoh, even a stable and successful one, was seen by those who followed her reign as too dangerous and unconventional to celebrate, or even to record. A woman out of place, in a landscape of men, is not someone to be revered, even if she had conquered the sea.

Non-royal women in the ancient world right through to the medieval period who lived near the European coasts did not tend to earn their living from going to sea; they weren't employed as shipwrights, and they weren't sailors. In later centuries, more women would become passengers on long sea voyages as routes to the New World opened up, and some women would even disguise themselves as men to run away to sea and work on board ships. But medieval women instead were restricted to roles in stories and legends, and to more prosaic work on the cliffs and beaches with the water never coming up further than their waists, as they laboured in the hard knuckle-shredding work done by fishwives to prepare the fishermen's catch for sale. For men, encountering women at sea was an event laced with dread or wonder. For the women themselves, magical or not, the sea was an even more ambiguous and dangerous place.

Women of the coasts have lost their husbands – and so their entire livelihoods – to the sea throughout history. Men went away on voyages to seek their fortunes, or just for a few nights' fishing in a storm, and were never seen nor heard of again. Women are rare in historical accounts of seagoing, and in many traditions it has long been considered bad luck to have a woman on board a ship. The reasons for men leaving women behind on sea voyages, except when they were needed as passengers on trips to colonise new lands (the Viking conquests of Britain and Scandinavia, for instance, and then, hundreds of years later, colonial ventures from Britain to America and Australia), were not purely superstitious. Going to sea before the age of steam and mechanisation, before decent weatherproofing and shelter on deck, and even before hammocks – only adopted for sleeping by European crews around the end of the fifteenth century – meant that anyone on board ship had to be fit and strong. Women often weren't considered strong enough to survive.

And when there are no women aboard ship, the sight of a woman in the sea – so out of place, so inexplicable, surviving against the odds – is thrilling and suspicious. Sea-women appear in sea legend and literature in some places as aggressive, like Scylla and Grendel's mother, and in others representing forces of trickery and wiliness more than pure aggression. Morgan le Fay, the witch of Arthurian legend, was said to have conjured mirages of fairy castles in the sea around coastlines to confuse sailors and lure them to their deaths. Mermaids are known for tricking men at sea to drag them underwater and drown them.

Mythical sea-women wreak their tricks and violence in different ways, but their most horrifying, unthinkable, chilling quality of all is something that they have in common: they're cleverer than the men. Mythical sea-women almost always have an understanding of the sea that transcends the knowledge of even the hardiest and most experienced male sailors.

Mermaids in particular are versions of women that play on old misogynist fears of women controlling men and leading them to their doom: mermaids are communities of women living without men; they are powerful athletes with sinuous strength, strong swimmers and accomplished divers; and they have the power to affect men's consciousness, singing them into deep sleep and removing all of their agency and power. Out on the water, they can be blamed for all sorts of male failings. Maybe Eve was a mermaid after all.

The supernatural omniscience of magical mythical sea-women is one possible explanation for ships being referred to as female and being given female names: ships are vessels like women are vessels, and they might possess a greater knowledge than man of how the sea operates.

In the *Odyssey*, the sea witch Kalypso captures Odysseus and keeps him prisoner as her sex slave, weaving on her loom and enchanting him with her song. Eventually she agrees to set him free with goods to aid him on his journey, though only after he has been at her mercy for seven years. The other enchantress who ensnares him, Circe, and turns his men into pigs, warns Odysseus about still more malevolent women of the sea, specifically the power of the Sirens' song:

> There is no homecoming for the man who draws near them unawares and hears the Sirens' voices; no welcome from his wife, no little children brightening at their father's return. For with their high clear song the Sirens bewitch him, as they sit there in a meadow piled high with the mouldering skeletons of men, whose withered skin still hangs upon their bones.

She tells Odysseus to command his men to stop up their ears with wax to protect them from the Sirens' song, and for Odysseus – if he wants to hear their song for himself – to lash himself to the mast, and to tell his men in advance that if the Sirens' singing causes him to beg his men to untie him, they should only bind him more tightly to prevent his escape.

When Odysseus does meet the Sirens, he has only just finished giving his men the instructions from Circe when the water becomes very calm. He cuts up a wheel of wax with his sword and softens it between his hands to plug the ears of his men, and then he is bound to the mast. Odysseus hears the Sirens' song as they call to him:

> No seaman ever sailed his black ship past this spot without listening to the honey-sweet tones that flow from our lips and no one who has listened has not been delighted and gone on his way a wiser man.

The women Odysseus encounters at sea know better than he does how to survive it. They give him advice. The goddess Athena guides his whole journey, and the journey of his son Telemachus to find out what happened to him in the hope of saving his mother from the predatory suitors who wish to marry her and take Odysseus's treasure. Mortal women do not spend time at sea, but the immortal, magical ones talk as if they own the place.

·

All of this writing and legend-making of mysterious sea-women that has lasted through history is told from the men's point of view. There aren't many first-person female accounts of life in connection with the sea.

One of the great voiceless presences of women in Shakespeare is Sycorax, the sea-witch mother of Caliban in *The Tempest*, who was banished to the island for her powers when she was pregnant and, once there, controlled the island's magical population and imprisoned the fairy Ariel. All we hear of her in the story is from Prospero's point of view. He describes Caliban:

> This mis-shapen knave,
> His mother was a witch, and one so strong
> That could control the moon, make flows and ebbs,
> And deal in her command without her power.

She's unseen in the play, which makes her magical powers seem even more mysterious than those of Prospero, who is a significant part of the stage action. We don't hear her tell her own story, and instead only hear about her horrifying magical abilities through her male foes, Ariel and Prospero.

Strange things happen when men tell stories about magical sea-women. Even though Homer's account of the Sirens has them as indistinct figures, describing them as female and horrifying but not specifying much beyond that, over the centuries they have suffered the same sanitised fate as Grendel's mother and Scylla, and we have come to imagine them as beautiful temptresses who are irresistible in body as well as in song. Herbert Draper's painting *Ulysses and the Sirens* (1909) shows the conflation between mermaid and Siren in the evolution of our mythology of magical women at sea.

In Draper's work, where the Greek Odysseus has become the Latinate Ulysses, the Sirens get much closer to Ulysses than they ever get to Odysseus in Homer. Ulysses is shown bound to the mast, eyeballs bulging, chest straining forwards towards the beautiful, naked and long-haired Sirens, his restraints having to be pulled even tighter to keep him back from reaching out to them. His crew are rowing with their ears blocked while the sea-women climb on board, hanging from the ropes and growing legs where glistening mermaid tails had been when they were in the water. The wind is whipping up choppy seas under a blank sky. The three Sirens – one blonde, one brunette and one red-headed – have woven little coronets of shells into their hair, like the capricious mermaid in Tennyson's poem, whose ringlets fall 'Low adown, low adown, / From under my starry sea-bud crown'.

They are overwhelmingly sexual and predatory, their skin so white that it almost glows. It's a scene of sexual fantasy, these women so beautiful that men have to be tied back from joining them, a fate which would spell their doom. These aren't women of outright violence, but they are women of beauty and supernatural power, which is – judging by the looks on the faces of the men in the painting – much more frightening.

•

Draper's other paintings are also full of seductive maidens curving their naked bodies knowingly in fantastical settings, many of them relating to myths of the sea. *A Water Baby* (1900) shows a woman opening up a giant, silky white oyster shell to reveal a tiny human infant inside. *Ulysses and the Sirens* is a companion piece to Draper's *The Sea Maiden* of 1894, where instead of nymphs clambering aboard a boat to torment the crew inside it sexually, a group of fishermen is shown dragging aboard a net in which is caught a young woman with golden hair and red lips, arching her back in an attempt to get away from them. The atmosphere is full of the threat of male violence. This is an image that recalls the darkest truth of the folk legend of 'The Maid on the Shore' song, where rape and male physical dominance are what awaited the maiden when she was hauled on board the boat.

Specifically, *The Sea Maiden* is inspired by an extract from Algernon Charles Swinburne's *Chastelard*, from 1866:

Have you read never in French books the song
Called the Duke's Song, some boy made ages back,
A song of drag-nets hauled across thwart seas
And plucked up with rent sides, and caught therein
A strange-haired woman with sad singing lips,
Cold in the cheek like any stray of sea,
And sweet to touch? so that men seeing her face,
And how she sighed out little Ahs of pain
And soft cries sobbing sideways from her mouth,
Fell in hot love, and having lain with her
Died soon? one time I could have told it through:
Now I have kissed the sea-witch on her eyes
And my lips ache with it; but I shall sleep
Full soon, and a good space of sleep.

Even this woman, found at sea seeming so helpless and afraid and
brought on board a boat, spells danger for the sailors. She doesn't
seek them out in order to torment them, and in fact she is
tormented and tortured herself by the men who capture her. And
yet, after these violent men rape her, feeling themselves so much
more powerful than her and revelling in destroying her softness
and sweetness, the sailors are the ones who die. Like the Maid on
the Shore, she manages to outwit the men in the end with her
own magical abilities that the men underestimated or couldn't
foresee: *She sang charming and sweet, she sang neat and complete, she
sang sailors and captain to sleep sleep sleep.* A woman who makes her
home in the waves is not to be trusted, is the paternalistic message
ringing out clearly from both Swinburne and Draper. Still, you

might just as easily say that the message to women at sea from folk legends and art should be, 'Don't trust sailors with drag-nets.'

•

The sea is home to magical women, and yet there is also an old superstition that witches can't cross water, or somehow find their powers overwhelmed by the superior supernatural power of the sea. Whenever you eat a boiled egg, you should poke a hole in the bottom of the shell when you're finished so that the witches can't use it as a boat, goes the superstition. The surest way for a medieval court to determine whether or not a woman was a witch was to dip her in water and see if she floated.

Women who knew anything about water, or displayed any unconventional relationship with it, were undoubtedly magical beings. In the ancient mind, there was a clear link between women's suspicious affinity with the sea and the ebb and flow of the tides, rhythmic yet chaotic and uncontrollable, in step with the moon. Men were creatures of the sun and earth, sure-footed and predictable, while women were shifting and mutable, profoundly and essentially in touch with the ever-moving water, moon and stars.

Franz Kafka gives a horror-movie twist to the legend of the Sirens. In his 1931 short story about the myth of Odysseus/Ulysses, 'The Silence of the Sirens', he writes that the Sirens have an even more fatal weapon than their song, which Odysseus, after all, managed to escape. The truly inescapable horror of the Sirens is the moment they stop singing. Someone might have escaped from their singing, Kafka said, but from their silence, certainly never. It's only when you realise the sea-song has ended, and the Sirens are quiet, that you know you're in trouble. That's when they grab you, eat you or drown you. The sounds and songs of the sea might have a dark dimension to them, but silence is worse.

FAIR MAID'S TRESSES

I DIDN'T EXPECT PREGNANCY TO BE an experience so infused with the fear of death right from the very start. Nothing reminds me of death as much as new life does. Every beginning suggests an ending.

There is a legend in the west coast of Scotland about two sisters who lived on an island. One of the sisters was very fair, and one of them very dark, and both were beautiful. Their father was a fisherman who had been lost during a storm, and they were brought up by their mother.

When the girls were teenagers, they both fell in love with the same local boy who also worked as a fisherman. The fisherman spent lots of time away at sea, but when he came to shore, he made it clear that he was madly in love with the fair-haired daughter. And she loved him too, even though her dark-haired younger sister was obsessed with him. He was a good-looking lad. And though he was always kind to the younger girl, he paid much more attention to the older sister, which, of course, made the younger one jealous.

Until one summer day, when the dark-haired sister picked her way along the stony beach, which was wreathed in tendrils of delicious edible seaweed, towards a house. There lived a wise old woman who was a herbalist (though some of the children whispered to one another that she was a witch, as children in small villages tend to do).

'I want you to teach me a song,' said the girl.

'What kind of song?' said the old woman.

'A song that will enchant whoever hears it, and make them fall asleep,' said the girl. So the old woman taught her an old Gaelic song, which she practised until she knew it by heart.

One day the girl asked her fair older sister to walk with her down on the seaweed-strewn beach. Her older sister was thrilled that the younger wanted to be friends again, and they went down to the rocks together, where the tide was out. They sat down on a rock, and the younger one took out a brush and began to comb it through her big sister's hair. And as she brushed her sister's shining blonde hair, she sang the song she had learned. Soon the older sister's eyes began to close, and she fell fast asleep.

The younger one started to weave her older sister's hair into intricately patterned plaits and braids. As she worked, the braids became more and more ornate, all twisting and knotting into one another. She began to weave the hair into the seaweed on the rocks.

The tide began to turn, and then to wash slowly in. The younger girl waited until all of her sister's hair was woven into the seaweed, and the tide was lapping around her ankles. And then she ran up on to the cliffs and watched as the warm summer sea swirled around her sister's sleeping body.

Just as water was about to close over her sister's unconscious nose and mouth, she saw a grey shape moving quickly through the sea to the shore.

It was a seal. When it reached the place where the sister, who was by this point completely submerged, had been, the seal dived under the surface. And then – the younger sister couldn't believe her eyes at this – *two* seals bobbed their heads up from the water. For a moment, both seals looked at the girl standing open-mouthed on the cliffs. She tried to speak, but couldn't. The seals turned, and swam out to sea together. And the girl – as girls at the end of folk tales tend to do – threw herself off the cliff.

As she fell, the wind caught her woollen cape, and lifted her up. And as she floated in the sky she became a cormorant, the ugliest bird of the sea, whose cry sounds like someone saying, 'I'm sorry, I'm sorry, I'm sorry!'

The two seals were long gone. To this day, you can hear the cormorant saying sorry to the seals, and whenever it gets too close you can see the seals snapping at the cormorant to keep it away. And the delicious seaweed on the beach is never eaten any more by the locals who live on the island. They call it fair maid's tresses.

The oldest stories of the sea involve songs and sounds, and the magical power that comes from combining the sea with human music. From Scottish legends to Biblical psalms, we've always understood the sea by singing about it. The legends also warn us of the power and danger of music when it comes to the sea. The song the younger daughter sings in the story enchants her sister, but it's overpowered by the far greater enchantment of the persistent Scottish sea-myth of magic: selkies who can turn into seals and live their lives half in water, and half on land, whose existence takes the shape of above and below, this life and the next. Their disappearance into the water is the end of one life, and the beginning of a new one.

SEA GLASS

WALKING ON THE BEACH ONE evening at dusk during that first holiday on Skye, carrying with me a small metal torch against the gloom, I noticed glints among the stones. Here and there were sparkles and flashes that I first assumed to be fragments of plastic, or just tiny rockpools catching the light.

On closer inspection at one flash, though, I realised it was something different, something with a definition somewhere in between a shell and rubbish. It was a fragment of glass, which must have been in the water a long while, worn smooth and soft like an old pebble by the sea, and not broken. It was roughly triangular, and a bluey-green colour that seemed to suggest the colour of the sea itself. It looked like a jewel.

From then on, collecting sea glass became a habit. I once read an article that suggested obsessive collection of sea shells and sea glass in children was a potential marker for neurological conditions. I can't assess my own brain, but I know that hunting for sea glass and shells feels like hunting for treasure, and anyone who isn't obsessive about it probably just hasn't tried it.

Chunks of sea glass are as glowing and ethereal as precious stones, and they are also worthless. As we fill up the oceans with discarded plastic that will never degrade, glass fills up the oceans, too, but in a different way: it rubs up along with the rocks and pebbles that are worn down by the restless movement of the currents and is reduced down almost to nothing. Glass is made from sand, and the sea does its best to get it back.

The most beautiful sea glass, the kind that looks the most other-worldly and worn, frosted long past transparency, stippled by salt water, and become rounded and tactile and luminous, its sharp edges just a distant memory, might be centuries old. It takes a long time to wear down. And so, if you find a fully rounded and softened piece of sea glass on a beach, it might have begun its life at sea as part of a gin bottle on an eighteenth-century ship of the line or a Victorian clipper, long-wrecked and lying on the ocean floor, its cargo splintering and softening with water and time. You can never really know for sure how it began. Pieces of sea glass are souvenirs of history, and people who go looking for them are a bit like metal detectorists, sharing the same desire to connect with the past, and a love of the idea of hunting for treasure. The difference is that metal detectorists may actually find real treasure, the kind with a cash value and a place waiting in a glass cabinet at a national museum. Sea glass hunters find something that will only ever be treasured by them, and them alone.

It's precious because of the stories it suggests to us, and the act of keeping and collecting it is the act of keeping and collecting imagined stories, though the full truth of them is lost to time. When my grandmother died she left behind her collection of recipes in dozens of notecards kept in an old tin box. The recipes on them are all written in her slapdash handwriting and called things like 'Chocolate mousse (Shirley's friend)'; 'Eggs in Aspic (Mrs Hunt's)'; 'Mrs Bevan's Starter for 6' and 'Lady Glock's Apple Cake'. I don't recognise any of these women's names or know how close they ever were to my grandmother. And yet at some point these recipes were gathered from all of these people and meticulously copied down and filed away. Other recipes have their own evocative names: 'Cut and Come Again Cake'; 'Apple tart with a difference!'; 'Three generation chocolate cake'.

Now that she has gone I can never find out the full stories behind the recipes. The recipes themselves are the only things left behind of past conversations and relationships. They seem important in themselves: artefacts with the remnants of stories attached to them, and you need imagination to fill in the rest.

•

Each piece of sea glass is unique, though like the glass bottles they come from, they tend to be green, or blue, brown or colourless. Other colours, such as orange or black, are highly prized by collectors. Transparent shards of glass eventually become white, almost completely opaque and moon-like from being buffed over decades. Pieces of sea glass absorb and diffuse the light, growing a warmth and gentleness. They are softened by the waves, and also hardened by them. You'll have a difficult time trying to break a sea glass nugget apart. This glass has been through too much to shatter now. Sometimes chunks of ceramic are also to be found on beaches having undergone a similar process to the glass, rounded at the edges, and these are beautiful too, sometimes showing snatches of patterns long since lost in their complete form. Because the same thing has happened to these artefacts that has happened to rocks, and shells, and small bits of coral and starfish and bone, they start to look just as organic as rocks and shells, too, and they become lost among them on shingly beaches. The natural and the man-made are the same as one another.

The best kind of beach for hunting sea glass is the rockiest, most uneven beach you can find. If there's a wrack line, a line of seaweed, driftwood and debris cast off by the sea at high tide, so much the better. Here you're most likely to find crab shells, feathers, plastic, bits of rope and other rubbish – and, hidden among it all, tiny ingots of sea glass. Little stars of beauty in the most dangerous of places, in amongst the rocks where ships are wrecked.

It's usually after a storm that you can find the biggest bounty of flotsam and jetsam on the beach, and this is also the best time to hunt for sea glass. Committed hunters can easily develop an obsession with the hobby that borders on dangerous compulsion. One sea glass handbook I read suggests, semi-seriously, that sea glass hunters, when setting out to search beaches in a new place, should not tell any of the locals what they are up to, and should even pretend they have no idea what sea glass is, to put others off the hunt. Most of the joy is in the discovery, anyway, and the excuse to walk on the beach.

The invention and surge of plastic use in the twentieth century means that future generations might not have as much luck hunting for sea glass as we do. It's hard to know what the oceans will eventually do to plastic over the centuries, though the huge amounts of plastic debris we cast into the sea every day won't ever completely disappear. One benefit of storing drinks and food in glass containers, the way we used to do, would be an increase in the number of sea glass jewels that might eventually wash up on beaches around the world.

And that would tell its own tale. Sea glass is proof that humans put themselves into the sea and were shaped by it. To pick up a piece of sea glass or sea crockery is to know the sea is a place of death and endings, stories and imagination.

III

KELAINO

Kelaino's name means darkness. In various myths she is a woman not to be trusted. She is loved by Poseidon and tied to the sea. As a star, she is only half as bright as Taygete, but can still be seen by the naked eye. A velvety brown moth commonly found in Britain and Europe, Haworth's Minor, is named after her: Celaena haworthii.

THE SEA CLAIMS THE DEAD

SOMEWHERE ON A BEACH ON the Isle of Arran more than a century ago, as the day dies away, a burial is taking place. A group of men – three or four – stand around the freshly dug hole. It's too small for the grave of an adult, too small perhaps even for a child. A little pile of freshly dug sand and earth lies nearby. The men have taken off their hats. They drop something into the hole, and share a moment, maybe just a few seconds, of silence. This done, one of them picks up the spade he had let fall to his side, and begins to fill the hole up with sand. And then the men turn their backs to the sea. They walk towards the grassy dunes, heading inland, and are gone.

·

Much further south of here, the landscape around the village of Brean in Somerset is well furnished with sandy beaches and caravan parks for visitors. The shore is sunny, welcoming, the area around it popular with tourists, and the village does a roaring trade in the local ciders and cheese. Still, no coastal tourist resort can escape a complicated history with the sea. As a local folk song – 'The Brean Lament', recorded by twentieth-century folk-lorist Ruth Tongue – relates, the locals traditionally had a particular way of dealing with the bodies of those souls who found them-selves washed up on the shore, with nothing to identify them.

> The waters they washed 'en ashore, ashore,
> And they never will sail the seas no more.
> We laid 'en along by the churchyard wall
> And all in a row we buried them all.
> But their boots we buried below the tide
> On Severn Side.

The dead were buried not within the consecrated ground of the churchyard itself, even though they were sometimes given Christian funerals in the church. Instead they were laid to rest in the Sailors' Graveyard down by the sea, carefully positioned just above the tideline. The superstition of the local community was that one day the sea might rise up and reclaim the bodies of the souls it had taken, in envy that they had been stolen from the water and buried in the earth. To appease the sea, and to prevent it from also taking back the bodies of non-sailors buried in the church graveyard when the tide rose in anger, the drowned dead had to be kept separate from those who had died on land. And a further precaution was taken, too: in the hope that the sea might be appeased enough to resist rising at all, and swallowing the coastal villages whole in search of its robbed corpses, the villagers buried the sailors' boots below the tideline, within easy and regular reach of the water, so the sea would be able to keep a memento of the dead – without stealing back the bodies themselves.

'The Brean Lament' tells us for sure that this practice was done in Somerset, though we know that it was done elsewhere in the British Isles too, and there are boots underground between the high and low tidelines around the country's edges from south to north.

•

In Scotland a murder in the hills, linked to the superstitions of the coast, remains not fully solved. Some of the crime's secrets are still known only to the sea and the dead.

In 1889, the Isle of Arran near the west coast of Scotland was becoming a popular holiday destination for outdoorsy Victorians, who enjoyed its combination of rugged hill-walking and lively local places to eat and drink. It soon got a reputation for something more than just fresh air, however, and the Victorians loved a scandal. In August of that year, a gruesome discovery was made in a howff, a shelter near the peak of Goatfell, the island's 2,866ft mountain. The severely damaged body of a thirty-two-year-old builder's clerk from Brixton, a man named Edwin Robert Rose, was found crammed under forty-two rocks and covered with turf at Corr-na-Fourin in Glen Sannox, close to a difficult route down from the highest point of Goatfell. His spine was broken and his skull smashed in. Rose had been missing for some weeks, and search parties numbering in the hundreds had been attempting to find him. The man who had been Rose's walking companion on a trip to Goatfell a few weeks earlier, on 15 July, one John Laurie, was nowhere to be found.

Quickly the story of Rose's mysterious death became a sensation across the country, largely thanks to the perceived spooky remoteness of the location and a general Victorian appetite for grisly murder, kept stoked by vivid reports circulated in the papers. Laurie remained missing, and it almost immediately became clear that he was on the run from the police. It emerged he had recently paid off all of the outstanding rent due to his landlady and resigned from his job as a patternmaker, also selling all of his tools. Laurie had been travelling under the false name of Annandale, checking himself into lodgings under this name, and had even gone to the trouble of having fake calling cards printed.

He didn't keep a low profile though. He seemed to have an urgent need to explain himself even while evading capture, and wrote letters to the *Daily Mail* and the *Glasgow Herald* while in hiding, insisting on his innocence and telling a rambling tale of botched robbery on the mountain involving unnamed third parties. One letter was postmarked Liverpool; the other, Aberdeen.

The two companions had met only very recently while travelling before Rose was found dead, though their friendship had developed quickly. They lodged together at a hotel in Rothesay and took the Arran ferry in each other's company before making for the relatively straightforward climb up Goatfell together. These are the last verifiable facts, bolstered by witnesses, that are known before Rose's body was found.

In September that year, Laurie was finally spotted by police, alive, in the town of Hamilton. After being chased into woodland by police with the assistance of some local miners, Laurie tried unsuccessfully to cut his own throat with a razor while eventually being apprehended, still claiming innocence: he admitted that he had robbed Rose, but insisted that he hadn't killed him. His trial at the High Court in Edinburgh would continue to attract the enormous press attention already ignited by Rose's disappearance and the discovery of his remains. Crowds gathered in the streets outside the courtroom to hear fresh pieces of news from the trial.

Several medical experts were called to give evidence. They contradicted one another on the manner of Rose's death. The jury were asked at length to consider whether Rose had definitely been murdered, or whether he might instead have died accidentally as the result of a fall part of the way down Goatfell's steep descent, as Laurie was now frantically attesting. The Arran-based witnesses were interviewed first, all together, probably so they would have time to catch the ferry home across the Firth of Clyde in the afternoon.

Eighty-six witnesses were called in total by the Crown to give evidence at Laurie's trial. A public frenzy was whipped up around the case, with mass public discussion over whether or not Laurie was guilty of murder, and queues outside the courthouse every day of people waiting to fill the public gallery. The *Scotsman* newspaper described Laurie's appearance at the trial as 'square-shouldered but slightly built, and [he] walks with a rolling gait. His teeth are a conspicuous part of him, and are remarkably white and regular. He is exceedingly fond of dress, and was often seen in knickerbockers.'

The jury deliberated for only forty-five minutes before a guilty verdict was returned, with a majority of one. Such was the public interest in the case that as soon as that night's edition of the *Glasgow Herald* was printed, police were called to the city centre to control the crowds crushing to buy copies at inflated prices.

•

Laurie was sentenced to death by hanging. His sentence was reduced on appeal on psychiatric grounds, and he lived out the substantial remaining years of his life in the lunatic section of Perth prison. He died in 1930 at the age of sixty-nine, still protesting his innocence.

There was an enormous amount of evidence presented on both sides, but the actual evidence that Laurie was guilty was purely circumstantial. Defence witnesses who had seen Rose and Laurie together on the mountain said that the pair had seemed on extremely friendly terms. Expert medical witnesses on both sides at first seemed sure of their opinions, but were all pressured to admit on cross-examination that the evidence could point in either one of two directions: Rose might have died because of maliciously inflicted trauma wounds, or he might equally plausibly have died as the result of a heavy fall. There was no clear motive for Laurie to murder him, other than the theft of Rose's belongings, which weren't worth much. No motive at all, in fact, for Laurie to inflict any harm whatsoever on his companion. The injuries sustained by Rose weren't obviously inflicted by any kind of battery. To add to the strangeness of the circumstances, the body was found in an inaccessible place on the mountain, not on one of the popular routes for ascent or descent – so it might, just possibly, have ended up there after Rose fell down from one of the more well-trodden routes.

And yet, Laurie's behaviour after Rose's death was manifestly suspicious. He was seen drinking alone in a bar in Brodick the night that Rose went missing, and then immediately left Arran and went on the run, well before the body was discovered. When he was found, he was in possession of some items belonging to Rose, including Rose's jacket, suggesting that he, at the very least, had known that Rose was dead. Laurie claimed that Rose had met two other men on Goatfell summit. He also maintained that Rose died in an accidental fall, which led Laurie to panic and rob Rose's corpse before concealing it thoroughly under a pile of rocks in the howff and fleeing. These could well be the actions taken by an unstable man, one who would inevitably end up in the care of a Victorian lunatic asylum.

•

Yet there were other mysteries about the death, too, that muddied the prosecution's case and fuelled the public's speculation about whether or not Laurie was guilty. There was the matter of the cap, for one.

Rose's cap was found in the gully where his body lay, but much higher up, folded neatly four times and placed under a stone. Had

Laurie placed it there calculatingly, intending to suggest it had become dislodged when Rose fell, as the prosecution claimed? And if so, why was it stored so neatly? Or had Rose put it there at some point for safekeeping before whatever events caused his death? Some of Rose's other possessions were found scattered nearby too, including his walking cane. Witnesses had seen the pair travelling up towards the peak, but nobody had seen them heading any of the way back down.

·

Importantly, there was a key piece of evidence missing from the trial, a piece of evidence whose absence continues to fuel theories about what actually happened to Rose. Rose's clothing, possessions and injuries were all subject to scrutiny by the prosecution and defence. One important prosecution expert witness, a Linlithgow doctor named Dr Andrew Gilmour who had been holidaying on Arran at the time, and had gone to inspect the body, stated that Rose's injuries could only have been inflicted by a heavy blunt weapon such as a rock. If he had fallen and struck his head accidentally, the state of his clothes and shoes might help to indicate how far he had fallen and in what position his body had landed.

But Rose's walking boots, the state of which might have told this story, were not there. When questioned in court about their absence, Sergeant William Munro of Arran's police was reluctant to say where the boots were and why they were not available for examination by the jury. Under questioning from the Lord Justice-Clerk, he finally admitted the truth. 'I believe they were buried,' he said. 'On the beach above the high-water mark.'

It turned out that the local police on Arran had prioritised superstition over evidence-gathering. In fact, one of Sergeant Munro's constables had buried the boots himself, in the presence of the chief constable, in what seemed to be an event fully sanctioned and overseen by the authorities. None of the police officers would admit to giving the order to bury the boots. But they had buried Rose's boots on the Arran beach. Even though the murder victim came from a faraway place with different customs and superstitions, the people of Arran had performed this sacrament so that the Londoner Edwin Robert Rose would be at peace, and not forever tormented by the tides and the hills attempting to tie his spirit to the earth.

When I come across this story in a newspaper archive, it's the matter-of-factness of the police officers' ritual that stays with me. There was no question in the reporting about whether it would have been the right thing for the police to do. For the police officers there was an acceptance that ritual in death was important and must be respected.

·

Rose's body's final resting place today is in the kirkyard at Glen Sannox, and is marked, in the kind of morbid irony the Victorians enjoyed, by a boulder, just like the ones that had concealed him up on the mountain. You can even spend a night in the same howff where Rose was found, if you're a hillwalker of particularly macabre persuasion. And the whereabouts of Rose's boots are still unknown, buried somewhere above the tideline, waiting for the sea to claim them.

A MIST MADRIGAL

A LL OF THESE THOUGHTS OF death, the fear and anxiety of pregnancy in its rabbit-in-a-hat half-state of unknown magic, existing and not existing, are suffocating. There's only one possible way I can imagine of feeling better, more open and positive, less weighed down by the burden of so many hypotheticals, and that is to go to the sea again. The city is too definite and finite a place now. Its buildings are drawn in lines too thick, all angles and corners, all dead ends and no haze, and even the skyline is a ceiling. I need water like a thirst. I need a sky that stretches on forever in an uncaring always, air and water that don't notice what my body is doing on land and will still be there long after I'm gone.

When the winter is over and the days start to lengthen I go away for a few days. I decide I'd like to see the Celtic carved stones at the museum in Whithorn on the west coast of Scotland, where they are held in an exhibition space built next to a replica Iron Age roundhouse. I spend three days on the Machars peninsula in Whithorn and Wigtown, the other side of the country from home, a thumb of land stuck out in the middle of lots of sea.

The museum of the Celtic stones is everything I'd hoped in a break from modern reality. The Iron Age roundhouse is comfortingly dark and enclosed, its air heavy with wood smoke as a fire burns in the central hearth, sending sparks up harmlessly towards the ceiling. The guides are dressed in woollen tunic approximations of authentic Iron Age dress – an effect only occasionally punctured by the crackle of a walkie-talkie message from the reception desk – and they answer any questions about rush floors and weaving.

The exhibition space is a contrast to the smoky old roundhouse. It's light and smells of fresh paint, with helpful information printed on the walls and a 'stamp your own Celtic design on to a bookmark' activity station in one corner. All around the walls are positioned large monument stones, collected from ancient sites around the area. Many of them have been found in a natural cave on the beach nearby, a site that had become a place of early Christian pilgrimage for centuries. The stones' edges are weather-beaten but on many of them the whorling designs of the crosses are still sharp.

One of them is given a more prominent position than the others. The Latinus Stone, discovered in 1891, has a story carved into it: a man and his four-year-old daughter had passed by, and a relative of theirs had made a note of their visit in the rock, like signing a lithographic guestbook in their honour. The ambiguous Latin inscription roughly translates as 'We praise you, Lord. Latinus, aged thirty-five, and his daughter, aged four, were here. Barrovadus, a relation, set up this monument.' The stone dates from around 450 AD, and it marks the first dateable evidence of a Christian presence this far north. I love the image of this man and his young daughter, making pilgrimage and taking refuge, and the little girl demanding that her presence on the trip is recorded too.

The exhibition is bright and clean, but the stones seem out of context here, pulled from the places they were supposed to be. One of the neat information signs, rendered in one of the unapologetic, bland, museum-notice typefaces of the glorified modern pillager, informs me that the stones were too precious to remain outside in the elements and so none were now left at a nearby sacred site called St Ninian's Cave, where most of them had originally been found.

In the time before St Ninian himself first arrived at Whithorn, the coasts to the west of Britain were vulnerable to raiders from the sea. In the early centuries of Christianity, monks brought their beliefs and their intent to set up missionary communities in boats from mainland Europe and from Ireland, up to Iceland and Scandinavia, and to the fringes of Scotland. In Whithorn they have settled on the date of 397 AD as the time that Ninian began ministering to Scotland. Ninian probably came to Scotland from Ireland about a hundred years before Columba built his monastery on Iona, the first missionary to attempt to spread Christianity among the heathen northern Pictish tribes. Bede's *Historia ecclesiastica gentis Anglorum* written in 731 AD mentions that a most reverend and holy 'Bishop Ninias' had already encouraged the southern Picts to forsake idolatry 'long before' Columba's time. (I remember Columba's face-off with the Loch Ness Monster, and wonder if Ninian faced any similar hazards.) For the first half of the first millennium AD, Scotland was cut off from the growing heartlands of early Christianity by the easily defended borderlands stretching in a line south from Carlisle to Berwick-upon-Tweed, and by the sea. The 'Northern Picts' in the Scottish Highlands were the hardest heathens to reach, being geographically obscured from the rest of the British Isles by 'steep and rugged mountains'.

·

The main part of the museum holds a café, gift shop and small audio-visual room, in which there is an opportunity to watch a ten-minute video history of the area and the intriguing St Ninian. Having paid for it as part of my ticket (there was no option to avoid doing so), I sit obediently in the darkened space and wait for the film to begin. It soon becomes clear that the film is mostly propaganda for the splendours of the region, and the pagan-busting achievements of St Ninian.

According to whoever had put together the film, and possibly the whole museum, before St Ninian arrived, Scotland had been a vicious, godless place, a place of darkness and terror, sorely in need of the firm hand and guiding light that only Christianity – and, along with it, a rigid new class hierarchy – could bring. Three cheers for St Ninian, according to this film, and down with the ancient Celtic culture that preceded him.

Where were the older rituals, the more ancient archaeological finds from the peninsula's shoreline, represented in the museum? Watching it now it's almost funny, this old-fashioned, Christianity-centric version of history presented as incontrovertible fact. It leaves out so much of the truth. I try not to catch the eyes of the museum assistants on the way out.

I leave the museum, nevertheless, wanting to see this place where St Ninian came ashore, to see his first impressions of Scotland, which to him was dark and unreligious and in need of rescuing, sorely wanting the touch of the divine. The old carved stones of the first Christian faithful may have been removed from where they were originally found to be brought to this museum, but maybe there is still something of the spiritual left in the place where they were first found. Maybe there is still some residue of whatever it was that made St Ninian stop, centuries ago, and think yes, here is where I can pause, and commune with God, and be nourished for my quest. Faith is what might keep me afloat in the weighty darkness and uncertainty of these weeks.

I make a plan. The next day I will wake up early, head out along the coast, and go and find St Ninian.

·

In the morning it rains hard. I decide to try to walk to the cave anyway as planned. I have tooled up against the weather: boots, raincoat, two pairs of socks, and a glint of determination that this rain and one pregnant body – thickening a little now, already feeling woozier and less certain of its steps – won't stop for anything. The dog, at least, is keen to get going. As I drive towards the little gravel car park that marks the starting point for the path down to the beach, a path which can only be navigated on foot, the rain seems to harden its resolve and lean in a little closer. This stout walk in the rain could only be more self-flagellatingly British, I think to myself, if I'd packed a couple of squashed ham sandwiches and a flask of over-brewed tea in the car boot. I'm beginning to wish I had.

Driving down the single-track road far into the fringe of the peninsula, we meet no other souls for almost all of the way, until the lights of one ghostly car start to shine blearily as they come towards us in the opposite direction. The rain is sheeting down so densely I don't see it until it's almost upon us, when it pulls rapidly into a nook on the wrong side of the road to let me pass, and then seems to vanish in the mist. Rain blurs the windows, spray throws itself up all around, and the tall arable fields wave silverly under the clouds either side, as if we are already at sea.

When we arrive at the car park, it's empty save for an honesty box asking £1 for parking. Large puddles spread across the mud, constantly speckling with still-braiding rain. I pull on all the waterproofs stashed in the boot, and let the delighted dog off the lead. I yank my hood as far down over my head as it will go. We set out along the path, the dog and I, and it soon turns into a wide farm track past fields, before winding down into muddy woods overhung with thickly leaved branches. This, when it comes, is a welcome development – the rain is falling even more heavily now, but it can't get to us quite so much down here.

The guide at the museum said that this is a very popular walk, being only a mile or so in each direction and picturesque all the way along, but the weather has apparently seen off most other tourists and we have the route to ourselves as we follow a stream towards the shore. The dog hurtles and spins through the under-growth, her tail bobbing like cotton above the murky grass, spotted here and there with the fringed blue baubles of sheep's-bit. The woodland is full of pale wood sorrel, sea aster and clumps of the first daisy-like sea mayweed of the year. Where the tree cover starts to thin, pointed clusters of sea lavender sprout from the sodden ground that's ridden now with rivulets flowing to the shoreline.

Soon the path widens out and the sky broadens above, the opening gap letting more water through, and the raindrops begin to crawl their way under my hood and down my neck. As the beach comes into sight, framed by long grass and scatters of candy-pink thrift, I can see that it must have been easy for the old pilgrims to find plenty of rocks to carve with crosses and symbols, making artefacts that would last for hundreds of years. The whole beach is built out of large, slippery boulders, and my feet slide over and down with every step. Instinctively my hand moves to cover my navel, and wonder if I am imagining it, or if my abdomen is already a little rounder than it was. I won't fall.

Under the thrash of the storm, the stones of the beach are coloured the vivid grey and orange of iron and rust, a vividly industrial kind of nature. Waves smash around in the distance. Slippery among the rocks are trails of dark red seaweed, edible pepper dulse that you can eat raw on the beach to taste the salt sea at its purest. In the rising dunes of boulders there is the end of the stream, pooling into the pebbles with a farewell burst of foam to mark its passing, presumably surfacing again closer to the tideline.

At first I can't see the cave, and am not sure of the direction to find it. The mist is closing in around, and the beach doesn't feel much like only a mile from the honesty-box car park. There's nobody else here but us. It's as if the beach is the shore of a lost island in the middle of a vast grey ocean, or the verge of a new world, or the edges of a video game where the programmer stopped coding the visual effects. It feels as though, if we went much further on, everything would fade to white and become impassable nothingness.

As I walk a little further along, though, a dark shape rises from the mist, framed by overhanging green and more steel-coloured crags. It's just when I've started to wonder what sort of cave I should be looking for that I realise I'm already looking right at it: a mousehole-like notch in the cliff face that looks small from this distance. The cave is set a little above the level of the beach. It doesn't look big enough to provide any real shelter from the elements.

Nonetheless I slide towards it, losing my footing every couple of steps, the rain coming down as strong as ever and the mist moving like smoke. Coming closer to the gap in the cliffside, I notice that the arrangement of the stones on the beach isn't so random as it was a few yards back, and now it looks as if their pilings up on the uneven shoreline are not in fact an accident of tide and time and weather. Some of the drifts of large boulders must have been placed there by strong waves, but on top of the piles delivered by nature there is something different about the composition of the scene. A more deliberate arrangement is detectable in the rocks, a shape that suggests the hand of a sculptor.

Perched on top of some of the biggest rocks are distinctive cairns of smaller stones. They reach, placed carefully on top of one another, one at a time, impossibly precariously upward in delicately balanced chains, looking for all the world as if they have been glued there. They stand like sentries guarding the cave's entrance. There's nothing human-made holding these stones together, just a trick of gravity and balance, held fast as tightly as small children hold hands. This act of balancing stones into cairns is becoming a trend visible on beaches all over the country. I worry about the scuttling beasties who make their lives among the shifting stones, and whose habitats are disturbed by clumsy human attempts at art. We damage the world in our eagerness to be remembered in it.

Most of the stones are blank iron grey or rust-coloured. Some of them have patterns formed on their surfaces, white lines as if drawn on in thin drips of Tippex, naturally made. The lines shine like veins, making the stones feel as live and sinewy as human muscle, glistening with a hard grey light. One of the largest stones on top of the cairns is a mingle of slate and orange in colour, slick-dark. It's about the size of a curled-up newborn, and its edges are smooth enough that they make you want to hold it between your hands to feel its weight and examine it close to your face.

Something stops me doing just that. Maybe it's the naturally occurring design on the front: two intersecting white lines, not made with any mortally manufactured paint, across its centre. It's a cross.

The cross-patterned stone is an accident of the beach, probably found by some previous visitor and lifted up from the rubble of rocks and seaweed washed clean twice a day by the incoming water, carried towards the cave, and perched delicately but securely on top of the other stones around it to mark the entrance to St Ninian's Cave. There's no typed sign to show me that we have reached our destination, but I know that we have, because the rock tells me. This must be the place.

•

The cave really is as small as it looked when I first saw it. At first I'm a little disappointed. Somehow I'd expected something grander, more Roman Catholic, something with opulent stalag-mites and stalactites hanging down like Stations of the Cross or sparkling Christmas decorations, or some ornate evidence of past divine glory. Ridiculous. This is Scotland, a country with its beauty cut by wind and glaciers, not Venice. Still, I'd at least expected enough space for a saint to light a fire and take his shelter. Later I learn that rockfall over the centuries has narrowed the cave down to a fraction of the size it was when Ninian knew it.

It's not even particularly sheltered. The opening is large, and the cave only goes back a few feet into the cliff. There's just enough space to keep out the wind and rain, but very little to help you conserve any warmth in the winter. The texture of the walls as you run your fingers over them is ragged with volcanic knots, worn away in places by long-dead hands, and sliced into and drawn on by previous pilgrims' pen-knives and biros. People write their names here, and prayer requests, and sneak little folded-up papers into the cracks. Some of the dates etched into the rock of centuries distant seem impossibly long ago, but their careful copperplate and serif-dipped writing does suggest they were written in an age gone by. It's a small place, heavy with relics.

When I turn my back on the cave's interior and its muted light, and look instead the way we came, out towards the beach, I get a sense of what St Ninian might have really found in this place. I feel alone, with a view of the whole world. The dog is tiptoeing through faraway rockpools. The beach is quiet, somehow, even though the sea and rain are roaring. To the left are managed path-ways, cared-for farmland, the car and the car park and the honesty box. To the right is the endless surging nothing, with the sea stretching out towards islands and horizons and who-knows-where. On the one hand domesticity. On the other hand the wild. And here I am, in between. Motherhood feels less like an ending in this place. It feels more like a series of possibilities, I am starting to think, as I try to work out if the shape that I can just make out in the distance is a ship.

I stay for about half an hour. I sing half a sea shanty to try out the cave's acoustics. It echoes just for a moment, and then the rocks drink up the sound. The rain is easing off a little now as the sea washes in. The beach curves round to the right to make a horizon of the sweeping coastline, lined by the low cliff under its fringe of green. The mist lifts and I can see more clearly the path that leads back towards the woods and farm beyond. The day is getting older, and warmer, and soon more people will be coming down that path to the beach and I'll no longer be alone. And surrounding the whole scene in a rough, tall triangle above my head are the walls and floor of the cave, with the stone cairn sentries in front of me. The sea and sky are a painting in a three-pointed frame. Father, Son and Holy Ghost.

TO WALK ON WATER

THE NEED FOR A VIEW of the sea is catching. My parents are moving to a new house, a whitewashed cottage right on the shoreline in the East Neuk of Fife close to where my mother was born. They tell me that the view from the upstairs windows makes you feel as if you could step over the sill and keep walking right across the North Sea, floating your feet on the crest of the waves. There's a small kirk in the village, too, they say, poised right on the cliff edge, and the congregants can worship to the sound of the waves on Sundays.

I make the journey up from the city to visit them. The landscape of the route, through Fife's flat fields with the sea opening out to the east, beyond clusters of higgledy-piggledy seaside villages with harbour-front cottages painted in pretty colours, all says that this is an area that was built for interacting with the sea. As the car winds into the village of St Monans, I decide to pay a visit to the kirk. I drive up the hill towards the cliff edge, the frothing sea on my left and yet more rain – or is it sea spray? – ploshing on to the windscreen.

It's just as they said. The kirk is perched right on the rocks, with the water lapping below and sea air swirling at the spire, and huddled in a small dip high on the grassy clifftop, as if sheltering there like a cormorant chick with its feathers puffed up against a chill wind. Leaving the car, and pausing to fill my lungs with a rush of the best sea air, alive and cool and wet, a shot of caffeine after the drive, I pick my way down through the steep green kirk-yard. The bodies have a sea view from their graves. I try not to think about what bones might be exposed, sticking out of the mud, if the sea were ever to wear the cliff edge away. Erosion is a problem on this coast, and there are sea walls built to hold back the inevitable all along the East Neuk.

The kirk door is thick and heavy, to keep out the seaside storms, but – unlike any other church door I've seen before – it also has a little glass porthole in it, looking for all the world as if it might have originally been found in the hull of a boat, and been plucked out to make the kirk's first window. Once you step inside, you can see that every wall is painted bright seafoam white. Two wooden models of traditional Fife fishing boats are suspended from the ceiling.

There is a plaque on the wall bearing the village's motto, *Mare vivimus*: 'We live by the sea'. As well as *Mare vivimus*, there is an English phrase, *Grip fast*. I pick up a leaflet about the building's history from a box near the door. This is a kirk that claims to be the closest to the sea of any in Britain. Its motto is said to have been adopted by the town because of a local story of the time Queen Margaret passed nearby on her journey through Scotland in the eleventh century. The story goes that she fell from her horse into the water, and a St Monans man threw a rope to pull her out, shouting 'Grip fast!' And she was rescued.

I'm tired after the journey, unusually so, but this nook of a church is somehow nourishing. It feels like a more complete realisation of the solace and shelter that St Ninian found in his seaside cave on the west coast, based on the same idea that rocky coastlines are places closer to the divine.

A church by the sea is constantly in conversation with it. When bells were first introduced to churches in the first 1,000 years of Christianity in Britain, in seaside parishes they were rung during storms, to ask God to calm the waters. Perhaps, they thought, people's cries were hard to hear over howling winds, and bells are louder than prayers.

It's not uncommon for seaside churches to be built like boats and refer to the landscape of their parish. The porthole at St Monans gives it the atmosphere of a ship of souls. Some churches on the Suffolk coastline have shells embedded in their stony walls. The Roman Catholic church of Our Lady Star of the Sea and St Winefride in Amlwch, on the island of Anglesey, was built in the 1930s by an Italian architect to a maritime design. The reinforced concrete ceiling, smoothed and painted pure white, is in the exact bowed shape of an upturned boat's hull, with porthole windows to the outside and star-shaped window lights surrounding the figure of Christ behind the altar. Amlwch is a port town with a shipbuilding history. The church needs to be a part of the sea, just as much as its congregation.

Amlwch and St Monans are sea-themed churches in the extreme, though all churches, really, are connected with boats. The word 'nave', meaning the central part of any church, is from the Latin *navis*, meaning 'ship'. Britain is peppered with folk tales about 'ghost churches' submerged by high tides, whose bells can still miraculously be heard ringing from beneath the water.

And the sea is scattered across the land. When I first moved to Edinburgh I rented a flat in Leith, small and shabby and on the second floor overlooking a busy road, part of a nineteenth-century tenement a little way away from the docks of Leith shore. I could tell that the original owners of the flat had been connected to the sea because the old fireplace surround – the original fireplace itself having been long ago blocked up and stripped out – was embossed all around with crumbling plaster moulds of seashells. The church on that road, a little further along, is called St Mary, Star of the Sea. And everywhere in Leith, from the church onwards, you can see fragments of the sea and its importance. The Leith coat of arms was granted in 1889, back when Leith was still an independent town rather than an area absorbed into the north of Edinburgh. It's painted on to signs on buildings, moulded on lamp posts and leaded into stained-glass windows, showing the Virgin Mary and her child seated together inside a perfectly symmetrical ship, bobbing on the waves, with a cloud in between the furled sails above them. In a scroll below, the Leith motto is written: *Persevere*. It's a motto that the people of Leith take to heart. There is a pub called the Persevere, as well as a cab firm and a housing development project, and the name of the Proclaimers' fourth album. It means you have to keep the faith.

∙

The link between perseverance and the sea surges through early Christian writings, monuments, and throughout the Bible, from Christ's recruitment of fishermen to be his disciples, to his ability to walk on water. In sea shanties, melancholy sailors often wish for the same gift to let them walk straight home across the sea to see their missed loved ones. Cyril Tawney's 'The Grey Funnel Line' is one of the folk songs that refers to 'St Peter's shoes', imagining that Christ blessed the footwear of St Peter the day that he calmed the storm and summoned him to walk across the waves. The song calls his enchanted path across the sea as he walked across it a 'silver lane':

> Every time I gaze behind the screws
> Makes me long for old Peter's shoes.
> I'd walk right down that silver lane
> And take my love in my arms again.
> It's one more day on the Grey Funnel Line.

Tawney said on his own website that he started writing the song in 1953 at the age of twenty-two, though he'd already been in the Royal Navy (nicknamed by sailors the Grey Funnel Line) for seven years. He finished writing it in 1959, just before leaving the service. It's a mournful song full of references to older shanties and folk songs, with the line 'It's one more day on the Grey Funnel Line' inspired by the structure of the shanty 'Rock and roll me over for one more day'. It's a newish song with an old heritage, a traditional shanty of romance and of work, an elegy for the boredom and homesickness of life in the

Navy and a longing for divine intervention to get back to the shore.

•

The sea flows right through the story of Christ. *Come,* says Jesus, *follow me, and I will make you fishers of men.* It's later that Jesus's control over the sea in the Bible is given as proof of his divinity. Outnumbered by the multitudes in Matthew 14, Jesus sends his disciples away from the mainland in a ship, and meanwhile goes up to the mountain alone to pray. When the disciples come into difficulty on board due to unfavourable winds, *in the fourth watch of the night Jesus went unto them, walking on the sea* (Matthew 14:25). The disciples are scared to witness this miracle, and Peter asks if he can walk on the water too:

> And he said, Come. And when Peter was come down out of the ship, he walked on the water, to go to Jesus. But when he saw the wind boisterous, he was afraid; and beginning to sink, he cried, saying, Lord, save me. And immediately Jesus stretched forth his hand, and caught him, and said unto him, O thou of little faith, wherefore didst thou doubt? And when they were come into the ship, the wind ceased.
>
> Then they that were in the ship came and worshipped him, saying, Of a truth thou art the Son of God. (Matthew 14:28–33)

Mastery of the sea, and the ability to walk firmly on its soft surface, is proof enough for the disciples of God's existence and that Jesus is his son. The moment that Peter sees the wind's power and becomes afraid, he begins to sink: the only way to be held up firmly on the surface of the water is to keep an unwavering faith in God's ability to deliver you safely to the other side. You have to respect the power, and believe in the magic and the benevolence of the tides and winds and waves in order to be safe from them. Resisting the deathly power of the sea requires a trancelike state of faith. God is like a mermaid, like T. S. Eliot's sea-girls:

> We have lingered in the chambers of the sea
> By sea-girls wreathed with seaweed red and brown
> Till human voices wake us, and we drown.

Human voices are the spellbreakers that can bring us back to the doom of the sea. As long as we believe in miracles, we will be safe from drowning, but the moment the trance is interrupted, the sea can claim us with the full force of its murderous power.

The Bible is full of the sea. In the beginning, before there is anything else in Creation, there is water. *In the beginning God created the heaven and the earth. And the earth was without form, and void; and darkness was upon the face of the deep. And the Spirit of God moved upon the face of the waters.* The Red Sea parted for Moses. In the Bible swims the Leviathan, a great whale with impenetrable hide that can churn up the seas and swallow man up in one gulp if it wants:

> He maketh the deep to boil like a pot:
> he maketh the sea like a pot of ointment.

He maketh a path to shine after him;
one would think the deep to be hoary.
Upon earth there is not his like,
who is made without fear.
He beholdeth all high things;
he is a king over all the children of pride. (Job 41:31–4)

He is unknowable, uncatchable, unpredictable, and so vast and powerful that when he moves, all the oceans move too, displaced by his presence like Archimedes in a colossal bath. His power over the sea is like God's power over all things. His vast movements spread foam through the water, a visible trail of his actions that trickles up to the surface so we can perceive them. *One would think the deep to be hoary.* God's control of the seas – the overwhelming, dominant, uncontrollable physical feature of the Earth's surface – is a Biblical proof of his power.

· ·

In the Psalms, the sea is a metaphor for the terrors and glories of God. In Scotland, Psalm 107 is most often sung to the tune of 'Loch Broom', a lilting folk melody with sweeping rises and falls that echo the rises and falls of the sea in the lyrics. In Psalm 107, God gives a command and the tempest at sea is stirred up; but when the sailors find themselves staggering helplessly and wretchedly across their decks and crying out for help, God changes the storm to calm, and brings them safely to harbour. The sea is the place where myth-making happens, and God is at his work:

They that go down to the sea in ships, that do business in
    great waters;
These see the works of the Lord, and his wonders in the
    deep.
For he commandeth, and raiseth the stormy wind, which
    lifteth up the waves thereof.
They mount up to the heaven, they go down again to the
    depths:
their soul is melted because of trouble.
They reel to and fro, and stagger like a drunken man, and are
    at their wits' end.
Then they cry unto the Lord in their trouble, and he
    bringeth them out of their distresses.
He maketh the storm a calm, so that the waves thereof are
    still.
Then are they glad because they be quiet; so he bringeth
    them unto their desired haven. (Psalm 107:23–30)

The constant movement of the sea and of God's power – *the Spirit of God moved upon the face of the waters* – is reflected in the Psalms through music, melodies that rise and fall, lyrics that progress towards a destination. The sea itself is a song.

Traditional songs from long before sea shanties revere the sea's power and see the divine in it. They take the music of the sea and put it into human mouths, making their own silver lane to walk across towards God. The 'Unst Boat Song' in the old Shetlandic language of Norn is one of the earliest folk songs from the British Isles, and having survived throughout the centuries is still sung today. Its exact age is unknown, but it is thought to be from around the seventh century. It's a prayer for the safety of those at sea during storms:

Starka virna vestalie, obadeea monye.
Stala stoita stonga raer,
O whit says du da bunshka baer?
Litra mae vae drengie.
Saina Papa wara, obadeea monye.

An exact translation is elusive given the loss of the language, though some of the words have similar modern equivalents in the languages of the north of Scotland. The first two verses of the song lament and curse the Westerlies, the strong weather from the west that troubles men at sea. *Whit says du da bunshka baer* asks if the boat will withstand the weather, and the final section – *Saina Papa wara* – calls on God to bless those at sea. It's a song to be sung by those left behind on shore as the tempest approaches, a prayer for the sea to be calm and not to harm the men at sail. It was probably sung by women.

It's a very different song from 'The Grey Funnel Line', but it has the same wistfulness, and longing for reconnection after the separation of the sea. Songs written in the voices of men long for the women they've left behind. Songs in the voices of women long for the men to be safe. They are more worried in tone, more desperate. The women left behind don't themselves face the dangers of the sea every day, but a storm that overturned a ship far away from land might kill the men they love and need, and so devastate them. Their songs reached out across the water in a show of faith.

Mare vivimus and *Grip fast* and *Persevere* all, really, mean the same thing. Music, water, magic and the divine are all one, and we have to hope that faith will stop us sinking.

STELLA MARIS

WALKING DOWN THE HARBOUR SLIPWAY in St Monans on the way to my parents' new house, I come across a row of pairs of children's boots, lined up in rows facing the sea. On closer inspection I see it's a welly boot garden, created and tended by local children. In the sheltered place where the concrete slopes down towards the boats, there are dozens of pairs of small wellies, many of them brightly coloured and patterned, some of them bought that way and further adorned by paint and glitter. And inside the wellies themselves are planted flowers that bloom in full summer: vivid pansies and geraniums, scented herbs and hardy coastal wildflowers lifted from the verges and given new homes here in the shoes, adding colour to the village seafront. The wellies come in every size and, I find out later when perusing the local Facebook group, are added to the garden when outgrown by children who once owned them. I can imagine on a sunnier day that the effect would be wholly heart-lifting, all this warmth and youth and greenery and growing, the jolly flowers moving gently in the breeze.

It's only on colder, darker days like this, when the rain is always overhead threatening and evening is soon setting in, and the tide is low, and the stink of seaweed at low tide is seeping into the streets, that the boots have an almost ghostly look to them. They look a little like the relics left behind of lost children who went away and never came home to claim back their shoes. Like imprints of children who aren't children any more, a record of tides that have come in and gone out, marking years as they passed. Just something else lost to the sea, lost souls in need of a mother.

·

Just as the strange and troublesome magical witch-women of non-Christian mythology offered guidance – trustworthy or not – to men at sail on the sea, since the earliest times of Christianity the Virgin Mary has been portrayed in theological writing, in medieval song lyrics, and in Christian folklore as a guiding star who helps sinners navigate the dangerous waters on their way to Christ.

> Heyl, levedy, se-stoerre bryht,
> Godes moder, edy wyht,
> Mayden ever vurst and late,
> Of heveneriche sely gate.
>
> Ave maris stella, the sterre on the see,
> Dei mater alma, blyssid mot ye be.

After seeing her image represented all over Leith, that vulnerable picture of a mother and child alone in a boat, accompanied by the word 'Persevere', I wanted to find out more about Mary's connection with the sea, and the sailors figured as children following her to safety.

The Leith image of Mary in the boat with her baby, looking so vulnerable, turns out to be an unusual representation of her. More often, Mary is associated with the sea because she is seen by Christians as powerful, constant and trustworthy, in touch with the divine in ways that other humans can never be, because she was chosen by God as a vessel for Christ. Because she is human, though, we can understand her, and relate ourselves to her experience. She is a sign from the heavens that can be comprehended by mortals, a clear line of communication with divine mysteries.

In Brazil, Mary is venerated as *Nossa Senhora dos Navegantes,* Our Lady of Seafarers, with her feast day celebrated on the second of February. Spanish and Portuguese sailors travelling from Europe to the Americas in the fifteenth and sixteenth centuries were particularly devoted to Mary as a divine protector on the long and difficult Atlantic crossing, and the sixteenth-century Spanish artist Alejo Fernández painted a magnificent altarpiece called *La Virgen de los Navegantes*, which depicts Mary reaching out her protective arms over sailors. Draped in rich brocade with a billowing dark cape around her shoulders, Mary is poised on a cloud while ships of all sizes float peacefully on the water below her, and storm-clouds part around her golden halo. The painting is peaceful, warm and optimistic, but there's a firm colonial element too: gathered closest under Mary's cloak, behind a group of prominent Spaniards, are a group of indigenous peoples from the Americas who have obviously been recently converted to Catholicism, and are shown praying piously. This vision of Mary shows her strongly approving of the colonisation of the New World, and watching over the colonists' dangerous sea voyages to get there.

The origins of Mary's title as Stella Maris, and how she came to be so strongly associated with the sea, are murky. There are other patron saints of the sea in Christian history. St Brendan is said to protect seafarers, and is particularly associated with Britain and Ireland. Italian sailors prefer St Francis of Paola, who spent six years meditating in a sea-cave. St Nicholas is best known in his legendary incarnation as Father Christmas, but in his spare time he is also said to protect sailors and travelling merchants. St Elmo, or St Erasmus, looks after men at sea during storms. St Peter and St Andrew, Christ's fishers of men, protect fishermen.

Different mariners turn to different saints. Mary watches over them all. She is shown, in paintings and prayers and church carvings, as more than just a protector. The fact that she is a mother seems to confer an additional level of protection, understanding and calm, her maternal qualities extending over all Christians. Milton's version of the creation story in *Paradise Lost* emphasises the feminine nature of the sea, when Milton finds Mary's mothering of Christ predicted even in the very beginning of everything:

> The Earth was form'd, but in the Womb as yet
> Of Waters, Embryon immature involv'd,
> Appeer'd not: over all the face of Earth

Main Ocean flow'd, not idle, but with warme
Prolific humour soft'ning all her Globe,
Fermented the great Mother to conceave,
Satiate with genial moisture, when God said
Be gather'd now ye Waters under Heav'n
Into one place, and let dry Land appeer.

Mary's initial connection with mariners may just have been a transcription error from early translators of Biblical texts into Latin, allying Mary's name with a connection to a Hebrew word for the sea, when in fact the etymologies should be separate. In Latin the words are similar: *mare, Maria*. Others point towards the meaning of Mary's name in connection with bitterness, a connection that extends to the bitterness of the salty sea. Whatever the origins for Mary's link to the sea, churchgoers and sailors across the centuries have seized an affinity between Mary, the sea, and bitterness, and prayed to Stella Maris for protection. Many a boat is called *Stella Maris*; many a Roman Catholic church is named after the Star of the Sea – it is a particularly Roman Catholic idea, after all, that Mary is the path for mortals to follow towards Christ, over the dangerous seas of sin.

Mary cried bitter tears over her dead son, bitter and salty as the sea. These connections and the wordplay they make possible are pored over in Middle English lyrics, the songs sung by the people in and out of churchgoing life, but Mary's connection with the sea is also at the centre of the eighth-century plainsong vespers hymn 'Ave Maris Stella' – 'Hail Star of the Sea'. In it are the words: *Vitam præsta puram, iter para tutum, ut videntes Jesum semper collætemur.*

'Show us a pure life, prepare a safe path, that we may ever rejoice in seeing Jesus.'

•

Female figures and their power over the sea are a mystery to mortal men. Male writers and artists, as well as priests and lawmakers, have often connected women with a great unknown, as creatures fluent in the mysticism of nature, the monthly cycle of female fertility conferring a rhythm that's echoed in the swell and fall of the tides, the wax and wane of the moon, the unpredictable movements of winds and storms that seem to have their own internal logical world of cause and effect. It doesn't matter if women don't find themselves mysterious, or that we think of our biology purely as a fact of inhabiting the world in a female body. And yet there is a pull there, an understanding between women and the sea that has fascinated and scared men for thousands of years. We can see it in the stories they write, and the songs they sing. Mary, the perfect woman, the route from the human to the divine, the only one who can understand both the land, the territory of humans, and the sea, the domain of unknown mysteries.

It's important that Mary is a mother. She is the pinnacle of spiritual and physical fertility. Like the Maid on the Shore, her virginity is protected even as she understands the sea so much more than the men who sail on it. Even the male saints who have connections with the sea – St Brendan the Navigator, St Columba of the island of Iona, St Ninian of the sea-cave – are subordinate to

Mary's ultimate power over the whole of the sea. Mary is both virgin and mother; the coast is both earth and water. I keep walking through the village, and leave the children's empty shoes behind in their garden, foaming with flowers.

DROWNDED

ABAD OMEN: SAYING THE WORD 'drowned', or 'drownded', on board a ship. To do so is to invite death. Drownded isn't really a word, although it has been used as one so often that the *Oxford English Dictionary* does list it, somewhat grudgingly, as an archaic form of 'drowned'. Drownded is a corruption, an error made by children who have already learned the words 'bounded' and 'grounded' and 'sounded' and thought that the D sound was a standard requirement for the past tense of verbs that sound like that. And adults continued in the error, and made it their own. Jonathan Swift used it in his Pastoral Dialogue: *In my own Thames may I be drownded, / If e'er I stoop beneath a crown'd head.* It's one of those words that is incorrect but sounds right, sounds like how drowning must feel. Drownded is final, complete. It sounds as if it means someone has been fully, completely overwhelmed, overcome, filled with water to such an extent that there can never be any return, that their lungs are forever filled with it. Drowned dead. It's all about the sound. 'Lord, Lord! methought, what pain it was to drown; / What dreadful noise of water in mine ears,' says Clarence in *Richard III*.

The truth is that I haven't only been thinking about death and the sea in abstract terms, in the glimpses of empty shoes and the reading of newspaper reports of beach burials. Even as I start to come to terms with the reality of new life, the lives I've known that have ended are beginning to haunt me, and the absences of people I've loved are becoming a constant presence. Here I am, witnessing the formation of new life – not just witnessing it but making it happen – and again and again – waves on the beach – I am pulled back to life extinguished. Life emerging, and life fading, tides in and out, shaping my dreams at night. The trauma of knowing this, that the first breaths of a baby and the last breaths of a person in pain bookend every story. The brutality of making new life when you've already seen how it must end.

•

The illness took my grandmother suddenly. One last bright Christmas five years ago, and then in the sombre blue of January she fell ill. A minor infection was mutating and rampaging into fatal sepsis before our eyes, in the intensive care ward of a dark hospital in Hertfordshire in the middle of the night. There was just time enough for the doctors to call us, for my father and aunt to make it to see her, to wait in the plain fluorescent overlight of the ICU family room.

Watching a person die is an intimate thing. It is like watching someone bathe, or seeing them talk sternly to themselves when they think nobody is there to hear. You wonder if they can see you, if they care you are there to witness them. You feel like a voyeur, even if the person dying is someone you have known all your life, someone you love deeply, someone who you know would want you there with them in their pain. Someone whose suffering you want to heal. You can't put on any artifice when you are dying. A dying woman is most completely herself.

In dark stuffy hospitals, in the intensive care ward that's kept too hot for healthy people and just right for the sick whose immune systems are struggling, death happens every day. Doors are closed on the dying in side rooms. Sheets are pulled carefully over them. Their families walk back out to the waiting room after it happens, staring at the floor as they go, carefully not making eye contact with anyone. The person they came with, the person they loved so much, has already gone somewhere they can't follow. And without really knowing why, the survivors always wait for someone official to give them permission to leave, like schoolchildren waiting for a teacher's dismissal at the end of the afternoon. What happens next, now that our world is changed forever? Can we go, now? Can we go home?

•

The day before they made the decision to turn off the machines, I had my last conversation with her. I was holding her hand in the low-lit room, and when she spoke the sound was muffled through the ventilation system they had put her on. The doctors had described what they were doing as a bit like pumping pure Dettol through her veins to kill the infection. Her internal organs were buckling under the weight of the sepsis.

'Oh, Charlotte,' she said with an exasperated sigh, apologetically, as if we were all here bothering over nothing. 'How are you?'

'I'm fine, Granny. We'll get you home soon.' And then I tried to think of something else to talk about. 'I made your mince pie recipe again at Christmas. They were delicious. The pastry was amazing.'

'You have to roll it out thin thin thin,' she said through the mask. 'That's the trick.'

'I know. I did.'

I told her she'd be all right. I told her she'd be going home soon. She looked at me directly, and for the first time that I could ever remember, she looked scared. And then she asked me a question.

'Am I going to get better?'

I gripped her hand tighter. I told her yes. Yes, of course she was going to get better.

The day before, I had believed that she would. But today her breath was ragged, and we knew she would not. The oxygen wasn't nourishing her lungs any more. It was as if she was trying to breathe underwater, her body burning with the effort. Now in the gaps between her breaths there was a terrible silence.

•

When support for life is withdrawn, it's done by a doctor in a different room, so that the family – we – don't have to see it. They work hard to make it look natural, inevitable, as if no decision has been made at all. The family sit around their loved one, holding her hand as her desperate lungs rake in the stale air.

A clergyman had been and prayed that flights of angels would sing her to her rest. I had told her that we love her. That we love her, so much.

We were all contorted by her pain. The gasps of breath became further apart. The beeping of the machines was turned off, so the room was silent except for the sound of those breaths. Breathing in and out, the last evidence of my grandmother's life, drinking down the dregs of the world that she loved to live in.

And then, at last, one of the silences was too long. Just too long, somehow. We all knew it, though we didn't say anything, and we could all of us feel that the others knew too. There could be no more breath after this. Her eyes were closed, and her threads of hair looked soft and fragile against the sheets of purest white. The room was more quiet than any room had ever been.

And we felt that she had gone.

The nurse who had been quietly with us for the last few days, a man with strong arms and a kind, constant half-smile of under-standing sadness, gently let himself back into the room. He glanced at the clock before he looked at us. The doctor was with him. They noted the time of death.

The nurse suggested we step outside and have a few minutes away from her while he and his colleagues washed her face, tucked her up in more fresh sheets, and made it look as though she could be sleeping. We could say goodbye, then. All the machines would be gone. It would be more like saying goodnight.

·

We walked out of the room together. I was holding my father's hand. We were staring at the floor. It had been so quick: a few days ago she had been teaching piano lessons in the cluttered music room at home. My mind, wandering wildly in the shock of this hour, travelled over to that music room, and remembered that there had always been a sign on the piano there, handwritten in elegant calligraphy and propped up in a plastic frame, asking for 'No objects please on Mrs Runcie's treasured piano'.

The sign had always been almost entirely obscured by a mass of objects flagrantly defying its request, a chaos of useful theory books and loose sheet music and exam syllabuses and thank-you cards from pupils, all piled high. Nobody, none of her pupils, ever dared to mention the irony of this to her. These were not just objects, you see. They were treasures too. Remnants of a life and endless stories. Seen from a different angle, sea glass becomes a jewel.

In amongst the clutter, a tiny keepsake box had always sat on top, beside the music stand and in constant use. It contained dozens of tiny gold star stickers on snipped-out squares of paper backing, all waiting to be pressed on to the workbooks of pupils who had done their practice, sometimes accompanied by a 'Well done!' in her proud, curling handwriting with its messy capitals. I thought of the piano, there at home waiting patiently for its player, the gold stars in the trinket box ready to be awarded.

Months later, when we had cleared the house and moved the piano into my parents' living room, I would discover that my mother had found and kept the little box and restored it to its place beside the music stand, its gold stars still waiting inside, though the rest of the clutter was long gone.

•

I had thought that death would be easy to spot when I saw it, like a switch flicked. Instead it's gradual, like a dimming flame. There was no definitive moment of loss in her death, no certain second when any of us in the room could say that yes, in that last moment she was alive, but now, in this moment, she is not. She did not leave suddenly or on her own. We were with her, holding her, helping her from the world as the light faded. It might not ever fade completely away. We can't know if it has. I let this thought comfort me a little. This tide has gone out, and one day another will wash in.

When we went back into the hospital's side room, my father's shoulders visibly lightened. The air seemed less stale now. She was there, and she was different with the machines pulled back from her, lying with the sheet tucked over her chest and her eyes closed, her lungs still and calm. There was no pain in the room any more. It wasn't so much that she could have been sleeping, but that she could be anywhere. She just wasn't here any more.

We said goodbye quietly; a last squeeze of the hand, a kiss of the forehead. We knew she couldn't feel our presence now. The women would wash and dress her. The men would carry the coffin. The funeral would be a bright winter day, and there would be lilies, and music.

LITTLE SNAIL

THE LITTLE CREATURE THAT GROWS inside me did not ask for my permission to be here. I am not very romantic about its abilities or properties so early in pregnancy: I do not believe that this baby has a soul yet, or even that it is really a baby yet. What is growing inside me is human in nature, in tissue, but it is not yet fully alive. It is in the ongoing process of becoming, an entity gradually acquiring the characteristics of life.

Death is a series of processes that shut the body down and ebb away. How do you know when someone is dead? I don't think, now, that there is any one definitive way. Is a dead person a person who isn't breathing? You can hold your breath for ten seconds and nobody would call you dead. A heart isn't beating? Defibrillators can restart hearts in the snap of a finger. A person is cold to the touch? So am I, most of the time. And still, when you see someone who is dead, you recognise that they are dead. You just know. You can see that life has left them.

I think it's the same with knowing whether or not someone is alive. A baby is born, and breathes, and cries, and everyone straight away knows it's alive, that it's a human being: a person in the midst of the unfolding, glorious, messy process of being. In pregnancy, things are murkier. Life is beginning to happen in the most central, deepest part of my body, the safest and darkest place that I can find to conceal it. The human thing that grows there depends completely on me being alive for it to come closer to life. And there aren't any guarantees that life waits at the end of this journey. One in five pregnancies ends in miscarriage, a statistic I keep seeing everywhere, weighing down my most morose thoughts. There are dangerous things that have to be borne before we are born.

You can find precious things on the beach, small things that can tell you the future. The religion of the Yoruba people, who have historically lived between south-western Nigeria, Benin and Togo, reveres the goddess Yemoja, water deity and mother of all spirits, a benevolent maternal goddess of fertility symbolised by the precious egg-shaped cowrie shell of the sea-snail, with its opening like a tooth-rimmed mouth on the flat side of its shining hemisphere. Yemoja protects travellers at sea, and though she isn't quick to anger, when she feels rage the waters surge. She is associated with women, the sea, and the moon.

There are many religions, including Yoruba, that see divine potential in the cowrie, the shells from a group of sea-snails in the Cypraeidae family. Handfuls of shells can be cast on to a table or cloth. The shapes they form, and whether they land flat side up or tooth side up, are interpreted as messages from the spirits. Cowries have been used extensively as a trade currency in many parts of the world in history, with industries springing up on the various coasts that meet the Indian Ocean, where the animals are found in abundance, to gather them from the sea, and export them to specific areas in West Africa and China where their value has vastly inflated. The shells are bounty from the sea, small and perfect relics of another creature who left them behind for us to make into treasure.

•

It is like a sea-snail, a not-yet, a question mark. And still it has the ability to change my body completely, the way I look, the way I feel. Politically I'm no longer my own. I am a 'vessel', a word which I can't stop thinking about and which implies something seagoing and man-made, a ship built to carry men and given a female name. Not something alive and sinuous and thinking and wanting on its own. Some would say my needs and wants are less important than the needs and wants of a thing that doesn't even yet have a working brain. It is like a sea-snail, dependent on its shell. And yet no, it's not like that. I reach for what it is like. It's like a small wave that might become a bigger wave if the right boat passes by.

The words people use to describe pregnant women are words from gardens and the moon: *blooming, glowing*. I feel neither. All I can think about, when I think about being pregnant, is how dangerous the whole experience feels. These people who say congratulations when you tell them you're having a baby, don't they know that producing a baby is how many women in history have ended their lives? Oh, childbirth is much safer now, here, in this country. It happens in hospitals, with antibiotics and anti-septics and stitches and drugs. And some women still die.

Since telling people I'm having a baby, every woman I know seems to want to tell me a story of a horrible birth that happened to them, or to their friend. I hear about women who lost every pint of blood in their bodies and were ripped open from throat to knees in an operating theatre and still somehow survived to hold the baby. People delight in these stories, and tell them with joyous horror in their eyes. They are like the stories that men tell of adventures at sea and fish that got away: *You should have seen the size of it. She almost died. She did it without pain relief, and she'll never get the feeling back in her right leg now, can you imagine?*

•

I notice, though, that people don't tell me the stories of when things went really wrong. They don't tell me about the baby who really did die, or the woman who slipped away from the earth the moment she became a mother and left her child behind. These are ghost stories too terrible to tell me, a vulnerable pregnant thing, too awful for me to imagine, in case doing so provokes the fates, and the same thing happens to me.

I am supposed to be thinking about the importance of life, to be resting, to be eating as well as I can. Thoughts of the dead keep rising up, bobbing back to the surface of my mind. I think of my grandmothers. I want to ask them how they had their babies, at their homes in a different time. Were they scared, too? Did they think about the dangers? My body will have to work hard to give this creature, this sea-snail stuck to the inside of my body, the things it needs for life.

A male friend asks me what it feels like to be pregnant. 'It feels so strange,' I say. 'It feels as strange and impossible to me as it would to you.' But it is woman's work, to make life in the midst of possible death, to provide safety in the middle of dangerous waters, spinning something golden from the dullness of the world, like magic, to give up your own life to the sea.

BYSSUS

I N THE LEGEND OF RUMPELSTILTSKIN, straw is spun into gold. Spinning is a process by which magic is done, an artistic and animal kind of magic. It happens in textiles every day: by harvesting the fibres produced by silkworm larvae, we make silk, a soft, shimmering fabric that catches the light like no other. And if you go diving in search of clams in the warm waters of the Mediterranean, you can achieve another kind of alchemy.

The art of making byssus, an especially delicate and ancient fabric also known as sea-silk, is dying out. It is made by turning the fibres produced by the large, endangered *Pinna nobilis* clam, found tied into the seabed by its own thin strands of soft hair, into glowing fabric as light as breath. The clam itself, native to the sea around Sardinia, is dying out after years of being gathered for use as food and a source of pearls, and the creature is now a protected species, carefully watched over by the Italian government. Its heritage is ancient: for thousands of years, divers – mostly women, passing down the secrets of the art through the maternal line – have taken the tiny strands of the clam's hairs and painstakingly combed them and spun them into threads, singing traditional Sardinian folk songs while they worked. The resulting material is a bronze-brown coloured fluff, a little like a ball of dark spun sugar.

The byssus material is so sparse to find and so difficult to spin that it can take a decade to work enough gathered material into one tapestry, the wool dyed with natural colourings and spices found in Sardinia and used by spinners across the centuries. It's possible to dye the sea-silk into many different colours, but the most beautiful finish comes from purely exposing it to the sun, when it turns a deep, burnished gold. Then, that done, it can be embroidered on to clothes in traditional patterns – religious robes and christening gowns are the most typical uses – and it shines, and takes on the appearance of intricate jewellery, sparkling in the light.

Mentions of sea-silk across historical texts are sparse, but easily recognisable, and significant when they do appear. The Rosetta Stone mentions a tax paid in 'byssus cloth'. 'For the sea withal yields fleeces, inasmuch as the more brilliant shells of a mossy wooliness furnish a hairy stuff', wrote the early Christian writer Tertullian, who lived from around 160–220 AD. 'Pinna wool' or 'sea-silk' is mentioned in ancient Egyptian and Roman documents as a valuable fabric, though details of its construction are scarce. Byssus pops up again and again as a valuable material, or a beautiful fabric with mysterious origins, in literature and records all the way to Jules Verne's *Twenty Thousand Leagues Under the Sea*, where the crew of the *Nautilus* dress in byssus cloth:

I quickly got into my clothes made of byssus fabric. Conseil made several comments on them, and I told him they were made from the shiny, silky threads with which the pinna, a kind of oysterlike creature very common near the shores of the Mediterranean, attaches itself to rocks. In olden days, people used it to make beautiful cloth, stockings and gloves, for it is both very soft and warm. The crew of the *Nautilus* could therefore dress at little cost and without having to take anything from cotton plants, sheep or silkworms on land.

Though it was always rare enough to command a high price once woven into fabric, the harvesting and weaving of byssus is now not so common as it once was, and it's even thought that there are only one or two women left making byssus fabric in the Italian islands today, passing on the knowledge, grandmother to granddaughter. It is a work that women do, weaving and showing fine skill with nimble fingers, and has been historically – as women's art so often is – generally dismissed for being more of a craft than an art form. Embroidery, tweed, and needlework have all suffered this fate, too. The women do not sell their wares, but give them to people who travel to visit and seem to have genuine need of blessing or good luck in their lives, such as a couple struggling to conceive, or someone seeking healing. Byssus has long been thought to promote fertility and good fortune. Its preciousness is beyond monetary value. When you hold the freshly harvested sea-wool, it's so light, you can't even feel its presence as it rests in the palm of your hand.

•

At twelve weeks, the app on my phone tells me, the being inside me is two inches long, and less than half an ounce heavy. So small, and so important. I have no way of knowing if this is true, though my body has already changed so much that I feel firmly disassociated from myself. From the outside, I know that my waist looks thicker, my skin is greyer, and exhaustion steals over me every day to the point where I can hardly get through breakfast without immediately wanting to go back to bed. I swing between ravenous and sick with extreme force and unpredictable speed, sometimes having to take an emergency detour in the car to the nearest supermarket to buy something, anything to eat, to stave off the nausea that will double me over and make my eyes swim in my head. I am a vessel; my body is not my own.

The hospital where I've booked in to have the baby is in the middle of the hills of the Scottish Borders, an hour from Edinburgh, countryside all around, fields of sheep and cows and horses grazing up the slopes. On the hospital site there is a helicopter pad and, bizarrely, a cricket pitch. The Pregnancy Assessment Unit where they do the scans is on the second floor, and the waiting room has a view of the cricket pavilion, and a sign asking you to make sure you haven't left your dog in your car. I drink a lot of water as we wait for our turn in the scanning room. It's a warm, yellow morning. Sean is here, holding my hand.

When a small and kind-faced woman calls my name, she can tell that I'm nervous, and is friendly in a brisk and upbeat sort of way. The room with the scanning equipment is dark and the air-conditioner makes a constant, soothing, whooshing sound. I lie on the bed as the cold jelly is smeared in a crescent moon shape below my navel.

One screen is turned towards the sonographer midwife, the other towards me. As she readies the equipment, it still feels so unreal, so impossible, that I am convinced that there will be nothing to show on the screen, just shifting black and grey lines and a gaping central emptiness in the dark. The pregnancy is all in my head. There is nothing inside me but blood.

We are waiting for the sound of the heartbeat. I think of the Sirens, of them being at their most dangerous when they stopped singing, the most profound horror of silence.

•

As the midwife presses the scanner hard into my abdomen, just above my bladder, a shape comes into view. She zooms in. I grip Sean's hand.

'There's a good fast heartbeat there,' she says. I'm breathing out. I can hardly hear what she says next because I've realised that I'm looking at the shape of a head in profile, taking up most of the dark, kidney bean-shaped space on the screen. There are wriggling arms and legs. The whole creature seems to leap upwards and land awkwardly on its face. And there, in the middle of the shape, there are what looks like two small grey beans pulsating together. There's no sound coming out of the machine – the speakers must be turned off – but I can see it, pumping the blood, strong and unmistakeable: a heartbeat.

Sean laughs a surprised kind of laugh. There is plenty of fluid around the baby, I hear the midwife say. She moves the scanner around some more. And then, eventually: 'That's everything we're looking for at this stage,' she says, her voice cheerful, and she hands us a printout of the picture from the screen. It's everything I'm looking for, too.

Walking back to the car park, blinking in the bright day, I stare at the shiny black and white printout in my hand, looking at the baby's blurred limbs. Its feet are smaller than my fingernails, its little body lighter than breath.

IV

MAIA

The shy goddess Maia is the oldest of the Pleiades. She lives alone in a cave, where she gives birth to the winged messenger god Hermes. Maia is the Greek word for 'midwife'.

HOW TO SURVIVE A STORM

IN HEAVY WEATHER, SAILORS HAVE to work hard to survive a storm. Hurricane-force winds can cause colossal walls of water to rise up and swallow whole ships, lifting them high and then dumping them low, pitching and rolling violently from side to side. The heavier the ship, the better chance it has of surviving the tosses and turns of stormy seas. Large vessels have more resistance against the whims of the wind. Modern cruise ships are several storeys high and carry thousands of passengers. They aren't too scared of storms: the captain might choose to steer around one in advance, but if not, usually the worst that can happen is a pitching boat and several seasick holidaymakers. The ships are equipped with stabilisers to stop them capsizing, but this doesn't stop the heave and roll completely.

Yachts and smaller craft have a harder time surviving. Modern forecasting is good enough that sailors of small boats can usually choose to avoid sailing during a storm. If you're heading out to sea, the advice is to learn the cyclonic patterns of the clouds so you can predict when bad weather is coming. Pay devoted attention to the shipping forecast and keep your wits about you. Preparation is important. Storm sails and a proper sea anchor can make all the difference. Across the centuries of sailing, crews of historical ships haven't found it as easy to survive as sailors today, and modern technology helps.

If you're heading into a storm, strap down everything so that nothing can fly around in the wind and cause damage. This goes for belowdecks too. Tie rigging lines everywhere around the deck so that you can hold on to them tight as you move about the storm-washed deck. As the waves move higher, pour barrels of oil – any kind of oil, olive, crude, whale – overboard to make the sea around you thicker and less likely to break over the hull and sweep everyone overboard.

If you have communications contact with land, let someone know your position. If the storm is still gathering and hasn't yet hit, give every crew member a hot meal, and agree what to do in advance if there's a man overboard. Make sure every hand is well rested and fed and ready to work.

'Any port in a storm', the saying goes, and if bad weather is forecast when you're already at sea, and a port is nearby, that's generally good advice, though some ports are better protected from storm winds than others. If you're far from land, you just do the best that you can. Sometimes it's best to stay as far out to sea as possible, well away from rocks or cliffs that the storm could hurl you towards. Otherwise, there are known pockets of shelter that can provide refuge in storms: Scottish sea lochs on the West Coast are good hiding places.

Once well away from dangerous obstacles, steer for the 'clean side' of the storm, the area of sea with the lowest waves. Keep the bow pointing into the waves to avoid them smashing you from the side: breaking waves can capsize you.

•

The worst-case scenario is that you drown. The next worst-case scenario is that you survive, cut adrift from your vessel, either in a dinghy or clinging to some chunk of your wrecked ship. Then you have to think as clearly as you can about the immediate steps you need to take to ensure your continuing existence. Find other survivors if you can. Find fresh water to drink. Find food. You may have none of these things.

Find a way to tell someone, anyone, where you are, and hope for rescue. Don't thrash around or try to swim. You'll waste precious energy. If you can relax, you will float, and if you can send up a distress flare or any other kind of communication signal, you're likely to be found before you drown. Unless it's winter in the far north, and you freeze to death first. If you do have to swim, doggy paddle is the best way to stay afloat while expending the least amount of energy. Breaststroke is better if you have to swim a long way.

If you have a life jacket and are awaiting rescue, try to float in the foetal position to conserve heat. Try to lash together as much debris as possible, so that you have more to cling to, and you'll make it easier for an aircraft searching above to see you. Raise a flag if you can. Make yourself as visible as possible. You need other people now.

Improvise a sea anchor from any material you can find to stop you drifting. You want to stay as close as possible to where you started, and the place from where you last managed to send a communication of your position back to land. Try to rig up a windbreak out of anything you have with you and try to stay as dry as possible to avoid hypothermia.

Stay calm. Calculate a rationing system for your food and water. Try to stop saltwater getting into any equipment you have that could stop working, such as radios and compasses. Keep a log if you can. Record the weather, record your rations, record anything you see that could help you navigate.

•

A vessel coming to rescue you may not be friendly. Pirates operate today just as they did 300 years ago. If you are in dangerous waters, and an unfriendly boat approaches you, submerge yourself as best you can: try to hide in the waves. If you know you are close to capture, destroy everything you have with you.

Fish can be a source of food. If you're far from land, the fish are unlikely to be poisonous. The closer you are to the coast, the more likely it is that the fish will be a danger to you. Sea snakes have a venomous bite and are to be avoided. If you are short of water, and can catch fish, you can drink the aqueous fluid from the fish's spine and eyes. Carefully cut along the spine and suck, then suck out the eyes. Do not drink any of the other fluids from the fish. In icy waters, old sea ice is almost free of salt, and you can melt it for drinking water. You can identify it by its bluish tinge, and how easily it splinters. Recently formed sea ice is a cloudy grey colour, and salty, and no use to you. Never drink seawater or urine.

THE HARMONY OF THE GALE

WHEN THE FIRST STORM OF the voyage hit, Stan Hugill slipped belowdecks. They weren't long out of the port at Liverpool. Ships as they rolled in bad weather were creatures he'd only seen before from the safety of Hoylake, where boats lifted and fell safely in the harbour like breathing lungs.

If you believe his stories from his American tours, his experiences of sea-storms were glorious from the first day to the last. Each storm was, supposedly, just another chance for Hugill and his crewmates to show off their sailing skills and tear through some shanties to drown out the thunder overhead.

That's not quite how it was. His first ever trip away from his family was a terrifying experience. Before setting off, he had never seen how the ships that he'd so loved as a small boy, and seen as places of safety and fun and stories told by his father, fared in the full thrust of a storm far from land. He had never seen how they pitched hard now at one angle into surging waves thick as paint, and now tumbled back over into another steep pitch on the reverse side. He had never seen men hurled from port to starboard with their lips and eyelashes salt-crusted from spray, in constant danger of being swept overboard and lost.

Ruskin called the storm-battered vessel in Turner's *The Slave Ship*, painted seventy years before Hugill's first voyage, 'the most sublime of subjects', evoking 'the power, majesty, and deathfulness of the open, deep, illimitable Sea'. There's a story of Turner conceiving his sea-storm paintings while lashed to the mast of an actual ship in an actual storm, like Odysseus against the Sirens, to know how the sea-storm would feel against his face. Another of those impossible-seeming legends that are formed at sea. It's probably not true, but you want it to be.

The reality of 'deathfulness' that Hugill faced was not sublime. He was there for work, not for art or romance. Music was part of survival and part of the grind.

The heyday of sail was ending and the push-button navy of steamer ships was beginning. Steamer ships coped better with storms than their sailing predecessors. For a sailing ship, the only way for men to survive heavy weather was for them to judge the conditions correctly, reduce the area of sail, lash their bodies (and, apparently, the bodies of any stowaway artists) to fixed objects to prevent men going overboard and to head below deck if possible.

The darkness of belowdecks warmed to the murmurs of the sailors as the storm began to whip itself up. Plenty of the men were old enough to be Hugill's father, and the sound of their talk was a comfort to him, even as the outside storm was beating its wings around the prow.

•

Hugill was thirteen. When I was thirteen, the closest I came to isolation from my family and everything I loved was a sleepover. How is it possible that Hugill took himself off to a life of intense risk, and storybook seafaring adventure, when he was that age? He was a child, and he was hearing sounds that most of us never encounter. The cries of the men in the throes of physical strength, hauling with muscles on the brink of tearing as the sea-storm threatened to drag them to death overboard. The wild yells as they spilled the wind from the sail to make the job of hoisting it lighter, to bring the ship closer to the wind.

Hugill's home life, though filled with all the trappings of his parents' passion for seafaring, was cut off from the reality of it until he left his school and home, seemingly with his parents' blessing, and began his first voyage. The cries of the men were really a new sound to him. Hugill would have known roughly how the shanties should have sounded from his childhood, and the versions he had learned from his sailor father singing them to him by the fireside with 'a fine bass-baritone voice, accompanying himself with a button-type accordion', as Hugill described his early musical encounters.

Or from his mother, a sailor's daughter who sang shanties to her children as lullabies. Or his grandfather, also a sailor, who wrote down the shanties he knew in a small book that Hugill came to obsess over. Their whitewashed cottage by the sea in Cheshire was filled with pictures of ships. There were so many images of billowing sails hung around the walls that his mother used to say that 'a good gust of wind in here would make us take off'.

Hearing the sea songs of his childhood on board ship, complete with the cry of the men and the accompaniment of the sounds of the sea, was utterly different. The shouting was constant in the orchestral communion of sea and storm.

Life at sea was hard for the boy, even a boy weaned on sea stories and saltwater. His fellow sailors drank, swore, fought and sung bawdily to keep their work going. When he writes about this time in his life, it's told briefly and breezily in snatches before entering into the more serious business of adventure on which he built the shantyman myth.

Hugill was sailing from Liverpool to New Zealand, a distance of incomprehensible size. He may have been excused from some of the most arduous tasks expected of a sailor due to his age, but he wouldn't have got away lightly from unpleasant work. And he wasn't the only soul on board who was scared of the unknown.

Sailing was risky. Disease could rattle through a whole crew; a storm could dash a ship to nothing; rocks could wreck her when the sailors could almost smell land. Only a few years earlier, the *Titanic* had sunk. Only a few years later, Hugill himself would narrowly survive a shipwreck in the South Pacific.

The shanties that were heard on sailing ships when setting off for voyages chose not to dwell on the darker possibilities of the journey. They were filled with excitement, bidding a fond farewell to sweethearts, and looking forward to exciting new destinations. They are jolly:

> *O say were you ever in Rio Grande?*
> *O, for Rio!*
> *It's there that the river runs down golden sand*
> *And we're bound for the Rio Grande!*

Then away, lads, away
Away for Rio!
And fare you well my bonny young girl
And we're bound for the Rio Grande!

'The Rio Grande' is an outward-bound shanty, most commonly sung by American crews in the nineteenth century but with roots in the Liverpudlian sailing tradition of which Hugill was a part. The sailors who sang it pronounced 'Rio' as 'Rye-O', rather than 'Ree-o', partly to differentiate it from the Rio Grande in northern Mexico. The Rio Grande in this song is the Rio Grande do Sul in Brazil, where the river does indeed run down banks of golden sand, and where ships used to sail from New York Harbour on well-paid missions to fetch prized South American coffee beans.

The other reason for changing the sound is because the refrain is generally sung over a soaring high note, and Hugill writes that the 'eye-O' sound was a clearer, more joyful open-mouthed sound than the more conventional pronunciation would be. If you are in the business of singing high notes, you know that it's easier to reach them on an 'aa' or 'i' vowel sound than on an 'oo' or an 'ee', because your mouth opens wider and the sound is louder.

It's a rousing, happy sort of shanty, sung while the crew were readying the ship for the voyage ahead, when all was promised, bellies were full, and there was the prospect of fat filled wallets on the sailors' return. Singing 'The Rio Grande' loudly and cheerfully as the first jobs on board were undertaken, the men were mythologising the voyage before it had even begun. They sang the journey ahead as if it were the most exciting treat, a feat of storytelling in the making, when in reality they knew it was to bring long, hard days and profound isolation from the loved ones left behind.

·

Hugill lets himself join the men in their singing. He doesn't know the words yet, but he can get the hang of the hitches, and maybe his teenage voice breaks as he sends it up soaring at the end of the lines. Death is in every storm cloud, but the singing is a spell of protection. Pain, joy, effort. The shanties keep the machine churning to hold back the gales, only letting them in just enough to guide the ship back to her course.

As he holds on to the rope and his mouth fills with the music he only half-knows, something about the salty songs in his lungs lifts him, draws him in, binds him to the work of a sailor. The storm and the work have been terrifying – but the story he'll tell will be wonderful.

The storm has ebbed. No one is lost. Waves that have spent the night in piles of froth, slamming into one another at colossal heights, are smoothed into innocent-looking, glossy-crested wavelets. The breeze is still sharp enough to pick up the hairs on Hugill's forearms as he stands on the deck, inhaling the autumn morning.

Screaming birds arrive with the dawn from the port the ship has left behind. Gannets and gulls, shaking memories of the storm from their feathers, call to each other as they forage the surface. They skim over the crests, turn, and fold out of sight in the sun as they head back to land.

THE SILVER LANE

AFTER THE SCAN HAS SHOWN that everyone is healthy, and it hasn't all just been in my imagination, the storm clouds seem to lift overhead. Spring warms into high summer. The days are long and light-filled. I drive down the east coast of the country to Essex for a long-awaited wedding of two friends one mid-summer weekend in June. The year is at its most distilled and golden, showing off in long hazy sunsets, and the wedding day bursts full of optimism. There are gathered bouquets of perfumed wildflowers, a music-soaked ceremony in a tiny stone village church followed by dancing in a tall, old barn, and a night spent in tents pitched around a fire pit in a freshly mown field. The pubs and churches of the south-east of England, in their warm haze as if seen through a jar of clear honey, call back to me about my own Hertfordshire childhood, more idealised the further away I get from it. Every settlement I knew when I was younger had a pretty little crooked church in it that felt sweet and quaint and familiar. They were nothing like the darker, damper kirks of the north, with all their ghosts and unfamiliarities.

The pubs in Essex are crammed under sloping Tudor beams and pitched roofs, the bars lined with rows of taps displaying the logos of the local breweries' dark, silty beers. Generally somewhere along the walls of any of these pubs there is a framed A4 piece of paper with a written history of the area and the building itself, which has probably stood for hundreds of years. St Albans had been full of these pubs, packed every summer of my teenage years with people attending beer and cider festivals, with blind eyes turned to under-age drinking to the extent that a sixteen-year-old could order a pint of anything if they asked for a plate of chips as well.

Hertfordshire and Essex give off an almost Mediterranean heat and dryness compared to the colder brightness of Scotland. The drive back north shows a postcard version of England in summer light, a managed landscape centuries old but so pretty and perfect that it looks as if it was built just last year for the benefit of tourists. I realise I've been going a long time without stopping for a break. On impulse, I turn the car and make a detour towards the Holy Island of Lindisfarne, a place I've seen signs for on several journeys but never visited. The land is flattening around the car, announcing the presence of nearby sea and the causeway to the tidal island beyond. Having started out in the beamed pubs of Essex, and being on my own physical journey towards a place in my life I don't yet know, I already feel like a pilgrim.

•

Tidal islands, and the journeys out to them across the mainland, are places where historic saints found the divine. There is something about a path that only reveals itself when it wants to, and that could at any moment cut you off and leave you stranded at sea with the water rising quickly above your head, that's Biblical. *Vitam præsta puram, iter para tutum.*

I love the walk out to tidal Cramond Island, with the winds of the Firth of Forth in your hair and a salt-matted wet dog scurrying about your feet. But it's just a Saturday afternoon jolly, really. Further down the east coast, on the other hand, Lindisfarne is a longer journey away from the mainland, the pathway winding you a little further out to sea. It has a stranger and more remote quality to it. Over centuries pilgrims have made their way to the Holy Island from the mainland of north Northumberland, striking out across the causeway from the saltmarsh and mudflats and dunes, racing against the twice-daily incoming waters that strand the unwary.

When you walk across to Cramond, you are taking a pilgrimage towards little more than a viewpoint, a moment in the middle of the Firth of Forth that gives you a panorama of Fife and Midlothian and the river becoming sea around you. There is wildlife, similar to the birds and mammals you find in the rest of the local coastline, and there are some small ruined buildings, but that's about it. I can already tell, as the car comes into full sight of the sea, that Lindisfarne is vaster. It's a place of greater spiritual significance, and to get there requires you to go right across the water like Christ and St Peter, taking a path across a plane that is often just sea and screaming gulls on either side, and reaching a destination which people before you have draped in spiritual meaning.

The island erupts out of the flat landscape. The seventh-century monastery founded by St Aidan, who came from Iona in the shadow of Columba, isn't visible: the Holy Island's main historic sites today comprise the medieval castle, the harbour populated by no-longer-seaworthy upturned herring boats, and the eleventh-century priory. The modern-day pilgrim to Lindisfarne will still see many of the same sights that the seventh-century pilgrim would have done: a wide-open landscape that floods the eye with sky sitting close to the surface of the earth.

•

Home is just an hour and a half of more driving. The sun is already making murmurs about setting, and I'm looking forward to stretching my legs and feeling a cold sea breeze in my hair to blow out the long journey already done.

I pull over to check the tide times on my phone and decide it's safe to head across. The drive out to the island along the causeway is long, with the world spreading itself out on either side of you like a cloth laid on a table. Like the walk at Cramond, the journey feels very exposed in the unnerving sense that where there should be solid ground around you there is only water. There is a sense of being watched, of the tide waiting to close in on all sides. Moses parted the Red Sea, but here the sea parts for any traveller twice a day.

The thick gold warmth of Essex has diluted and cooled the further north I've come. The light is tinged with blue now, looser and more delicate, as if a painter has flooded the palette with water and run all the colours into one another. It's colder, too, with the salt tang of the wind sharpening the beginning of the summer night.

I park the car and walk along the narrow roads into the village, and without having much of a purpose in mind beyond breathing more sea air I take some time to wander the ruins and graveyards that are still open. I'm too late for the tourist attractions; by now, most of the island is closing its doors and winding down towards sleep. I find the harbour and pick my way beside the wrack-draped rockpools of the stonier side of the island. I admire from a distance the medieval castle built solidly on the Whin Sill, the thick ridge of igneous rock that shapes this landscape.

Only 160 people live on Holy Island today, shaping their lives by the tides, but 650,000 strangers visit every year. There are no emergency services, except for the coastguard, and no doctors or dentists, but there are pubs and churches and coffee shops, and an all-pervading sense of quiet as I walk along the empty roads. Supermarkets deliver from the mainland when the tide allows. Drivers get caught out and have to be rescued by the coastguard. There's the sixteenth-century castle to visit as well as the more ancient Benedictine priory, but the place is best known as the site where the ethereal *Lindisfarne Gospels* were inscribed and illuminated around the year 700 by the monk Eadfrith. They form one of the greatest masterpieces of early Christian art in Britain, the sacred text lifted and woven through with colourful Celtic whorls and blocks of gold leaf. The book isn't here now – it's kept in the British Library – but the Holy Island has everywhere in its stones the memory of its most holy work of art.

The small and friendly-looking church of St Mary the Virgin, nestled in trees and a neat rocky graveyard to the south-west of the village, stands close to the site where St Aidan built the monastery that would anchor the island to its long-felt connection to the spiritual world as a place of pilgrimage, yoking it to British Christianity for the rest of its history. Like most of the village, it's locked up for the night already, but the porch is open, and I shelter from the cold wind inside it for a few minutes and watch the rainbow pattern the light makes through the glass above the parish cork noticeboard. It sweeps over the printed-out paper sign bearing the church's name, inked on to separate pieces of paper pinned up together, bordered with a black pattern of Celtic knotwork and bookended by Celtic crosses.

The church of St Mary predates the priory. It is one of the oldest holy sites on the island, one of the 'thin places' where the boundary between the spirit world and our own feels most translucent. The ghosts of the past are just a fingertip away, or so the pilgrims who come here have always felt. St Mary, Star of the Sea, has her representation here in this church and on this island, guiding pilgrims across the sands in the safety of low tide, as they walk impossibly on the water's home.

In the churchyard, the wildflowers are windblown and the sound of the sea is ever-present. It follows me around. I keep catching sight of it, lurking over the stone walls, waiting beyond gates, and peeking through nature-made porthole cracks in the rocks and in gaps between the buildings.

The sea throws up the sand in strange shapes all along this coast. This is the place to find rosary fossils, the small circular stones known as St Cuthbert's beads, which look like little serrated bolts, or miniature coins with holes through the middle. Really they're the fossilised remains of the stems of feathery prehistoric crinoids, an ancient marine creature that looks more like a plant than an animal, similar to a fronded underwater fern. Its fringed stems are really dozens of feeding arms, waving out from the point where its spidery body sits down on a rock to rest the many tentacle limbs that it uses to crawl along the ocean floor. It was once a tiny sea monster. Long dead, it's now a tool for worship.

The calcified nuggets the crinoids leave behind are prettier than the creature they came from, like little stony jewels forged by the sea. Medieval people who lived nearby, and pilgrims too, created the association with St Cuthbert that led to their name when they foraged them and threaded them on to rosaries. They touched them daily in prayer and felt God's presence in their hands, sensing something sublime in treasure from the sea.

Everything is closed and the night is gathering, but I'm glad I visited in this twilight in-between time. Holy Island is a thin in-between place, an island that visitors can reach only sometimes, and you have to know the trick to get there safely. I feel like a spectral visitor, coming and haunting alongside centuries of ghosts, half on land and half in the sea, halfway between day and night.

I decide to come back, I tell myself as I head back to the car in the gathering gloom, hoping I haven't misread the tide timetable before heading out along the causeway again. And when I come back, I'll come in the full sunlight of the middle of the day. I'll bring the baby, too, to this in-between place, and it will be proof that something real and solid can grow from the intangible. And in the meantime, with sea air in my lungs, I head for home. The sea yields up its little stony prayers and I go across the water.

INSTEAD OF THE CROSS, THE ALBATROSS

FAITH KEEPS US AFLOAT, BUT bad omens can drown you. The idea of the sea as a malevolent force was so strong in early medieval European mythology and Christian theology that there was a prevailing belief that when Judgement Day came there would be no more sea on the Earth at all. It would be drained and vanquished as a sign of God's conquering glory. Augustine wrote that at this time there would be 'no more of the surgings and restlessness of human life, and it is this which is symbolised by the sea'. The Book of Revelation is more dramatic when it comes to describing the conquering of the sea: *And the second angel poured out his bowl into the sea, and it turned to blood like that of the dead, and every living thing in the sea died*. (Revelation 16:3) When the end comes, the monsters won't be able to trouble anyone any more.

'The very deep did rot' is another way of putting it. That's what Coleridge writes of the eerie stillness of the sea in 'The Rime of the Ancient Mariner'. After the mariner shoots the albatross, the ship on which he travels is cursed, and the dead albatross is hung around his neck by his doomed crewmates as a sign of the mariner's own evil and the mischance at sea that he has brought. It replaces the crucifix that should be hung around the neck of a lucky, godly man.

Getting under way and heading out to sea on board ship has historically been such a dangerous venture, so at the mercy of the capricious winds and sea swells on the journey, that sailing has always been a highly superstitious endeavour. Woe will betide you if you bring bad luck aboard. Albatrosses are good luck, so the mariner shooting one was a terrible omen, and the bringing of a curse to the ship. There are other ways to curse your voyage. Whistling any tune can be deadly, as it's a challenge to the wind, one that you are destined to lose. Never wave goodbye to a sailor about to head off on a voyage, because your hand will be a challenge to the waves. Never wash a sailor's clothes on sailing day, because submerging them in water enacts drowning, and will bring that fate upon the clothing's owner. Re-naming a boat will doom it forever, while leaving harbour on a Friday is risky. Bananas are bad luck on board.

Women, we know, are just asking for trouble, unless they are in the form of the naked body on the ship's figurehead, a mermaid to ward off other mermaids. There is a story recorded by the maritime historian Suzanne Stark, a woman who pioneered modern research about the history of women at sea, about a ship that once ran into trouble in a violent storm off the coast of Cornwall while carrying a mix of male and female passengers. The crew men, believing strongly that women were bad luck on boats, started throwing the female passengers overboard. Sixty women were murdered. The ship sank anyway.

Coleridge's Mariner has a bloodcurdling vision of a devilish woman on his cursed voyage:

> And is that Woman all her crew?
> Is that a DEATH? and are there two?
> Is DEATH that woman's mate?
>
> Her lips were red, her looks were free,
> Her locks were yellow as gold:
> Her skin was as white as leprosy,
> The Night-mare LIFE-IN-DEATH was she,
> Who thicks man's blood with cold.

The cross and the dead albatross are two sides of the folklore of sailors' luck at sea. Christian faith and its trappings can drive out evil omens, so the superstition goes. It's the best weapon against the mysterious unknown, the strange magic that governs the behaviour of women and the moon and the tides. In *Moby Dick*, the otherworldly great white whale is set against the crew of the *Pequod* and their Biblical, Christian names: Ahab, Ishmael, Elijah. Stories at sea are most frightening when the sailors give their all to their Christian faith in the hope of ensuring good luck on their voyage, but the magic of the sea is too powerful, and the monster triumphs, Moby Dick sinks the *Pequod*, death proves to be the winner after all, and no superstition can stop or delay it.

•

Pregnancy is full of omens. You can tell if you're having a boy or a girl, so the superstition goes, by lying down, taking off your wedding ring, threading it on to a length of string, and letting it dangle above your belly, allowing it to move freely, trying not to influence its direction. If the ring moves in a circle, the baby is a girl. If it moves back and forth, like a pendulum, the baby is a boy.

If your baby bump is high up on the body, the baby's a girl. If the bump is round and defined, it's a boy. When the midwife listens to the baby's heartbeat, if it sounds like a fast-moving train, it's a boy; if it sounds like a galloping horse, it's a girl. If you pick up a key by the roundest part, instead of the pointy bit, the baby is a boy.

Some of the superstitions are based on old-fashioned sexism. If your skin becomes dry and spotty while you're pregnant, you're having a girl, because she is already stealing your beauty. I've seen no noticeable difference in my skin.

I want salt all the time. Salt and vinegar crisps, the cheaper and flimsier the better; the salty maize Chipsticks that come in bright blue packaging; Monster Munch and French fries from McDonald's and Snackajacks and all the saltiest, most unhealthy snacks I loved as a child and now urgently need again. I load up my trolley in the supermarket and it looks as if I'm planning to open up an Eighties-themed corner shop. Obsessively Googling this symptom I find that it's a common belief that craving salt means you're having a boy; if I'd been craving cupcakes and sugar that would mean a girl. This seems too neat, and too based on questionable gender stereotyping, to be true. Sugar and spice and all things nice; slugs and snails and puppy dog tails. I'll hit the internet again if I find myself craving slugs. I hope it doesn't come to that.

Every year of my life until the year my grandmother died, she made me a chocolate cake for my birthday. It was always the same rich and dark recipe of two sponge cakes sandwiched together with thick fudgey icing. She owned only two trusty old cake tins, and they were two different sizes. This meant that the top half of the cake was always much smaller than the bottom half, making it look mad, a bit like a lopsided bowler hat. She made up for this failing by dolloping lots of extra chocolate icing on top so nobody ever minded. This ridiculous chocolate cake is the only sweet thing I find myself craving, even though I know I can never have it again.

The sickness has been incredible, coming in waves of nausea that have swept over my body from the moment I woke up in the morning until I went to bed each night, making me feel pale and weak, meaning that I couldn't stomach even one mouthful of some of my favourite foods. I feel constantly as if I am rolling on board the deck of a ship in a storm. The sickness is worst in the evening, when my stomach seems to flip over again and again, and it feels as if some monstrous fish is thrashing around inside my guts. I think of lines from Rupert Brooke's bizarre poem 'A Channel Passage', read long ago and only half-remembered, as I run to the bathroom at midnight:

> And still the sick ship rolls. 'Tis hard, I tell ye,
> To choose 'twixt love and nausea, heart and belly.

In the morning, I look up the poem and find that I'd forgotten its central story, that it's about Brooke concentrating hard on thinking of his longing for a lover to distract him from the seasickness he feels while crossing the Channel. They say the sickness is supposed to be easing soon, the 'glow' of pregnancy beginning instead, but it's taking its time. I have always had ice-cold feet, but now my feet burn hot all day and night. I ask my mother if pregnancy will ever be really enjoyable. 'I think there were about eight weeks in the middle that weren't terrible,' she says, not reassuringly.

GRIP FAST

J ULY COMES, AND WITH IT the Diving World Championships
on TV. Confined at home by sickness, I watch little else while
it's on. I love it all. I love the blue-green water, the ritualistic
twitches of each diver approaching the podium, the impossible
heights, the pursuit of the splash-free entry into the water, the post-
dive jacuzzi to keep the muscles warm. It's the most dramatic sport
I can imagine. All those years of training for just seconds of action,
just one colossal fall from a high place into a wet one, into the deep,
a disappearing act performed by wizards with muscle magic.

The best bit is the part in the dive when the divers are perched
on the edge of the board with their back to the crowd, just about
to commit themselves blind to the inevitable, their toes gripping
fast to the edge, gravity just beginning to pull their bodies slightly
off centre into the water below.

Then there is the moment of tipping, the only just perceptible
point of no return when the diver's whole body tenses, the pull
becomes stronger, and all at once they tumble over into the blue
air beneath them, into somersaults and spray.

And so the heat of summer really and truly comes, bringing change to my body and the way that strangers treat me whenever I walk down the street. I'm gripping fast for as long as I can to this year and everything it's filled with, until the seasons tense and pull and we all turn over towards autumn, and then into the deep white winter, and the promise of newness, waiting under frost.

•

'At this stage there is a good chance your baby is experiencing REM sleep in the womb, and is therefore already dreaming,' says the pregnancy tracker app on my phone. My baby is apparently the size of a bunch of grapes, or a chocolate yule log. My body still doesn't really want to eat anything except crisps, else nausea creeps in. In the night I can feel the baby as it shivers and stirs.

Lying on the sofa in the heat, drifting in and out of restless sleep, I sing to myself, and I hope that the baby hears me. In the dreams that flutter over me as this nameless, sightless being rolls in the blood-red gloom of my body, I try to fathom what it can be dreaming of. This creature has no past to distort and re-imagine in its subconscious mind. Is it having prophecies of the future? Or does it dream about the things that I can already see, filtered down through my blood somehow – the grey morning, lightening its eyes that are, according to the apps and the books, already open and blinking within me? Does this growing human brain already somehow know the feeling of dry air? Of spring?

Maybe the baby's dreams are actually more real in their texture than mine. They might be more based on solid experience: a dream of the feeling of nutrition, of blood flow, the in-and-out swell of my breathing. Or they could be based on the melodies I find myself singing now, every day, in case they make the baby respond, to see if tiny hands and feet will press into my muscles and organs in kickback to the noise. One day, when Sean drills into the bathroom wall to install a new shower, the sudden loud sound makes the baby jump so violently that I briefly worry it might be having some kind of seizure. But its movements soon return to the vaguely constant rhythm of staccato jab and roll, and I am reassured that the DIY home improvements haven't had any terrible, lasting effects. Not on the baby, at least.

At night sometimes I try, with an uncharacteristic belief in telepathy, to send a dream down to the place where my baby sits and turns and grows. My brain and this new, second brain in my belly exist in the same body, and so I tell myself I can communicate with it in some definitely impossible, faux-primal way. In the twilight dream-logic of those borderline minutes of almost-sleep, I silently talk to my baby, and catalogue the things that I see each morning, patterning the wallpaper of my life that this person-in-waiting will soon see too. I talk in detail about the pretty mess of the heather and the buttery gorse as it spreads up the hills in the distant borderlands that I can see from the kitchen window when I stand at the sink, holding a coffee in the morning light.

And I feel that our dreams are in step. Together in my body we dream of my mother, and her Fife house by the steely flat sea, and the swoop of the bats in the garden at night, and the lick of the rain. And my face, my hair, my arms, and this life that means home for us both.

It turns in the waters inside me, a mermaid. This animal will breathe liquid until human voices wake it, and it will not drown. All of my muscles grip fast. Even if all that the baby dreams is the beat of my heart, again and again in the dark, I am amazed that we dream before ever we breathe, before we have ever seen light.

INSTRUMENTS

A SEXTANT IS AN OLD NAVIGATIONAL instrument used by sailors. It measures the distance between any two visible objects. My sister bought an antique pocket-sized one and gave it to my dad as a present once. I liked the way that it looked – it seemed to have a personality of its own and its own alchemic secrets – and I started reading about the whole enormous, world-changing history of the people who travelled the world navigating in this way. It's small, and brass, and pointed, and if you have never used it to navigate, it's very hard to figure out how it's supposed to work. The mixture of circles and angles in its construction and the symbols along the side look like they are made to communicate with stars. In a sense, they are. It is reassuringly heavy in the hand. A pocket sextant is something you can rely on. And it is something that connects three elements together, the water and the earth and the air, speaking of a history of the pre-computer past when navigation was something you had to calculate yourself with your hands and eyes and mind; tracking lines across the surface of the world.

•

My belly is getting so much bigger that I'm convinced it will rip itself apart, like bread dough pulled too far apart between the hands. How could a body expand so quickly without breaking? If we were made of fibres, they'd wrench into nothing under the weight of a growing mass. I feel like a flimsy paper bag stuffed with too much shopping.

The first NHS antenatal class I go to is run by a midwife called Pat, who seems to delight in saying the most unhelpful things she can think of. We are a group of seven women sitting nervously before her, fanning ourselves in the stifling room, some of us sitting next to men that we've brought along for the ride, and all eyeing a jug of cold water and a stack of plastic cups that have been placed on the small coffee table. Nobody helps themselves. The chairs are low, doctor's waiting room chairs, and there are brightly coloured pictures of cartoon characters and posters about health in pregnancy pinned on the walls. I feel as if I'm back at primary school. The air tastes faintly of antiseptic.

'There's hundreds of you!' says Pat. 'What happened nine months ago?'

Nervous laughter. She moves on. 'How's pregnancy been going for you all, then? You're all in the third trimester now? Do you think that expecting a baby has brought you and your partners closer together?'

I sense that the correct answer is yes, though there isn't time to give any answer at all before a dark look falls across Pat's face. She pounces on her next words with glee.

'Yes, well, that'll all change when the babies are born. You won't even be speaking to each other.'

Was that a joke? It's hard to tell. Then, as quickly as it came, the dark look is gone from Pat's face, and she is studiedly sunny once more. A ripple of uncertainty passes over the gathered women. Are we supposed to laugh?

'Now. This week we're going to talk about normal birth, and the three stages of labour. We won't go into anything that can go wrong or anything dangerous that might happen. That's all covered in week four.' I begin to dread week four. 'First, we'll just have a little getting-to-know-each-other session.'

The men and the women are split into two groups – perhaps mirroring what'll happen after labour, according to Pat's prophecy – and we're asked to make a list of all the positive and all the negative things about pregnancy. The men are nervous, but the women launch straight into a well-rehearsed list of complaints: heartburn, feeling hot and uncomfortable, worry about whether the baby will be healthy. The negatives list flows along easily. We all have a lot to complain about.

'Stretch marks?' I suggest, thinking of the torn purple lines spreading across my abdomen and thighs, deeper and angrier every time I look at them in the bathroom mirror, long tracks engraving themselves forever into my skin.

There are blank looks.

'I don't have any stretch marks,' says a woman who had introduced herself as Kirsty at the beginning of the session, with a shy smile.

'Me neither,' says Laura, sitting to her right.

'I rub vegetable oil on my skin every day and I've never had a stretch mark,' says Marion, from somewhere on the other side of me.

'Oh,' I say. 'Well. I've got loads.'

There is a pitying silence.

'You should try vegetable oil,' says Marion.

'I won't put it on the list as most of us haven't had it,' says Sarah, who has commandeered the pen and paper.

I decide not to say anything else. Maybe, under my clothes, I am a different species from the rest of them. A mermaid covered in scales. A hag whose ugliness is a malevolent force to be feared by other pregnant women. Diseased, and possibly contagious.

When we come to sharing our responses with Pat and the rest of the group, it turns out that the most positive thing any of the men have to say about imminent parenthood is that at the moment they can have a few pints at the pub and rely on their pregnant, non-drinking girlfriend to drive them home.

The rest of the class passes in a series of flip chart cross-section images of an unfeasibly large baby progressing slowly along a birth canal, rendered in eye-watering anatomical detail, and stern instructions from Pat not to bother the hospital too early when we're in the first stages of labour, and ride out the pain at home with a bath and a couple of paracetamol. There are further forbidding references to the complications that will be covered in week four, in the context of caesareans, haemorrhage, and forceps. I catch a glimpse of a poster with an ominous selection of glinting silver instruments on it, all designed to haul a stuck baby out of a broken mother. I decide to bunk off week four. I'd rather not know.

•

That night, I run a very deep bath and pour into it decadent, obscene rivulets of three different kinds of bubble bath, scenting the swirls of the water with clouds of lavender, mint and sandalwood. After climbing tentatively in, my growing body becoming increasingly difficult to manoeuvre, I press my fingers into the angry purple welts on my skin, the stretch marks that nobody else in the world, apparently, has ever noticed on their own body. They run in streams across my abdomen and thighs, like old shipping routes on medieval maps, tracking distances from one country to another, with a few sea monsters along the way.

This baby is going to change my body forever, I think. It already has. I choose deliberately, in this moment, to think of it as 'changing' and not 'being ruined'. When I move in the bath, shifting my position a little to find somewhere more comfortable, the frothy water laps at the edges of the bump. Under the white foam, the marks remind me of the sandy ridges on the beach at Portobello at low tide on a cold day, the sand wet and compressed, life waiting under its surface.

Later, in wakeful sleep, I dream about walking on a beach on a sunny day in a swimsuit past groups of women looking at me with pitying eyes. My body is changed, but it is not ruined. It's still my body. The lines that appear are just a map for where I'm going next.

•

It's only weeks later that I realise some of the women were probably lying.

'Of course they were lying!' says my mother when I confess my stretch mark shame to her over coffee at her kitchen table. 'Or, if they weren't lying, the minute their babies are born and they look at themselves in the mirror, they'll realise they are covered in stretch marks they haven't noticed before. And they'll be much worse than yours.'

Not for the first time, I'm flooded with gratitude for the women in my family and their brisk view on things. I feel stupid for caring this much about the way my body looks, and yet this is just one more thing chipping away at my identity, marking a change that can't be reversed. A friend who already has a baby tells me, lovingly and reassuringly, that the marks fade to white in the end, and nobody ever notices them except you, and only because you know they are there, your own private reminders of your body's power and possibility, painted on skin.

WHY THE SEA IS SALT

I N THESE LONGEST DAYS OF the year I start thinking about the wide stretch of the Firth of Forth again, and of salt. On my next visit to my parents in St Monans, I head out of the village east instead of west. The landscape here is shaped by its history of salt pans, and as I walk a little unsteadily – my centre of gravity is changing drastically – along the Fife Coastal Path, the walking route that curves around the serrated outline of the East Neuk, I go in the opposite direction from Elie to the south-west, towards Pittenweem and Anstruther in the north-east. I will reward myself with fish and chips at the end of a long queue at the Anstruther Fish Bar as dusk blues the harbour.

It's just a few hundred yards to the north-east of St Monans along the path that you first see them: the soft-mounded grassy dunes, nestled a little below the windmill and the fields beyond, the muddy path edging around them with a couple of billboard signs up to tell you about the history of the industry here.

After the 1707 Acts of Union between Scotland and England, there sprang up an increased demand for Scottish salt in English homes and for English exports, to preserve food and fish for transportation across the world. Salt has been a precious commodity since the age of the Roman Empire, when the word *salarium*, meaning pay, was linked to the ability to buy salt. It's where we get the modern English word 'salary'. Salt had been extracted from the sea in St Monans since medieval times, but to meet the new demand in the eighteenth century the East Neuk became one of the places that began to process salt in huge quantities, and in 1772 Sir John Anstruther and the Newark Coal and Salt Company constructed the saltworks comprising the mill and nine stone-built panhouses on this shore.

The panhouses, low sandstone buildings with pitched slate roofs, were built into dips in the foreshore close to the Fife coalfields, and a wagon route from the mines near Pittenweem provided fuel for the furnaces that extracted the salt crystals from the brine. Under the eye of a master salter, many of the employees of the saltworks were women and children, whose job it was to carry fuel to stoke the boiling saltpans, where the brine would evaporate to leave the crystals of salt behind. The mill pumped seawater up into the panhouses from sea-fed reservoirs cut directly into the rocks of the coast. It was a tough life at the saltworks, calloused with sweat and smoke.

•

By 1820, the saltpans fell out of use, when changes in English tax meant that rock salt mined in England was cheaper to produce. The panhouses are just ruins now, outlines of stone walls that look more ancient than they really are, as if they could be the stunted remnant walls of excavated Roman villas. The mill on the raised dunes above has been restored and re-roofed to help it better withstand the biting coastal winters, but there is nothing left here of the industry that once drew the salt from the sea.

St Monans is one of the best preserved sites of the old salt industry in Scotland, and the mill that so efficiently pumped seawater meant it could produce salt on a huge scale. In the late eighteenth century, the coastline would have been thick with black smoke from the coal-fired panhouses every day of the week except Sunday. There were other towns along the Firth, too, that had a history of salt production shaping their economy and landscape. Prestonpans, in East Lothian less than ten miles east of Edinburgh, gets its name from the saltpans that supported the town's economy from the Middle Ages onwards, when twelfth-century monks extracted salt from the sea there and the area became known initially as Salt Prieststown and later as Prestonpans. Its Royal Warrant to produce salt was granted in medieval times and was only lifted when the pans closed in 1959. Like St Monans, the salt processing was supported by small-scale, pre-industrial local coal mining. And like in St Monans, it was mostly women who did the work. The *Topographical Gazette of Scotland* recorded in 1853 that:

A race of females known as salt-wives and second in notoriety only to the fishwives of Fisher-row and Newhaven used to carry the salt in creels to Edinburgh and dispose of it in the city and its suburbs.

The salt processed by these panhouses wasn't always drawn directly from the sea. Sea salt contains impurities that need to be refined out, something that can be complicated and expensive. Before 1820, demand for salt processing from Scotland was so high that some Scottish saltworks imported mined rock salt to refine along with sea salt. Now when I walk along the coastal path beside the bumpy, tufted remains of the panhouses, the only trace of the salt industry is the smell of the sea.

•

If you spill salt, you're supposed to throw a pinch of it over your shoulder for good luck. Scattered over the threshold, it keeps witches away from your door. In superstition and in old medicine, salt is used to cleanse and purify, to preserve and to heal. As a child I wondered why the sea is salty. I find myself wondering again now. It's a natural thing to wonder, I think, because we are salty, too. Tears are brine, and if you lick a cut on your hand you'll find that blood tastes like the sea. As a baby grows, it twists in the saltwater of the fluids of the womb. The saltiness of tears and amniotic fluid is a useful antiseptic, with the salty conditions making it more difficult for microorganisms to grow, and so protecting our eyes and the environment of the growing baby. Salt nourishes and protects us, and keeps our blood flowing and organs functioning. The question shouldn't really be why is the sea salty, but why salt is in everything we are. The panhouses drew salt from the sea, and we find ourselves drawn back to it.

There are fairy tales that spin origin stories for the saltiness of the sea. They are attempts to answer a question we don't know why we were asking. 'Why the Sea Is Salt' is the name of a Norwegian variant on a tale that exists in many European languages, about a poor man who desperately wants food to feed his family for Christmas. He goes to his rich brother, and asks him for food, but his brother will only give him enough meat for Christmas if he goes on a quest to the underworld. The poor man accepts a joint of lamb from his brother, and sets out for the underworld as he promised. He soon meets a man on the way, who tells him that when he gets to the underworld, the devils there will offer to buy his food from him, and offer him great wealth in return. But, the old man cautions, he should not sell the lamb in exchange for anything except the magic mill that hangs in the hall of the underworld.

The poor man travels on, and finally reaches the underworld. Sure enough, the devils there greet him, and offer to buy his food. 'You can have this lamb,' says the man, 'but only if you give me the mill that hangs on the wall.'

The devils agree, and hand over the mill. The poor man goes back home to his wife and family, and begins to grind the mill. To his surprise, when he grinds the mill it grinds out endless delicious food and drink, enough for a whole feast. The family have a lavish Christmas with plenty of food and wine. The next day the poor man's brother comes to visit and asks him how his journey to the underworld went.

The poor man, perhaps having drunk too much wine, shows him the mill, and tells him that he had the most wonderful

Christmas feast. His brother is a jealous man, and after the poor man falls asleep drunk by the fire, he slits his throat and steals the mill from him, and takes it back to his own house. He starts to grind out soup, but he is a greedy man as well as a jealous one, and grinds and grinds until the soup that comes from the mill floods his whole house. His wife is furious, and tells him to get rid of the mill.

The rich man wanders through the town, down to the docks, where he meets some sailors. The sailors tell him that they need salt to preserve meat on their long voyage, and the man tells them that the mill will grind out as much salt as they want. They take the mill from him in exchange for fish that he can eat with his soup, and set out to sea with the mill on board. Halfway across the North Sea, they begin grinding out salt when the ship is hit by a terrible storm. The ship breaks apart and is wrecked on the waves, and the mill falls overboard and sinks down to the bottom of the sea. It remains there to this day, still grinding, turning the sea from freshwater to salt.

•

If you want a more scientific explanation of why the sea is salty, you might prefer to hear that salt in the sea comes from minerals in the land, washed out into the oceans through rivers and from coastal cliffs eroded by the acids in rainwater, and is joined by salt that seeps out into the sea from the rocky ocean floor. The heat of the sun evaporates water up from the oceans, leaving salt behind, so the salinity of the water is more concentrated in some parts of the sea than in others.

Seawater is salty because the land is salty, and salt is in everything. The salination of the sea is a continual, circular process, salt moving from the water to the sky to the land and back around again in eternal balance. As more minerals from the land are washed away, the sea has become gradually more salty over time. The scientific explanation is, in its own way, beautiful.

•

The amount of salt that's in the water matters to how we talk about it. There are different words available for describing how salty a body of water is, going down to very specific degrees. Freshwater, which is not necessarily to say drinking water, has less than 0.5 parts per 1,000 of salt. This is the water of underground aquifers, overground glaciers, ice caps, rivers and streams and burns and ponds and lochs and springs, high on the mountain. Brine is the saltiest water. Sea water is not always brine; in fact only the saltiest bits of it are. There are brine pools, depressions on the ocean floor, that form deep lakes of saltier water that doesn't mix with the less salty sea water above it. This is the saltiest water of all. These places can have a similarly salty composition to the hyper-saline salt lakes on the earth's surface, such as Don Juan Pond in Antarctica, where the water can be up to 50 per cent salt.

Sea water, on the whole, is only around 3.5 per cent salt. It varies a lot around the world depending on proximity to estuaries, and times of significant rainfall or intense heat evaporating more water and leaving more salt behind. Estuaries and rockpools, and the Baltic Sea, are places where the salinity of the water is so low that its proper term is brackish, the word for mixed saltwater and freshwater. Most plants and animals on Earth find it hard to survive in brackish water. The environment is too variable, too inhospitable.

Some creatures do thrive. The Firth of Forth stretches from the Isle of May inland to Stirling, and along the way brackish water settles into mudflats, where oystercatchers and redshanks hunt at low tide.

The saltiness of the sea makes a difference to its behaviour. The saltier the water, the lower its freezing point. Don Juan Pond is so salty that it never freezes, despite temperatures regularly twenty degrees below zero.

Saltiness makes a difference to the human body's behaviour, too. It can mean the difference between life and death. It's better to almost drown in saltwater than in freshwater, if you have the choice. Almost everyone who drowns does so in freshwater: in baths, rivers and lakes. That's not just because you're more likely to find yourself in a bath than in the Atlantic. It's because, once you find yourself in distress in water, you're much more likely to survive if the water contains salt.

This is because of the difference between the saltiness of the water and the saltiness of the blood pumped through your lungs. When you get into trouble in saltwater and begin to drown, it's usually because you can't get enough oxygen. As you struggle, you inhale water and your lungs fill up with it, so you can't breathe because there's no space in your lungs for air. If all the saltwater could be removed from your lungs, you'd be able to breathe again. Pressure is still put on your body, though: seawater is saltier than blood, so, when your lungs fill with saltwater, water is sucked from your blood towards the salt in your lungs. This makes the blood thicker and more difficult for the heart to pump. You might die from cardiac arrest or from a lack of oxygen to your brain, and either of these will take around ten minutes. If you are rescued quickly and given freshwater to rehydrate your blood, you're likely to recover.

Drowning in freshwater is faster and more violent. Freshwater is much less salty than blood so, as the water fills the lungs, it rushes into the blood to equalise the concentration of salt. It swells blood cells and bursts them, and tissue is damaged beyond repair. Your blood pressure rises quickly. Without these red blood cells, the blood can't carry as much oxygen, and the haemoglobin from the burst blood cells can overwhelm the kidneys and cause them to fail. The extra water in the blood puts a strain on the heart. You'll go into cardiac arrest and die within five minutes. If you're rescued before that, you'll still have tissue damage from the blood cells bursting in your lungs, oxygen deprivation from the lack of red blood cells, and kidney damage. You're much more likely to die.

Cold freshwater will travel even faster towards the heart, chill it, and stop it, giving you a heart attack, and killing you. If you're still choosing which way to go, choose a cold sea. The iciness of it is likely to give you hypothermia, and induce a last feeling of warmth and euphoria before you die.

FISHWIVES AND COCKLE WOMEN

You ARE NOT SUPPOSED TO eat shellfish when you are pregnant. It's one of many things you're not supposed to do. There aren't any actual laws about it, and nobody is about to send you to prison, but the rules for how pregnant women behave are enforced by a strict social code of tutting, disapproving glares, and deep-felt internal guilt. *Of course you're unlikely to get listeria from eating houmous or soft cheese*, say the other mothers at the antenatal groups, with a pitying stare, *but why take the risk?*

Why take the risk? Your brief moment of freedom and pleasure is unimportant as you nurture the being that depends on you utterly. Why risk a moment of pleasure, which you almost certainly do not deserve? If anything happened to the baby, the suggestion is, you would be as good as a murderer, simply allowing death to happen from atop your fancy throne of houmous and Brie.

As with everything forbidden, I find myself wanting to eat it more than anything. Now that the sickness has finally subsided, my ideal meal at this point consists of all the things that I am not allowed: rare steak and Gorgonzola, with a hoard of mussels in shallots and garlic and white wine on the side, and a mug-shaped pint of strong bitter ale. Poached eggs, runny in the middle, and duck liver pâté smudged thickly on warm sourdough. And the last three items included in the NHS booklet of foods to avoid in pregnancy, delicacies which I have never had occasion to try but to which I now find myself powerfully drawn: shark, swordfish and marlin, creatures that sound as if they are more likely to eat me than the other way around.

Cockles in particular are a delicious and earthy British kind of shellfish. They taste of sweetness and distant, sand-flecked mud. I dream of scrubbing the grit and the barnacles clean off their fat little heart-shaped shells and eating the innards, steamed or cold, with lots of vinegar and salt.

The mixed salt and freshwater of the Firth of Forth, and its gradual increase in salinity, makes it a rich habitat for wildlife and has given it a fertile history as a source of food to be gathered and traded on the banks and in the towns. Cockle picking is also an old trade in Penclawdd, to the north of the Gower Peninsula in Wales, over the Burry estuary at the mouth of the river Loughor. The men of the area have traditionally mined coal, while the women have fetched cockles from the beach. Now derelict, the once-white-painted Mount Hermon Chapel stands above Penclawdd, where it was built both as a landmark to guide sailors on the estuary and, so the story goes, to tempt children who used to play in the hills on Sundays to come to church.

The female cockle harvesters worked here from Roman times into the twentieth century, gathering the cockles from the beach, cleaning them, and loading them on to carts for ponies to take them to be sold at Swansea market. The cockle women wore a distinctive work garb of layers against the biting winds that whip across the beach, and you can see them in old photos from the 1900s, dressed precisely in thick, heavy cotton skirts, covered over with woven woollen aprons and wraps, and fringed plaid shawls. On their heads were felt hats, pulled down firmly to keep the cold from their eyes, and held on tight with a scarf. They carried their wicker baskets down to the rocks. Further into the twentieth century their outfits were updated to brightly coloured shirts and boyish caps, more slimmed down and practical for work than the elaborate shawls of the past. They are proud women, skilled and strong.

It's easy to assume, in imagining women's history, that women's work has always been domestic. That it has been about cooking, and cleaning, and looking after children, skilled physical tasks in themselves. When you look to the seas and the fields, you see there's more to it than that, that women have been required by society to do all of the labour of home and childrearing on top of the labour of earning money in the outdoors in all weathers. Women have been at work in the landscape and seascape for as long as men have been, and they pick cockles, and process salt, and gut fish, and stand with the cold water swirling around their bare legs and feet, and say goodbye to men on whose livelihoods they equally depend, and hope that a storm doesn't kill the ones they love out on the open ocean.

These days, the work of cockle picking is mostly done by men, and helped by machinery, though it's still a hard life built around physical labour and fresh air. Things have changed a lot since the old photos of the women cockle pickers in their thick shawls. Since 2005, cockles in the Burry Inlet have been dying off before they reach full maturity, so they are now smaller than they were before, and cockles of edible size are fewer in number. Nobody really knows why.

The balance of natural life in the area is crucial to sustaining the food we draw from it. To make the industry sustainable, enough cockles have to be left on the beaches for migrating birds, and they can't be over-hunted, so you can only gather cockles today if you hold a licence with Natural Resources Wales. The ecosystem of the estuary is difficult to control, and a significant reason for the decline in cockles could well be the spread of a disease from non-native parasites washing into the fishery. The cockles are dying out, and so is the heritage of women's work. Seafish (the public body for the seafood industry) reported in 2015 that, while 250 women from Penclawdd were gathering cockles here in the early twentieth century, the future of the cockle fishery at Burry Inlet could be limited, and the area 'may have passed an ecological threshold and the ecosystem may no longer be able to return to its previous state'.

•

Reading about the way it used to be in Penclawdd, and looking at old pictures of the resilient women working on the shore, reminds me of the fishwives of Newhaven in Edinburgh, close to where I've been living for the last two years. The fishwives of Newhaven in the nineteenth century attracted a considerable reputation as formidable. They were hard workers, beautiful, and skilled at selling their catch for the best price. The nineteenth-century Scottish journalist James Glass Bertram wrote that King George IV, on his much-celebrated visit to Edinburgh after which one of the city's central road bridges was named, called the fishwives 'the handsomest women he had ever seen', and noted that Queen Victoria was also said to admire them.

Bertram wrote a detailed account of the trade of the fishwives in his 1866 book *The Harvest of the Sea*, and described the fishing trade in the Firth of Forth as a 'gynecocracy', where all the men had to do was catch the fish, and the women organised the rest of the business, from cleaning the catch to being in charge of sales and accounts. The women would carry the catch in creels on their backs up to the Old Town from the shore, and once they reached the markets they would call out to hawk their wares: 'Caller herrings', was the cry, or for the women selling oysters – the 'oyster-wenches' as Bertram called them – it was 'Wha'll o'caller ou?', a sound that created a 'prolonged musical aria' echoing through the streets. The women would routinely ask for double or triple the price of the fish that they would be willing to accept, telling buyers: 'Fish are no fish the day, they're just men's lives.'

Bertram's interest in the attractiveness and dress of the fishwives – to whom he casually refers as 'Nereids' – isn't, perhaps, purely objective. As well as a social documenter and writer of non-fiction, he was also a sort of literary pornographer: he wrote an enthusiastic and surprisingly detailed history of whipping called

Flagellation & the Flagellants: A History of the Rod in All Countries from the Earliest Period to the Present Time. He shows his nose for human interest even in *The Harvest of the Sea*, which could have been a sombre account of the nineteenth-century fishing industry in Scotland, but which is actually rich in snippets of personal and familial detail: he observes that the close of the herring season is often celebrated with a flurry of weddings among those working on the shore, and says, 'I have seen at Newhaven as many as eight weddings in one evening . . . the evening winds up, so far as the young folks are concerned, with unlimited dancing. In fact dancing at one time used to be the favourite recreation of the fisher-folk. In a dull season they would dance for "luck", in a plentiful season for joy – anything served as an excuse for a dance.'

As the railway took on more of the load of carrying fish to market, and carried them more quickly, the fishwives' burdens were lessened, and though initially it allowed them to travel further to sell their catch, eventually they were required less often in person to hawk the fish, and so their trade began to die out by 1900.

The Newhaven fishwives and the women of Penclawdd were hard workers. They knew what it was to push the physical limits of the body. As my body reaches its own limits – my skin stretching purple over the baby as it grows, my ankles swelling and no longer fitting into any of my shoes, my spine unable to bend forwards quite so far – I wonder at these women, who worked in an age before reliable contraception, and before antibiotics and safe caesarean sections. Did childbirth still seem like a life-changing physical process to them, an ordeal that could kill them, a higher power to which they might, at any moment, have to surrender? Or was it nothing, a minor physical exertion compared to their daily work on the seashore?

•

President John F. Kennedy had an old fisherman's prayer written on a bronze plaque on his desk: 'O God, thy sea is so great and my boat is so small!'

I have started to feel like an impostor, a weakling, for being so scared of giving birth and unnerved by the changes I'm experiencing. I am lucky, I know, not to have struggled with infertility. I am lucky to have access to my country's health service. In every respect, my experience of procreation is straightforward.

And yet, how can anything about this be straightforward? Having a baby means watching your body mutate and change at a rapid pace. Your body begins to prioritise something else over its own health. The baby gets first dibs on all of your vitamins, iron, blood flow and nutrition. Socially, it's accepted that mothers put the welfare of their child above their own. Biologically, your body has been doing the same thing since conception.

There is cognitive dissonance in feeling such a profound change and feeling as if I shouldn't talk about it. Nobody likes a moaner. Friends don't want their friends to change when they have children. And, in any case, parenthood is nothing new or special. Women have done this before me for thousands of years. And you're not supposed to talk about it, because people don't think women's work is important. Men's work is the work that pays. But the work of creating a child, of standing exposed to the elements on the borders of life and death, is work nonetheless, and work that women have been told to play down, to act as if nothing has happened. Working mothers must pretend they are not mothers, and mothers must pretend they do not work.

Women's art and craft, needlework and embroidery, the singing calls of the fishwives. So many of these ancient crafts are really just seen as busywork for idle ladies, not as art.

The enemy of art is the pram in the hall, so goes that old toxic saying from Cyril Connolly, an Etonian Oxford graduate whose sneering aphorism has proved to be more lasting and memorable than any of the rest of his writing. He did not think that parenthood was art, and his opinion has made so many parents wary of mentioning parenthood in their work, lest it be considered self-indulgent, boring, mundane. *You think you are the first person ever to have a child*, we imagine the criticism to be. And there's truth in that. Every parent feels like the first parent. It feels impossible to make something totally new and completely familiar from the flesh of our own body. Creating life makes humans feel like God.

And we are supposed to behave as if it's nothing, as unremarkable a process as making toast in the morning. Mothers who go back to work feel under pressure never to mention the change that motherhood has made to their life and to their sense of purpose on Earth.

We all have parents. One of the markers of growing up is the realisation that our parents are human, capable and guilty of mistakes, with their own desires and forgettings and moments of self-sabotage that haunt them long afterwards. The soul of creation is making a child, feeling it grow, watching it become alive in a delirium of pain and danger. Creating a child is profound, and it changes you, and we have to write it and paint it and never ever, really, to understand it. Parenthood isn't the enemy of art; it's art.

THE LIGHTHOUSE

EVERYTHING ABOUT PREGNANCY AND BIRTH seems to involve calculated risk. How much I eat, how much I weigh, if I drink at all, if I do too much exercise or not enough. And all of these risks start to feel inconsequential compared to the grand risk that is coming at the end of it all, the risk of childbirth, and the moment that will be one of the most dangerous and precarious of my life, and the life of the child I've yet to meet. I am treading a rocky path, and I deal with this by treading actual rocky paths in places where the freedom of the sea feels strongest, the rockier the better, to convince my feet that they still know how to navigate difficult ground. I am getting slower, my lungs more squashed and shallow, and any uphill path is already becoming a struggle.

A few summers ago I walked to the lighthouse at Neist Point on the Isle of Skye. The way is short and clear, though steep and winding and spectacular. It starts looking down on the lighthouse itself from a high cliff at Durinish, the westernmost point of the island, and descends down a rocky path into a great dip before going around the land as it juts out into the Minch, the last stretch of water of the Hebrides before the Atlantic Ocean begins. Then it bends around to see the lighthouse again.

On the way down, there is an aerial wire pulley system that was once threaded all the way along the path, used to send supplies to the lighthouse without the delivery person having to make the rocky, slippery trip along the headland in all weathers every time they were needed. The pathway is easier to navigate now, having been mostly concreted over or levelled, but once would have been a daunting prospect in the least bit of rain or mist. A sturdy metal handrail leads the way through the common grazing land on the tops of the cliffs either side and over to the lighthouse. These cliffs are called An t-Aigeach: the stallion. He rears a dark head out of the water halfway along the path.

Turning a corner, the lighthouse comes into view, with its squat black-tipped tower perched like a gannet on the stacked grey rocks edged with green, surrounded by the empty former keepers' cottages. Built by David A. Stevenson in 1909, it's automated now.

The water to the north-west of Skye, off the coast of Durinish, is one of the best places in the UK to see dolphins, whales and basking sharks. It's also home to wilder creatures of mythology, the Blue Men of the Minch, a variation on the legend of water kelpies. These human-sized water-dwelling men are said to lurk in caves near to An t-Aigeach, to speak in rhyme and to lie in wait to wreck ships that come too close to the island. They are called the Blue Men because they are the same colour as the sea, and are sometimes invisible as they move through it, the green and blues of the water blending with the colours of their skin. The Scottish folk story collector Donald Mackenzie wrote that the Blue Men of the Minch were the marine counterpart to the Green Ladies of the land, also human-like creatures of myth, who would live hidden by day among the forests and the long Scottish grasses, in the midst of knolls and rivers and waterfalls, and approach travellers by night on deserted roads and cause mischief. They are shape-shifters, appearing both as comely young women and as hags, and also enjoy appearing to shepherds as dogs and tormenting them by driving their sheep apart over the hills. Sometimes a Green Lady's mischief is more malevolent: she lures travellers over cliffs and into rivers to drown. One of her powers is linked to speech. She can ask a man what weapon he is carrying, and if he names it, she can render it powerless, a gift of all-encompassing impotence.

·

When you reach the lighthouse at Neist Point, after carving your way through the headland, there are scatters of stone cairns, a little like the ones that had been left by visitors and pilgrims at St Ninian's Cave, stretched out along the rocky clifftop. This isn't a site of Christian pilgrimage, but a popular walking route for outdoorsy sorts: steep and breathless-making, but not too far a distance from the car park at the start of the route to the view from the lighthouse across the Minch at the end.

Lighthouses are places of metaphor, of light shining in the darkness, and of human help standing against the dangers of the sea. There is a story of a Victorian heroine who lived in a lighthouse, one whose heroic deeds earned her a sensational following in the Victorian press, a gold medal of bravery from the RNLI, and £50 from Queen Victoria. Her name was Grace Darling, and she was immortalised in portraits painted of her deeds. The public loved her, and a rose was named in her honour.

In 1826, a storm was breaking six miles off the coast of Bamburgh in Northumberland. William Darling was the keeper of the Longstone Light, the lighthouse built in 1826 on Longstone Rock in the Farne Islands, to the south-east of the Holy Island of Lindisfarne. Today you can still see it as bold as ever, the lighthouse, coloured brightly in candy-cane red and white stripes against the blue of the sea and sky. At high tide, the lighthouse sits only three feet or so above the water line.

When Grace Darling, the lighthouse keeper's daughter, found that she couldn't sleep that night because the sound of the storm was so loud, she was increasingly concerned for any ships navigating the rocky waters around the island. Looking out to the sea at quarter to five in the morning, in the light from the lantern she saw a ship – the *Forfarshire* – in trouble and being tossed on the waves, headed dangerously close to nearby Big Harcar Rock. She knew that nothing could be done, in the toss and violence of the storm, to save the vessel. Though Grace and her father, William, looked together through their telescope to see if there were any signs of survivors around the doomed ship, they couldn't see anything in the stormy night, and resigned themselves to waiting until morning to get a better view of what had happened to the souls on board, checking their telescope glass as often as they could in the meantime.

When it was light enough to see better, at about seven o'clock, the waves were still churning from the winds of the storm and the sea was still dangerous to navigate. Looking again out to where the ship had last been sighted, however, Grace and her father now thought that they could see the moving shapes of three or four survivors, waving desperately to be seen, and pleading for rescue. William was moved by their plight, but he initially thought that the sea would be far too rough for any small boat to attempt to save them. Still, Grace ran down to where the little flat-bottomed coble fishing boat was moored, and he followed.

Together they heaved a course of nearly a mile, taking the long way around the rocky obstacles of the shore to get what shelter they could from the full blast of the storm, towards the rock where the survivors of the shipwreck were still clinging. William jumped across to the rock while Grace used all her strength to steady the coble in the swelling and falling water. When they came ashore, they discovered nine people clinging there.

Not all the survivors would fit on the boat, and so some had to be left behind. One woman was clutching her two small children. They were dead. She had to be persuaded to leave their bodies behind on the rock so that more living souls could be accommodated on the coble. The initial trip carried only the woman and four of the men back to Longstone Lighthouse.

Steering her small boat into the rising waves, Grace and her father headed back towards the safety of the lighthouse. William and two of the surviving male crewmen would return to collect the remaining survivors and the bodies of the dead children.

The dangerous waters raged for days more and provisions at Longstone were scant, there being no safe way of getting more supplies over from the mainland while the sea was still so dangerous. The Darling family and the survivors of the wreck of the *Forfarshire* would have to wait out the storm as best they could, with limited rations and no change of clothes. The survivors included *Forfarshire* crew members John Tulloch, the ship's carpenter, firemen John Kidd and John Nicholson, ship's cook Jonathan Thickett, three male passengers, and passenger Sarah Dawson. Her children, seven-year-old James and five-year-old Matilda, had both died of exposure on the rock. Their bodies were collected, and they would be buried in unmarked graves in Bamburgh churchyard.

Later on the day of the rescue, the lifeboat from the mainland at Seahouses, with Grace's own brother among its crew, arrived at Longstone. They had attempted to reach Big Harcar Rock, where the wreck of the *Forfarshire* had been sighted, but the waves were far too rough for them to get anywhere close to it. Mooring instead at Longstone and intending to wait until the seas calmed, they were shocked to meet with the rest of the Darling family and hear about the rescue that had already been completed at dawn that morning, with the young Grace playing a crucial role in steadying the boat through the dangerous conditions and comforting the traumatised survivors on their journey towards safety.

By the time that the men of the Seahouses lifeboat arrived at Longstone, conditions had worsened even further on the water, and it was now too dangerous for them even to attempt the trip back to the mainland. So these seven men joined the *Forfarshire* survivors and the Darling family to wait out the storm with dwindling supplies and limited space. Space was so scarce, with the wreck survivors injured and in need of rest and care from Grace and her mother, that the lifeboat crew slept in outbuildings away from the lighthouse itself. They were there for three days before being able to head home safely.

When the lifeboatmen were able to reach the mainland, so too were a small group of other survivors, who had leapt aboard the ship's quarter boat when it became clear she was in trouble. The quarter boat survivors spoke to the press of the scale of the disaster, and assumed there had been no other souls rescued. But the lifeboatmen told a different story, and when those who had been rescued by the Darlings were able to make it to shore and to start to travel home towards their families, they did so telling a story that captured the Victorian public imagination.

They had been stranded, soaked and injured, on a craggy rock in a raging storm, they said, and salvation had come to them in the form of a young girl determinedly steering a small boat towards them over colossal waves. Though Grace had been accompanied by her hardy lighthouse-keeper father, soon the story was being told that she had acted alone in a mission of supreme bravery, risking her own life for the lives of strangers on a wrecked ship. Her age – twenty-two – was revised downwards. It was suggested that her deeds weren't those of a strong, fit and capable woman who was well used to assisting her father in manual work at the lighthouse, and all the general activities of living in inhospitable island conditions, as they really were, but instead the prodigious talents of a frail young girl, possibly divinely inspired through some miracle.

Reports in local newspapers, and soon in *The Times* of London, stressed the fact that Grace had urged her father to make the decision to strike out to rescue the people they had spotted on the rock. 'Is there in the whole field of history, or of fiction even, one instance of female heroism to compare for one moment with this?' asked *The Times* report of 1838. Circuses and theatre companies offered to pay Grace to appear with them. She turned them all down. As young single women thrust into the public eye tend to be, she was inundated with offers of marriage. She turned them down, too. People wrote to her asking for locks of her hair, living relics. She granted some of those requests. She was a modern saint in their eyes.

William Wordsworth, poet laureate of the time, commemorated Darling's actions in a poem named after her. 'Grace Darling' captures the public outpouring of admiration for her actions, and riffs on the Biblical resonances of the name Grace:

> Among the dwellers in the silent fields
> The natural heart is touched, and public way
> And crowded street resound with ballad strains,
> Inspired by ONE whose very name bespeaks
> Favour divine, exalting human love . . .

He goes on to describe Grace Darling as 'A guardian Spirit sent from pitying Heaven, / In woman's shape', and to paint her as 'Pious and pure, modest and yet so brave, / Though young so wise, though meek so resolute' and – in flourishing Romantic style – to command that once the survivors were safely borne home:

> Shout, ye Waves!
> Send forth a song of triumph. Waves and Winds,
> Exult in this deliverance wrought through faith
> In Him whose Providence your rage hath served!
> Ye screaming Sea-mews, in the concert join!

And on and on, to 'carry to the clouds and to the stars, / Yea, to celestial Choirs, GRACE DARLING's name!'

Wordsworth wasn't the only one who was to become enraptured with the legend of Grace's deed. Funds were gathered from well-wishers to raise money for her, and so many artists wanted Grace to sit for them to paint her that she and her father entertained seven painters in twelve days for sessions at Longstone. The resulting portraits show a young woman with a composed, determined expression, wide-set eyes, and dark hair plainly parted in the middle.

More dramatic visual interpretations of the rescue itself were painted by artists including William Adolphus Knell, whose painting shows Grace standing tall and brave, dressed in red, in the boat as it crests a wave, gesturing towards the survivors on the rock. Francis Sebastian Lowther depicts her reaching towards the huddled group of terrified victims, including Sarah Dawson and her dead children. Thomas Brooks's painting, *Grace Darling*, gives the most radically revisionist version of the story by completely omitting William Darling and showing only a calm and composed

Grace, alone in a small rowing boat in a storm with her sleeves rolled up and her hands on the oars, her eyes searching out-of-frame for people to rescue.

Grace and William Darling were bemused by all the attention, it seems, as the official lighthouse keeper's log doesn't record any of it, except for brief mentions of the visiting artists. The newspapers had spun what really happened out of all proportion, and by and large forgotten the role that Grace's father, mother and brother had also played in rescuing the survivors of the *Forfarshire* and nursing them to health.

Grace was an ideal outlet for a Victorian desire to exalt young women as beatific, pure and kind-hearted examples of the best of humanity, a desire that would, throughout the century, also find its way into pre-Raphaelite paintings and little girls modelling for the emerging technology of photography. Queen Victoria had been crowned only the year before Grace Darling's heroics, at the age of eighteen. The nation was ready to exalt young women. Living out on the rock where Longstone was built, Grace Darling embodied a post-Romantic ideal of the innocent bucolic maiden called to Christian duty. In an age where shipwrecks were common, and the seagoing life was seen as something so dangerous it should only be attempted by men, a young woman's interaction with the sea at its most stormy and dangerous was remarkable. This was another woman with an inexplicable, ethereal command of the sea, and she deserved worship.

Sadly, Grace didn't live a long and healthy life befitting a national heroine. Only three years after the wreck, she contracted tuberculosis, and in 1842, the year that Wordsworth composed his poem in her honour, she died at the age of twenty-six. At the time it was rumoured that the frenzy of media attention caused her so much anxiety that it contributed to her early death. She is buried in St Aidan's churchyard in Bamburgh, near the unmarked bodies of the two children who died in the wreck. Today there's a museum dedicated to the story of her life in Northumberland. Grace's headstone is a proud carved monument, engraved with more verse by Wordsworth, describing her and her lighthouse as 'like the invincible rock itself that braves, / Age after age, the hostile elements'. She had become famous for successfully navigating around dangerous rocks, and now she had become a rock herself, strong and unyielding and eternal.

THE EAGLE WITH THE SUNLIT EYE

It's as i'm walking back from the lighthouse at Neist Point, back towards the car, sweating and breathing fast shallow breaths, that I see them: large, black, fluttering, almost still in the sky as if pinned there. In my distracted state, they look to me like the ragged cloaks of spirits of the dead on the wind. There are two of them, I think, circling around each other in the sky and buffeted on the swift wind, easy to tell apart from the zanier spiralling movements of the gulls. Even from all the way down here on the ground I can tell they're enormous, these two, with their wings making long, oval blocks of shade in the sky.

They can't be golden eagles, not this far from the mountains of the highlands on the mainland. And anyway, the movements of these birds are far jerkier than the smooth soars of the golden eagle that I know from watching wildlife programmes, but have never seen for real. These look more like vultures, scavenging for sea-carrion from far above.

That's how you spot them, the sea eagles. You know them by their huge, hulking presence in the sky, impossibly aloft, and their lurching flight that seems to resist physics. Britain's biggest bird of prey goes by many names, appropriate to a creature that looms large in our collective myth and memory. To modern wildlife watchers they are the white-tailed eagle. In Old Norse they are known as the *erne,* a word preserved mostly in place names from the areas they once lived in high numbers. In Gaelic they are *iolaire mhara*, sea eagle, or *iolaire chladaich*, shore eagle. Or, most romantically, they are *iolaire sùil na grèine*, the eagle with the sunlit eye.

I watch them as I stand a few feet away from the car park, near to where the land falls steeply away into water. The eagles are flying high above the cliffs of the headland, using their detailed magnifying-glass eyesight – many times more powerful than ours – to spot fish glinting near the water's surface. Even before glimpsing their prey, they move with precision and purpose, drawing straight lines in the sky with thrust and speed as if engine-powered, before moving quickly in a moment of dainty ballerina pivot that quickly collapses into clumsy, lolloping swerves. They plot a slow and thoughtful course, their fringed wingspan, more than eight feet across, like a great black paintbrush washing the sky around and around. I stretch out a hand, pointing them out to nobody in particular. Their flight feels as though it shouldn't go unwitnessed, like an apparition. Like an omen.

And then, all at once, one dives towards the water. The dive of the sea eagle isn't anything like the gannet's cannonball drop and its precisely measured, slicing plunder; it's more blunt and brutal than that. The eagle swings at the water with its stout, bare legs like a drunk thug with a hammer: swoop, dip, seize. Like in Tennyson's 'The Eagle':

The wrinkled sea beneath him crawls;
He watches from his mountain walls,
And like a thunderbolt he falls.

There's a thunderbolt surge of energy as it dips inches above the surface of the water, down below where I'm standing, and I can see the shape of it contract as it pushes its legs forwards, finger talons outstretched, ready to grab the fish from the wave. And then, prey snatched, it mounts up again, climbing the winds with the fish still writhing in its talons, yellow knuckles knotted thick and gnarled around it like the hands of an old sailor. Its wings stroke and push the air down as they compress it to go ever higher.

The eagle only takes fish from near the sheen of the top of the water. There's an old legend that the sea eagle uses magical powers to hunt, that it can charm the fish up from the deep to drift near the surface of the water, lie belly-up and await their own doom at the eagle's talon. The eagle I've been watching folds out of sight towards the headland. It'll take its catch far inland now, and find a quiet spot to pick it apart and swallow it down. Maybe towards its nest, high on a treetop somewhere, or sheltered in a cliffside haven. It meanders back with its dinner the way a tipsy student might wander home with a kebab.

When I get home, and settle my feet into a plastic washing-up tub full of hot water to bring the feeling back into them from the day's walk, I watch videos of sea eagles hunting on YouTube. I think they are the most wild and beautiful birds I've ever seen. Watching them close-up, tagged and numbered in their

CCTV-rigged nests so they can be constantly monitored by conservationists, makes me feel like a voyeur.

I notice the way their long necks end in the sharpened faces of murderers, their muscled shoulders hunched below a hooked chunk of yellow beak and the calculating eye of a Tudor nobleman, pale and watchful, expressing determination and a slight, meaningful smile of intent. The chocolatey-brown plumage of the young in the nest gives way to a cream head in their mature parents, a white crown above speckles of iron and chestnut, shaking down towards the lace-white tail of a bridal train, or a christening gown. Rain-feathered, they feed on fish or on the hares that run over cliffs, and often on fulmars. In winter they're more likely to eat carrion of sheep or deer. They've been known to take lambs, mostly dead, sometimes alive.

That makes them unpopular with some sheep farmers, especially as sea eagles were extinct in Britain for the best part of the last century, and are only found in Scotland again today after a labour-intensive reintroduction drive. The last native sea eagles were seen in Britain in the north of Scotland in 1918, having been hunted to extinction for sport, their nests disturbed and their eggs raided by collectors, until they faded from our shores as the First World War was won. From the mid-1970s, young breeding pairs from Norway were reintroduced in the Hebrides to the Isle of Rum, and eventually began rearing chicks which successfully fledged and spread out across the west of Scotland from the mid-1980s. Though they're still victims of illegal killing and egg-collecting now, they're becoming more established on the west coast, and there are efforts on the east coast to introduce them there, too. Their nesting sites to the east are kept secret, to protect them from human raiders. Human efforts to protect them are an act of penance for mindlessly driving them out in the first place.

The sight of the sea eagles above the headland stays with me for days. Even from the distance between ground and sky, these birds seemed to have a plan and purpose beyond any other I'd seen among the wildlife on the coasts. Maybe it's because they are birds on a human scale. Their enormous wingspan means that they're wider than we are tall, but the males weigh only between seven and eleven pounds, roughly the weight of a newborn human infant. Their faces and their hunting show planning and ambition. They are larger and far rarer than the golden eagles of inland, which soar so elegant and still on the air currents above the mountains and glens, feeding steadily on birds and mammals of the hills. The sea eagle, on the other hand, is a bird of the tide, an improviser and a thief, taking whatever it finds for its own.

Sea eagles appear in the most ancient poems and carvings of our islands. The eagle is one of the creatures that feels most at home in old folk tales, with their wisdom and mysticism: the eagle, the serpent, the salmon, the stallion, creatures of British myth. Near Strathpeffer, in Easter Ross, there is a carved Pictish stone of blue gneiss showing a swirl-patterned sea eagle, recognisable for its long neck and unfeathered legs. There are others, too, painted and carved into stones and caves, commanders of the air preserved and revered in earth and rock, once and future monarchs. Creatures of the coastline, they swap from land to sea constantly, over all human borders, forever hunting the waves, white-coated custodians of old magic. In the past the British skies were thick with them. Now it's rare and wondrous to see them on the wing; a gift.

V

MEROPE

Merope is the faintest of the Pleiades. She is said to have hidden her face because of the shame of marrying a mortal. She marries Sisyphus, who is punished for his crimes of deceit and self-aggrandisement by being forced to roll a boulder up a hill for all eternity.

THE TIDE CLOCK

THERE IS A TIDE CLOCK in my parents' house in St Monans. It is mounted on the wall beside one of the windows that looks far out to sea. It tells the time, and in addition has one more hand than a traditional wall clock, a hand that swings slowly from high tide to low and back again, twice a day. It's a useful tool when you're looking out of the window towards the horizon, where the sea falls away into grey mist and becomes sky and blur, and you are planning a walk on the beach, and you want to know if the tide – currently halfway up the rocks – is coming in or going out.

Once I had romantically and naïvely assumed that tides operated outside such a thing as precisely predictable time. This was an idea that grew out of noticing that the high and low tide seemed to happen at subtly different times each day, which made childhood beach holidays enjoyably unpredictable, not knowing if that walk out to the sea-cave to look for shells that I'd been craving would be possible before lunch or if it would have to wait until teatime.

I had seen tide tables on the beaches, but at first I'd dismissively assumed them to be loose guesses, and not to be relied upon completely accurately. It came as a surprise to learn that tide times are predictable with a high degree of accuracy, and the only unpredictable factors tend to be storm surges which bring tides much higher than usual. Even these are predictable to an extent, just like any storm, and the weather forecast will tell you a few days in advance when they are on the way.

The timings of the high and low tides are the same, but just how high and how low they are on the beach is what changes. The biggest factor affecting them is the moon. At a new moon, or a full moon, the high tide is higher and the low tide lower than usual. This is called a spring tide when the difference between high and low tide is at its widest, or a neap tide when the difference between them is narrower than usual. They are especially pronounced close to the spring and autumn equinoxes of 21 March and 21 September. The difference in height between a high and a low tide on any particular stretch of coast is called the tidal range, and steep beaches might have a low tidal range, while shallow beaches, where the shore descends gradually downwards, have higher ones, as the tide races up and down them. The Severn Estuary in the UK has either the second or third greatest tidal range in the world, depending on who's measuring, with around fifty feet of difference in depth between its high and low tides. Its competitors the Bay of Fundy in Canada, as measured by the United States' National Oceanic and Atmospheric Administration, and Ungava Bay, also in Canada, are similarly dramatic in range.

Around most of Britain, there are two tides a day, and high tide occurs every twelve hours, twenty-five minutes and fourteen seconds. That refusal to operate strictly alongside the precise twelve-hour divide of day and night is what makes high tide slightly later each day, and gives the tides the impression of unpredictability, or at the very least of operating according to their own mysterious schedule, one step beyond human control.

Geographical factors can change the timing of the tides slightly, too. Features such as rocks and small islands, as well as bathymetry – an ancient-sounding word for the water depth of a location – can lengthen or shorten tide times. To own a tide clock is to resign yourself to forever re-setting its accuracy slightly, if you're determined to keep it right. You set it when the tide is high, and it counts down the tides endlessly until it falls out of sync with the sea, and at the next full moon, when the tide is highest, you set it again.

The certainty of the tide and its twice-a-dayness starts to strip away the mystery of the sea a little, to make it, like time, seem less like an unknowable force, and more like something with rhythms that can be observed and predicted. The sea finally becomes something that can be measured in units of time, like music.

·

I am not, at twenty-eight, young to be having a child; in fact, compared to the women of earlier in the last century and even further in the past, I'm on the old side to be becoming a first-time mother. I shouldn't be naïve about what it involves.

And yet it feels young. Not very many of my friends have children yet. When I first told some of them that I was going to have a baby, several asked if it was planned, a question which startled me in its nosiness and its irrelevance. Women like me, who have jobs and ambitions, are not supposed to have their children in their twenties, these days, or at least, not before they've built a solid career and seen the world and bought a house and met their soulmate. Women are not supposed to have children after thirty-five, either, according to tutting newspaper lifestyle supplements that warn darkly of dropping off a 'fertility cliff'. I don't know when the right time to have a baby is supposed to be – perhaps some time during the fortnight after you turn thirty, when the planets align – but having a child now, and particularly hoping to continue working after doing so, starts to feel somehow transgressive.

All of this means it's hard not to get swept up in the suggestion that having a child means that you throw something away. I think of the women I am sacrificing to be this woman, a woman having a child. There are very different women whom I have desired to be, my desiring in the past now: beautiful, funny, clever women, women with expensive perfume and an insouciant air of freedom about them, bohemian, their shoulders not burdened by commitments or relationships or the drudgeries of life. Women who are smartly dressed, always to be found smoking with excellent men and sharing wry jokes and making art, and never to be found cleaning bathrooms or looking after children or doing a supermarket shop. I don't know if it was ever possible for me to be the kind of woman I am imagining, a life lived in homage to Virginia Woolf and Vanessa Bell and Sylvia Plath, or even if it's possible for any woman to be like them. They are a fantasy of womanhood, a misleading photograph with the yet-to-be-folded laundry out of shot, or blurred into the background. If you look at them from one angle, these women are all art and daring and brilliance. I don't know what you see if you look at them from the other direction. That seems to be the direction I'm staring in right now.

I think of Sylvia Plath in the photograph on the cover of a recent edition of her poetry, blonde and glamorous and on the beach in a bikini, an image that doesn't tally at all with the facts of her existence: someone who was sometimes troubled and sad and abused, a single mother and a suicide victim, and with powerfully articulated and complex thoughts about being a woman and being a parent. Her poems on becoming a mother make the transform-ation seem so acutely emotional that they drown out all reason. She writes about the ache of feeling the world isn't good enough for the small miracle of an anything-possible child you have made. These realities of her life are submerged by the myth of her, by the image of the beautiful blonde woman on the beach, washing over the darkness with a crystal blue tide.

I think of the glamorous Bloomsburys with their relaxed atti-tude to biological parenthood, Vanessa Bell and Duncan Grant and their various children all growing up against a backdrop of the bright-painted walls and fireplaces of Charleston, and running wild in the gardens. And I think of my newly lost ability to drop everything and spend the weekend in Paris – something which I never did, but something I always could have done. I could have been the kind of person to do this.

Fatherhood must be easier, I think, maybe unfairly. Male writers can become fathers and barely notice, with no blood spilt or skin stretched out or scarred in the process. When their children grow up and start speaking to them, and sometimes stop speaking to them, is when their anxiety seems to begin. At the beginning, though, the differences between mothers and fathers are sharp. When the baby is coming, a man can run. Wherever a pregnant woman goes, the baby goes too. Your body traps you in itself.

We have to pretend this isn't the way it is. As young women we have to pretend to be relaxed and carefree, to be Sylvia Plath laughing on the beach, and not Sylvia Plath with the dark ceiling without a star looming over her. For a woman artist, if you are to be taken seriously, you have to pretend that motherhood doesn't matter to you, that it isn't itself an act of creation.

Artists do motherhood painfully and in detail. Mary Shelley's *Frankenstein* is all about creation, the madness of it, the fact that staring into the eyes of another intelligent being that you have formed can be so great and terrible a responsibility that it can ruin you, can lead you on a chase across the world to the ice of the Arctic. I realise that it's not just my body that I'm afraid of losing control over. It's my mind, too.

I feel the conventionality of it all stealing over me. Wasn't I supposed to resist this, the expected life? The conformity of having children with a partner and living steadily in one place? And yet there is nothing about this experience that feels safe or familiar or dull to me. I am starting to think there is a wildness and a craziness in this ordinary. I am tipping forwards voluntarily, diving headlong in surrender to nature's inevitable, overwhelming supremacy over me and my desires. How dare I think I am in charge? She will beat me in the end, through birth or through death.

Before, I wanted to be the kind of woman that I thought men wanted, mixed with the kind of impossible, glorious, high-achieving fictional woman that I wanted to be for her own sake. Things are changing, now, and shrinking, becoming clearer and more exquisite when I look at them in miniature. And I think that now I want to become, most of all, a woman strange and new. A woman I do not know, with a face I wouldn't recognise, and talents I've yet to learn: the woman that my child will need.

SEASICK

IT'S IN THE LAST THROES of high summer, with Sean on the drive back from a visit to my in-laws' house on the border of Wales and Shropshire, that I start to feel as if something is wrong. It has been the hottest weekend of the year and I have spent the nights in complaining discomfort, much too hot, sweating just to breathe through my new, heavier body, still so unfamiliar to me.

We are only a few miles away from home when I feel so sick that I have to ask Sean to stop the car. Nausea is nothing new in this pregnancy – it has come and gone since the moment I found out I was pregnant, and has been joined by the unwelcome addition of heartburn as well for the last few months – but this feels more intense, more urgent, more terrible. I know I'm going to be sick. I've been lucky in this pregnancy not to have suffered from extreme pregnancy vomiting, completely debilitating for those who do get it, like the worst day of a norovirus bug, over and over again, for months. Some women end their pregnancies, and choose never to have any more children, because of it. I have only had, in comparison, very little.

It's probably just a stomach bug, but because I've spent the weekend with family visiting an open farm, the paranoid anxiety starts to rise in my throat with the vomit that I've caught some kind of disease from the animals, something that will endanger the baby. There had been signs all around the farm advising pregnant women not to touch any of the animals, especially not the sheep. I had been careful not to touch them. Maybe, though, I shouldn't have gone at all. The responsibility for another human life still feels too heavy on me.

When I get home, I am sick violently and repeatedly and for hours into the night. My body feels as if it is purging itself of something. The sickness comes in surges, and though I tell myself this must just be a bug, in a self-pitying moment close to midnight with the perspex mixing bowl full of sick balanced on the duvet beside me, I wonder if I might actually be dying.

I haven't had many such illnesses in my life, but one of them swims back to me: I was about eleven years old, at school, and had been feeling strange all day. The locker room where I went to get a textbook out of my bag between classes smelled thickly of teenage sweat, mouldering old gym kit and the acrid fake bubblegum scent of cheap body spray. Normally I wouldn't even notice these smells. Today they rammed themselves down my throat and I doubled over, breathing hard. I took a minute to stick my face under the water fountain, told a couple of classmates I was going to miss the next lesson, and headed straight over to the school nurse.

She looked at my pale, clammy face and asked if my parents could come and take me home. They're both at work, I said, but my grandmother doesn't live far away – maybe we could call her?

She came to pick me up in her little red Honda, looking mildly inconvenienced, not pausing to remove her smart leather driving gloves when she collected me from the waiting area. She nodded at the school nurse and briskly escorted me outside.

'Are you just pretending to be sick to get out of school?' she asked as soon as we got into the car.

'No,' I said, sulkily.

Admittedly I had done that before, which she knew. She had had little sympathy for me feeling 'under the weather' last time, when she assigned me reading and writing exercises and set me to organising one of her huge heaps of crossword books. This time I didn't say anything else for fear words wouldn't be the only thing coming out of my mouth in the car if I did.

I was very quiet on the short journey to her house. When we arrived, she unlocked the door and walked in ahead of me. I took one step through the door, on to the blue-and-purple patterned mock-Persian rug that was laid out in the hall, a long-beloved family heirloom, with uneven and frayed white edges, and patches where the pattern had been worn smooth by generations of shoes. The decades of use had only made this rug more loved and precious, the blue and purple more earthy in texture, but still the colour of jewels.

I vomited all over it.

There was a moment of silence. I was frozen, terrified: my granny's house was elegant and pristine, a house containing a grand piano and old paintings on the walls, and dozens of prized ornaments on every shelf and sideboard.

I looked at her. She looked at me.

She sighed. 'You poor old thing,' she said, finally. 'Go and lie on the sofa. I'll clean this up, and bring you a bowl and a hot water bottle.'

Inside I was overcome with love and gratitude. Outwardly I just smiled in a pale sort of way, and did as she said. As she scrubbed the rug cleaner than it had ever been, I was sure, I slipped into a fevered sleep.

•

Now in my midnight bed which seems to eddy and swirl underneath me, I wish she was here. I crave someone who, quietly, with unconditional caring and without fuss, could clean up after me and tell me I don't need to worry, that there's nothing else I need to do, that I can just lie down somewhere quiet and concentrate on getting better.

And now I realise for the first time that I am going to have a child in my life who will depend on me, in exactly the same way I depended on my grandmother that day, when I was sick for hours and hours, and she brought me water and sang quietly around the house and intermittently played the piano. I think of the hundreds of times my own mother looked after me the same selfless way. I can't just let myself go limp now, and allow others to care for me. There's someone else I have to care for. If I'm feeling rotten, it's likely the baby is, too.

The next day, the sickness is worse. Sean is at work and it's all I can do to lie on my side, as still as possible, to stop the room from lurching, crying quietly with the pain of my cramping stomach muscles. I can't eat or drink without the food and water resurfacing again straight away. As the day goes on, the pain of the cramping gets more intense, and other worries start to cluster together in my mind. The cramping pains are now so sharp that each one makes me convulse and cry out. Surely this couldn't be it, I think. I am only twenty-seven weeks pregnant, only just in the third trimester, only two weeks past the point where 'viable delivery' is even possible – and even then the baby would be extremely premature, and likely very unwell and in need of intensive neonatal care for a long time.

I phone the labour ward at the hospital and tell them my symptoms. I tell them that the painful cramps are so strong that I can't tell whether I can feel the baby moving or not. They ask me to come in and I'll be seen straight away. Sean comes home and we set off together.

When we arrive, the doctor feels my abdomen, takes bloods and gives me an anti-emetic. She hooks me up to a foetal movement monitor, thick plastic pads over cold jelly, and instructs me to press a button every time I think I can feel something, and they will check that it corresponds to the heart rate they are recording. She does a scan, and shows me the baby: bigger than it was at the last scan, more recognisably baby-shaped. I can see its hands move in the darkness in the exact way that a newborn baby's hands open and close in the light, testing their grasp. I'm not in labour. The baby is safe.

I am more of a problem. My liver isn't coping well with the virus and I'm very dehydrated. A drip is brought in and I stay for two days, being presented with a series of hospital meals and told that I have to eat them without vomiting before I can go home. This is no easy feat when the hospital kitchen produces mashed potato that is dolloped on the plate in the precise size, shape and lurid yellow colour of a tennis ball, and tastes as if it's made out of glued-together wood shavings. The cramps subside and I can feel the baby's swaying, jerking movements again, and I am lulled by them.

Eventually, I eat a small bowl of porridge. I have never been happier to go home and fold myself into bed, which is where I stay for days, drinking raspberry Lucozade and hoping that the birth is still far in the future.

A FAIRY HALL

I DON'T THINK MY GRANDMOTHER WOULD have thanked me for remembering her as a grandmother. She always wanted to be seen as her own woman, a person in her own right, not obscured by the lives of those around her. And yet it's not right to say that she wanted to be the centre of attention. It's more that she was, as the wife of a clergyman, expected to perform a certain role: to minister to the sick and needy, to support her husband and look decorative at church events, to be quiet and pliant and wear decent hats.

She supported her husband in other ways than this, in humour, in good conversation, and in making him wash dishes and fetch her tea. He wasn't a figure of royalty to be scurried around, the unimpeachable head of a household. He was her partner, and she was his. Her work, and her creativity, were just as important in their house as his vocation to live his life in communion with God, shepherding congregations towards the divine. She found divinity in music and in laughter. As I find myself struggling to work out how I'm going to be a mother, and devote my soul and care completely to the wellbeing of a child, I consider again the way she lived her life, the distance she had from her family, the preservation of her love of music and its vital role in nourishing her heart. My memories of her when she was alive are all filled with music: after a long day together out shopping and running errands, she would ask me to bring her tea, and then take off her shoes, lie back in her comfiest leather armchair and put on a CD of Bach. Sitting back, closing her eyes, she would let the music wash over her and let her hands move, almost of their own volition, conducting the recorded performance.

I remember playing with the toys she kept at her house for the sole purpose of grandchildren's visits – my father's worn old teddy bears, and an inexplicably large cuddly toy blue lion – while she played the piano freely in her music room, practising every day, the way she told her pupils that they must do. She played much less after my grandfather died. I didn't really understand why at the time. Now I think I do. Music was love to her.

•

My grandmother used to drop me in the bath and ensure that bathtime was conducted with efficiency and practicality, in her belief that all children spent the day getting grubby and should therefore be scrubbed as thoroughly as possible come evening, ideally with a bar of strong-smelling soap and a stiff brush. I used the time to admire her extensive collection of shells, some glisten-ing on the windowsill, some perched on the side of the avocado-coloured bath. She scrubbed my head so firmly that it felt as if she thought that the first layer of a child's skin should be removed each night ready to grow back soft and new in the morning.

'If you don't wash behind your ears, you'll grow potatoes back there,' she said every time, and every time I said I thought that sounded like a great idea, because roast potatoes were my very favourite thing to eat. I never bother to wash behind my ears now. I don't know when I stopped. No potatoes yet.

I was in the Brownies group that met every Wednesday evening in the church hall, and one day the Brown Owl asked us if any of us had any collections of keepsakes or curiosities at home. If we did, we could bring in our collections to show to the group, and explain what we knew about our chosen collected objects, and then we would be given the Collector Badge to sew on to our ugly mud-brown sashes.

'Why don't you take in the shells you've picked up from all the beaches you've been to?' my mother had said to me in the car on the way home when I'd told her about the badge. 'You could have a collection like the one on Granny's bathroom windowsill.'

I thought of the large, inviting conch perched on the bath. My mother went to the bookshop that weekend and bought me a Collins guide to the British seashore. I gathered up all the shells in the pockets of my coat and trousers and the bottoms of ruck-sacks, and the ones that had fallen down into toy-boxes and been stashed away in the sock drawer, and laid them all out together. I looked up what each one was, and made a label for each shell. My mother found me a length of yellow-gold fabric that I could spread on the floor in the church hall and display the shells on. I had one razor clam, and a few treasured spiralled whelks. Scallops and mussels and periwinkles. A prickly urchin. Dozens of limpets. One oyster.

All laid out together, I was proud of what I'd managed to collect, almost without trying. Years of foraging had led me to a natural history collection of which a keen Victorian lady naturalist might be proud. And yet I wasn't quite satisfied with what I'd managed to gather. It all looked very British, very seasidey, not as exciting and inspiring as I had hoped it would be. The shells, shorn from their natural context of the wet beach and live waves, looked as muted as the driftwood I'd tried to paint red on Skye.

That weekend, staying at my grandmother's house, at bathtime I again marvelled at her collection of enormous shells drawn from around the earth's equator. Seizing a moment of confidence, I asked her if I could have the conch, the biggest of them all, the shell almost the size of my head that would let me hear the sea if I put it to my ear.

The answer, of course, was no. The conch was too precious. She thought for a minute as she scrubbed with what felt like extra rigour behind my left ear. I wondered if I'd have any skin left at the end of it.

In the end, she let me borrow a Mexican sand dollar. I pretended to Brown Owl that I'd collected it myself. She didn't ask where from.

·

When I left for university, my old childhood shell collection ended up being stored on the bathroom windowsill in my parents' house. I don't know what it is about shells and bathroom window-sills. I wonder if it's strange that a lasting memory of my grandmother after she is gone lives on in these shells and treasures of the sea, in the sand dollar that's mine forever now, and think of *The Tempest*:

> Full fathom five thy father lies;
> Of his bones are coral made;
> Those are pearls that were his eyes:
> Nothing of him that doth fade,
> But doth suffer a sea-change
> Into something rich and strange.

One weekend I went to Edinburgh's Botanic Gardens where there is a small building, a folly really, though they call it a pavilion, at the back of the Queen Mother's Memorial Garden which was installed in 2006. The garden is split into four, to represent the 'four corners' of the world – a strangely old-fashioned idea – and accordingly planted up with specimens from Asia, Europe, North America and the Southern Hemisphere. In the centre is a laby-rinth formed of bog myrtle. The pavilion is made from Caithness stone. As I stepped inside, it was as if I'd walked into my dream shell collection: the walls were encrusted with thousands of pris-tine shells in blue and white, mussels and scallops in repeating patterns around tiles painted with the Queen Mother's initials, ER. It was like a shrine, both to a queen and to the sea.

Shells have long been used as wall decoration. Shells were first stuck on to stone walls, wedged into cracks, in ancient coastal shrines, caves that became worshipping places to Greek gods, places like St Ninian's Cave where contemplation and meditation felt closer because of the sea. Aphrodite, who grew in a scallop shell and was born through sea foam, had shell caves dedicated to her, and in the coasts of Ancient Rome, too, where she was Venus.

Shell grottoes became more deliberate and elaborate in Italy during the Renaissance, shell decoration becoming used more in garden follies and fountains, and the first British shell rooms and grottoes emerged as aristocratic indulgences in the seventeenth century. Chatsworth House and Woburn Abbey were early sites, and Skipton Castle in Yorkshire. Woburn Abbey claims to have the largest surviving shell room in the country, orchestrated by the French architect Isaac de Caus and including mother-of-pearl and green ormer shells from the Mediterranean and the waters around the Channel Islands.

Shell rooms and grottoes reached their full height of popularity in the eighteenth century, the golden age of the extravagant nobleman with a lust for showing-off. A shell grotto inside a garden folly became a must-have accessory for the discerning British aristocrat.

At Goodwood House in West Sussex, there is a shell house that was created by the second Duchess of Richmond and her daughters, Lady Caroline and Lady Emily, in the 1740s. The shells that encrust the walls and ceiling and flare around the oval windows are collected from around the world, and have been stuck into grand shapes that echo the scrolls and florals of the intricate plaster mouldings of the finest Georgian ballrooms, and sculpted into approximations of Greco-Roman vases. Some of the shells were donated to the Duchess by sea captains who knew the family's love of shells, and brought them exotic specimens in pink and yellow from around Jamaica and the South Seas. Others – pale blue British limpets and mussels and shimmer-white twisted spirals of dogwhelk – were gathered by the family themselves during jaunts to nearby Sussex beaches. Having naturally crumbled and degraded over 250 years, in the early Nineties it was restored to pristine beauty with over 55,000 extra shells.

One of the surviving eighteenth-century shell grottoes that claims to be among the biggest in the country is Scott's Grotto in Ware, in Hertfordshire, created by the Quaker writer and poet John Scott in what were then the grounds of his estate, Amwell House. Scott completed extensive design and landscaping of the park there, and excavated a grotto of six interconnected rooms stretching twenty yards into the chalky hillside, their walls all encrusted with fossils, glass, Hertfordshire puddingstone and black knapped flints and most of all shells: silver ormers and oysters and conches and fifty more varieties besides. The display of full-hearted decoration was completed much to the disapproval of Scott's puritanical brother. Scott wrote lovingly of the stimulating, creative, and restful experience of walking through his garden and grotto:

Where, 'midst thick oaks, the subterraneous way
To the arch'd grot admits a feeble ray;
Where glossy pebbles pave the varied floors,
And rough flint-walls are deck'd with shells and ores,

And silvery pearls, spread o'er the roofs on high,
Glimmer like faint stars in a twilight sky;
From noon's fierce glare, perhaps, he pleas'd retires,
Indulging musings which the place inspires.

Scott enthusiastically welcomed visitors to see his creation, and kept a visitor book which recorded more than 3,000 names. Samuel Johnson is said to have visited the grotto several times, and called it 'a fairy hall'. There's a sense of humour to the design, too: a seat inside the chamber is inscribed with the word 'FROG' written in shells, in reference to Scott's first wife, Sarah Frogley. Much decayed, like the shell house at Goodwood, it was almost demolished by bull-dozing developers in the 1960s who were building a new estate of houses, but was saved by a council preservation order at the last minute – the bulldozers had already flattened the porch, but stopped short of venturing further. In 1990, it was restored by the Ware Society and opened to the public. Now the grotto is concealed in the middle of a residential neighbourhood, surrounded by suburban houses and gardens, hidden away like all of the most magical places. Ware is close to water in the form of Lea Valley wetlands but miles from the coast, and yet its hidden cave of shell-covered wonders connects it directly to the sea through the imagination.

•

We know how Scott's Grotto came into being, and its whole history. There's another shell grotto in England's south-east whose origins are much more mysterious.

In 1835, on a windswept day in the coastal land beyond the Kent Downs near Margate, a schoolteacher named James Newlove was out in a field with his young son. They were digging ground to make a new duck pond. While digging in a new spot, the younger Newlove's spade hit far softer ground than the land around it, ground so yielding that it seemed to give way completely underneath him. Digging away a little more, he realised that if just a little more earth was cleared away, some sort of gap would be revealed below the superficial grass and mud of the Downs.

He called his father over to have a look at the strange phenomenon. Together they removed more earth, until there was a hole big enough for a young boy to fit through. The cavern that lay under the earth seemed large; a well perhaps, or maybe some long-buried structure. James Newlove fetched a rope, and to sate the pair's curiosity, he tied it around his son's waist and lowered him into the cavern to have a look around.

When he pulled the boy back to the surface to hear about what he'd seen, at first James thought his son was making it up. He reported an ornate underground grotto, with curved walls covered in intricate mosaics made out of sea shells, whelks and mussels, scallops, limpets and oysters. The shells are arranged in patterns depicting trees, hearts, flowers, diamonds and stars, owl faces, a turtle, Greek gods and anchors, and, in one place, a womb and umbilical cord. There are around 4.6 million shells in total. Almost all of them appear to be native to British shores, and collected locally rather than imported.

The grotto was opened to the public to view in 1837, and has been maintained as a privately owned visitor attraction ever since.

There isn't any documentation, however, about who built it, or how it came into being. Given the number of shell grottoes and follies created by artistically minded aristocrats in Britain in the eighteenth century, it seems most likely that the grotto also dates from this period, though the number of pagan symbols drawn in shells on the walls has made some visitors conclude that it's a pagan shrine dating from much earlier than this.

Something about the atmosphere of the grotto, its art of mysterious origin in the darkness, makes people reach for spiritual explanation. Groups have held seances in the chambers to attempt to contact the spirits of the builders of the grotto and ask them why and how they created it – though, to date, no definitive response has been forthcoming from the spirit world.

AGAINST THE ROCK

THE LAST FEW WEEKS OF pregnancy take a toll on my body, making me feel heavy and awkward, incapable of functioning like a human being. They also affect the mind. I am returning to the in-between feelings of those earliest weeks of pregnancy. I am not only myself – there is another being that I am already caring for – and I am not yet a mother. The difference is that now everyone who looks at me can see the state I'm in. It feels like the last stages of a journey, the in-between point before reaching the destination. I'm not yet swimming deep in the sea of parenthood and all that it means. I'm paddling in the shallows, getting a sense of the temperature, getting my goose-pimpled skin acclimatised to the coming change.

The beach has this area of almost, too, the zone of the intertide, also called the littoral, from the Latin *litoris,* shore. It's the part of the beach that extends from the high water mark of the tide at its fullest point, all the way down to the low tide.

This area is a special kind of ecosystem. It is full of creatures that depend both on salt water and on the lack of it, equally, to survive.

The zone of the intertide takes many forms and can be a scape of rockpools, mudflats or saltmarshes, large stretches of waterlogged land where curlews hunt for worms and sea lavender blooms.

The intertide is the land of the not-yet. There are two hearts beating and two brains sparking inside my skin. And I am not yet a mother. I and my child are at the borders of life, paddling in the shallows of the water in the greeny opaque waves hung underneath the surface with seaweed, at the point where you can feel the shudder of uncertainty as an unknown object brushes against your leg. The weeks feel very long. This is a place where time closes down and opens up, operating at completely different speeds from normal.

The imminent arrival of my own child is making me think, almost all the time, of what I remember from my own childhood. The beach seems to be a stage where the happiest moments played themselves out. I start to look forward to beach activities I might be able to do with this child, all the activities of a British seaside holiday: rockpooling and crabbing and sandcastle-building, ending up with an ice cream and a warm towel wrapped around shivering shoulders. I remember buying a crabbing line from the shop of seaside bric-a-brac on the island of Herm in the Channel Islands one summer, with family friends, and baiting it with a bit of bacon rind saved from breakfast. We hauled up crabs from the little pool beside the jetty to put in a bucket and count, and then put them back at the end of the morning.

There was endless rockpooling in Fife, too, where blennies and butterfish abound in the busiest pools closest to the water, tiny eel-like creatures that dart into the dark corners if they see you coming. There are sea slugs, and pipefish that look like miniature elongated seahorses, and the strange, leathery pockets of mermaid's purses, capsules for dogfish eggs which have since hatched and swum away.

Waving underwater, but just as able to tolerate being out in the hot sun, are the squat reddish brown flowers of the beadlet anemone. When they're submerged, you can see over a hundred tentacles arranged in six circles around a mouth, waiting to sting and attack anything that touches them, and have it for lunch. Sometimes the long, creepy legs of the spider crab reach out from the murk.

It's a house full of bad-tempered roommates, the rockpool, different characters all living on top of one another and getting in the way, and eating each other's food, and when you look down into it you can see the sea in all its variety.

I've never experienced the soft white sand and warm clear waters of the tropics, so my frame of reference for the seaside is all stinging cold shallows, and sharp crunchy shingle underfoot, and bone-like bleached driftwood, far removed from balmy paradise and coconuts. As well as the Channel Islands, I came to Uist as a child. We stayed in a cottage that was close to a path taken by a herd of Highland cows, who tramped from their grazing places back home through the front garden every evening in the rose-gold light, bells clonking around their necks. It's the only place I've ever been where you could use the expression 'until the cows come home' and mean it literally as a measure of time.

The sea butts up against the fertile and grassy machair plains of north-western Scotland and Ireland, and their islands, Lewis, Harris and Uist. Machair is an unusual type of landscape, low-lying dunes made of sand blown further ashore than the tide-line reaches in windy and wet conditions, on to marshland and grass. The air here smells of sand and grass and your hair crunches with wind-blown grit by the end of the day. It's home to animals that are picky about where they set up their homes. The low, grassy plains are green and tufted over the sand and undulating in tiny hillocks on the wide flatness, and you could believe they are little mop hairstyles belonging to trolls and fairy creatures that live submerged in the seaside bog.

Machair is a landscape that's home to scarce animals. There are large numbers of ringed plovers and the much rarer corncrake, with its long legs and tawnyish feathers and its loud and distinctive creaking corkscrewing call. They sound halfway between a door opening in a haunted house and a music-box being wound up. They sound as if they have a sore throat after smoking too many cigarettes. They sound a lot like their scientific name: *Crex crex*. They sound as if they've lived a life. Corncrakes are small and hard to see, because they like to hide among the tall waving machair grasses when they visit the west of Scotland in the summer months, so you're likely to hear them before you spot them. Even though they're hard to find in this part of the world, they're easy to hear.

The creatures that live here in the machair have to be hardy, and able to cope with a variety of different conditions, from being completely submerged in cool seawater to being fried by the hot sun. The sand that shores up the machair has an exceptionally high concentration of broken-up shells – 80 to 90 per cent of the sand is made up of shells, rather than of worn-down minerals and stones. In winter, the machair is windswept and desolate, without much plant life to be found. Often the plains become waterlogged, which protects the fine sand from being blown away, and allows them to become home to wading birds and the aquatic annual plant *Najas flexilis*, the 'slender naiad', with thin green hairs that love to drink the brackish water.

When spring and summer come, though, the grasses froth with colourful wildflowers. Tough marram grass digs down into the sandiest parts of the dunes, closest to the water, and provides cover for more plants to grow beyond. Rare bees thrive, particularly the great yellow bumblebee, the Platonic ideal of the bumblebee, round and fuzzy, its body striped in topaz and onyx, with detailed wings of black lace.

Once, in a school biology lesson, we were told to look at little piles of sand under a microscope. I expected that what I would see when I looked through the lens would be the same identical yellow grains that I saw with my unaided eye, except bigger. I was surprised to find that the particles of sand looked, instead, like full-sized shells in a hundred different colours, not alike at all, but easily discernible fragments of real creatures and skeletons long dead and left behind on the shore. Here was quite clearly a large chunk of what had once been a limpet.

Limpets are animals of the tide, their lives shaped by the timing of it washing in and out, their existence dependent both on the sea and the lack of it. They cling with their one foot so tightly to the rocks of the shore – avoiding becoming the prey of seabirds – that to remove them is difficult and murderous. On soft rocks, they use their hard shells to carve out a space for themselves that's the perfect fit, and on harder rocks, they wear down their own shells to slot into the contours of the stone. They grip the rocks with enormous tensile strength, making a bond stronger even than spider silk. Once they've found their spot and adjusted the fit, when the tide is in they wander around under the water's surface to feed on seaweed, before returning back to the exact space they occupied before and locking themselves into place again when the tide is on the turn. Detaching them in this state is likely to injure them so severely that you kill them.

I had thought of limpets mostly as just as shells in themselves, but I started to learn about the creatures that live inside the little ridged pyramids that stick themselves like pimples all over rocks on the shorelines of British beaches, to be kicked off by children who don't understand or care that they were alive. I had thought that they were brittle, and I learned that they are strong. I learned that inside each limpet are kidneys, eyes, muscles and a three-chambered heart.

STORMALONG

IN THE GOLDEN DAYS OF sail, as Stan Hugill recorded them, there was one figure who encapsulated every myth going, and his name was Stormalong.

Lots of sea shanties mention Stormalong, from the early nineteenth century onwards. Hugill claims that some of them at least have origins in African American song, their tunes taken across the Atlantic on slave ships and then popularised and spread through African American crews for the next 100 years, centred around ships that set off from Massachusetts. There are songs about a giant called Stormalong John, or a shadowy character called Stormy Along, or even Alfred Bulltop Stormalong. Most of the Stormalong shanties are halyards, sung while hauling the ropes that raised or lowered ladders and sails aloft, a physical act that is close to the opposite of lowering a coffin into a grave. That's relevant because in the songs the character of Stormalong is usually dead and being mourned, his legend sung:

> He was a sailor bold and true,
> *To my aye storm a-long!*

A good old skipper to his crew;
Aye, aye, aye, Mister Storm a-long.

He lies low in an earthen bed,
To my aye storm a-long!
Our hearts are sore our eyes are red;
Aye, aye, aye, Mister Storm a-long.

He's moored at least and furled his sail,
To my aye storm a-long!
No danger now from wreck or gale;
Aye, aye, aye, Mister Storm a-long.

The crew would rest during the verses, and heave with all their strength during the refrains. The legendary sailor is dead and gone, but the work involved in keeping a ship at sea goes on. The legends of the man Stormalong that survive in the shanties are vague and shifting. He was a giant, three fathoms tall, according to some. The White Cliffs of Dover are only white, the legend goes, because Stormalong's ship was so vast that it got wedged in the English Channel, and his crew had to grease the hull with soap to ease it out, and as the soapy ship scraped out the cliffs were washed clean in the process. Stormalong is also said to have battled a Kraken, survived a hurricane, and saved several boats from a deadly whirlpool by lifting them from the water on to his own ship with his bare hands.

His feats are the feats that every sea-thirsty adventurer would want to be true. They're tall tales from an age of sail that seems so impossible, so glorious in itself, that when it's remembered in song it seems as though the life of Stormalong might really, truly have happened. After all, strange things did happen at sea: the hallucinations and visions of sailors who had gone a long time without proper food could spawn whole myths in themselves, and there were real-life strange sights too, odd-looking fish and birds in bright colours and unfamiliar shapes were encountered by young men who, before going to sea, had never even left their home town. Their families back at home would never believe their descriptions of the things they had seen. In this age of missionary travel and the slave trade, whole cultures unseen before by Western travellers would have seemed alien to these boys too. In a time when sailing the world meant you could happen upon paradise birds and cultures who worshipped entirely different religions, who was to say to these boys that a giant Kraken-fighting sailor of legend couldn't be true, too? The sea was full of marvels.

I think that Stan Hugill, collating his sea shanties long after the days when the sea was full of sailing ships, saw himself as a bit of a Stormalong figure. There was nobody alive, by the time he was telling his stories of his own exploits to rapt crowds, who could dispute the adventures he said he had when he was a teenager, climbing aboard a ship and making his way in the world, surviving only on pluck. Was he really shipwrecked? Did he really speak all of those languages? Or was he just another Stormalong John, a man made entirely out of myth created from wondrous things that seemed as though they could be possible 100 miles from land? I want him to be the real deal, this relic of the high seas. I want the sea to be magic.

CANDLES

THE BABY IS SIX DAYS late. Not that it knows it: in the darkness and quiet of its current dwelling-place, time has no real meaning. It inhabits a dark and always-moving world somewhere behind my navel, a place the baby and I had grown together, somewhere that didn't know anything about times or dates or the expectations of a frowning midwife. The baby will come when it is ready, everyone says. And it is not ready yet.

It's dark and quiet here, too, in my bedroom in the middle of the night, another night that finds me awake. I am very big now. At the midwife appointments at the doctor's surgery in town, I turn my face away when they ask me to stand on the scales. I know that the weight I've gained is a good sign, a sign that the baby is growing properly, and that my body is laying down stores ready to support and nourish it even after it's born. And still I can't shake that old feeling that for women any kind of weight gain is bad. None of my clothes fit me now. I am all bulk in front, all baby, all new life ready to burst out. 'It's going to be a girl,' says the older woman in the changing room at John

Lewis to her young assistant, with a satisfied smile, when I carry in yet another maternity dress to try on. *Crone*, I think cruelly, my venom invisible. I'm being bad-tempered and unfair, but none of my shoes fit me, and I am extremely grumpy about the red marks cutting into my heels and comments on my body from strangers.

I am happy to be getting so much bigger, to be so visibly pregnant, to have this outer sign that everything is going well. And yet, when a friend tells me I look 'huge', I'm upset. It's irrational. I supplement my diet with lots of digestive biscuits and Dairy Milk, embracing the problem.

At night I don't sleep. If I lie on my back, I can feel the weight of the baby pressing down on to veins and arteries that don't want to be compressed, and I get lightheaded and breathless. So I lie on one side, until the weight of my body and bump start to press too heavily on my bones, and then I have to begin the long and complicated task of turning over on to the other side, which requires significant planning. I grab my belly with both hands and lift, shifting my pelvis all the while, gradually moving on to my back, and then over to my right, easing the weight down into the mattress, my joints clunking back into place. The baby protests, kicking upwards into my lungs, and makes me jump. I close my eyes, and hope we can both get a little sleep, and pray I can last a few hours before needing a wee. This is unlikely.

The evenings are beginning to draw in, the nights getting longer between evening and morning. The leaves on the trees are flaming with autumn. And I have started to light candles, tealights and cheap little scented votives from the supermarket, in every room, every day when the twilight begins, to guard against the dark, little offerings to something I can't name.

•

Light can mean death or life. The sea is prone to causing weather phenomena that shine light in the darkness out of nothing. Storms and whirlpools come on suddenly and overwhelm you, while strange lights in the sky make themselves known in quieter ways, and can unnerve you with their premonitions of death and fear to come, the qualities we attribute to things that we don't understand and can't predict.

St Elmo's fire is the name for the luminous plasma that appears in an atmospheric electric field, such as a thunderstorm, around ships at sea. Sometimes ball lightning, where glowing electricity in the air during a storm collects in strange orbs, is mistaken for St Elmo's fire, but St Elmo's fire looks more like the light captured in glass tubes and made into neon shop signs. It always attaches itself to an object, maybe the mast of a ship at sea, which can look as though it has caught fire, but doesn't burn.

Both ball lightning and St Elmo's fire, when seen out to sea, can be either good or bad omens. The sight of 'death fires' is a sign of dark magic and an evil, superstitious omen in 'The Rime of the Ancient Mariner':

> About, about, in reel and rout,
> The death-fires danced at night;

> The water, like a witch's oils,
> Burnt green, and blue, and white.

St Elmo's fire is part of the family of mysterious natural light phenomena that also occur over inland wetland, including the Scottish legend of the will o' the wisp, the flickering lights that appear above marshes and boggy ground at night and are said to lure travellers away from the path and into danger. The light has intelligent, independent properties, the legends say, and malevolent aims.

Sometimes, though, electrical weather events like these, and the glowing lights they emit, can be peaceful omens. The distinctive purplish light of St Elmo's fire is named after St Elmo, or St Erasmus, one of the patron saints of sailors, and originally was seen by sailors as evidence that he was protecting them. Strange lights at sea are sometimes called corposants, from *corpo santo*, holy body.

St Elmo's fire has been observed across the centuries, and has been given supernatural explanations by seagoing peoples from all over the world. In *The Tempest*, Ariel claims responsibility:

> I boarded the king's ship; now on the beak,
> Now in the waist, the deck, in every cabin,
> I flam'd amazement: sometime I'd divide
> And burn in many places; on the topmast
> The yards and bowsprit, would I flame distinctly
> Then meet and join. Jove's lightnings, the precursors
> O' the dreadful thunder-claps, more momentary
> And sight-outrunning were not; the fire and cracks

Of sulphurous roaring the most mighty Neptune
Seem to besiege and make his bold waves tremble,
Yea, his dread trident shake.

I prefer the traditional Welsh folk explanation for St Elmo's fire. It's a true ghost story with a soothing heart to it. In Wales, there is a tradition that strange lights appearing most often along deserted roads by night – sometimes, according to the legend, specifically along the roads that funeral processions take to graveyards – are called corpse candles, or spirit candles. The Welsh phrase is *canwyll yr ysbryd* or *canwyllau cyrff*. These lights, which can be in the form of glowing blue and purple auras, or small yellow balls, or in the shape of actual candle flames, are said to signify the souls of the recently dead, as they travel in a straight line, over hills and fields and streams, towards their grave site. The appearance of many such lights gathered in one place, where nobody has recently died, indicates that a death is imminent. *Canwyllau cyrff* are sometimes observed alongside the *cyhyraeth*, a disembodied moaning voice whose sound was also said to herald death coming soon.

These ghostly lights have been seen most often by the sea. The Victorian writer and natural historian James Motley – who was born in Leeds before making a career as an industrialist in South Wales – wrote in his 1848 book about Welsh lore, *Tales of the Cymry*, about the *cyhyraeth*.

There are many who relate [he says] who when they have been watching by the sea shore for wild fowl or foxes, or may be for a wreck, on a dark windy night, they have heard its moan; at first at a distance, gradually approaching towards them along the edge of the waves, and then dying away as it were upon the gale . . . Frequently too, upon such occasions, a dismal light is seen hovering on the waves, but this is not looked upon as in any way belonging to the Cyhiraeth, though it occurs as the same time, but as a sort of Canwyll Corph or corpse candle.

The Victorian gothic novelist W. H. Ainsworth included a poem about corpse candles in his 1834 novel, *Rookwood*:

> Through the midnight gloom did a pale blue light
> To the churchyard mirk wing its lonesome flight . . .
> . . . Is it the soul, released from clay,
> Over the earth that takes its way,
> And tarries a moment in mirth and glee
> Where the corpse it hath quitted interred shall be?

There is an origin story for the corpse candle legend. It's said that when St David was dying, one of his last prayers was that God would send a sign to the congregations in Pembrokeshire that their spirits were watched over in death, to bring them consolation, and from that day onward, the Holy Spirit would light the path of spirits of the dead in Wales. It's possible that this is a retrofitting of Christianity to a more ancient myth, one which chimes with a family of similar myths of ghostly spirits haunting empty roads and marshes by night. Like all supernatural signs that are said to fore- shadow death, they can be taken either as the darkest of all possible omens, or as a sign of positivity and change, peace and brightness, the death of an old way of life and the beginning of a new.

•

In the kirk at St Monans, on my very first visit, I lit a candle for my grandmothers, an offering to the dead against the night. I paused to remember them, the pain they suffered and the work they did to bring me to this place. I miss them sharply. Grief comes in waves, each one different, always moving and never finished. I wonder how they would have taken to being great-grandmothers, and I think of the women who dive for delicate byssus in the Mediterranean, passing on the skills and the tradition from grandmother to granddaughter, down through centuries. In the kirk the model boats had made ghostly shadows against the walls in the gloom. Places to buy nautical supplies used to be called ship's chandlers, because they also sold candles from the same place, lights spreading out across the world over the sea, and sending messages from the dead to the living.

VI

ELEKTRE

Elektre is sometimes depicted as an amber-tinged cloud. She is often conflated with another Elektre appearing in Greek mythology, one of the Okeanides, the 3,000 sea-nymph daughters of the Titans Okeanos, personification of the sea, and Tethys, daughter of the sky and earth. This Elektre marries the sea-god Thaumas and is mother to Iris, rainbow goddess.

Or who shut up the sea with doors, when it brake forth, as if it had issued out of the womb?

— Job 38:8

RISEN FROM THE SEA

BEFORE 1837 THERE WAS NO obligation for anyone on a British registered ship, Royal Navy or merchant ship to record any baby born at sea. After that date, the government asked people to send records of all births or deaths at sea to the General Register Office, from where they would then be recorded in the Marine Register:

> That if any Child of an English Parent shall be born at Sea, on board a British Vessel, the Captain or Commanding Officer of the Vessel on board of which the said Child shall have been born shall forthwith make a Minute of the several Particulars herein-before required to be inserted in the Register touching the Birth of such Child, so far as the same may be known, and the name of the Vessel wherein the Birth took place, and shall, on the arrival of the Vessel in any Port of the United Kingdom, or by any other sooner opportunity, send a Certificate of the said Minute, through the Post-Office, to the Registrar-General.

The message didn't always get across in the chaotic aftermath of a baby actually being born at sea, though. Who has the time to send off a form, when you've just returned from a voyage which gained an extra passenger? When you look through the census records of the nineteenth century and come across details of people who claim to have been born at sea, it becomes clear that there's no really consistent way of recording how and where they came into the world. Sometimes the name of the ship on which a person was born is given as the place of birth; in other entries, the port that was nearest the ship at the time is listed; in some cases the place of birth is as broad and vague as 'Pacific Ocean' or 'On British Seas'.

These short, factual entries glimpse vast personal stories gone untold. There aren't many records of what it was really like to give birth at sea in the age of sail and before. Government records don't tell the story of the mess and chaos there must have been at a sea birth: the danger and the lack of nearby medical aid; the infection risks; the experience of a woman at her most vulnerable trapped in a ship full of men.

Deaths at sea were much more common than births. They include the deaths of women and babies during labour only recorded as small, sad footnotes in the official record of a ship's voyage. Almost excised from history are the births and deaths of enslaved peoples aboard ships crossing the Atlantic during the slave trade, the horrors they suffered in torture hidden from official records, their souls deemed null by those who traded them. The enslaved peoples' relationship with the sea was marked by pain and injustice. Their stories are their own and not mine to tell. The sea's darkness came for them with human hands.

Most of the stories we do have of sea births are the stories of white American families. United States records show that a baby was born on board the *Mayflower* ship that first brought pilgrim settlers from Britain to America; the infant boy who met the world in the middle of the Atlantic was named Oceanus. Centuries later, American whaling ships were some of the few types of vessels that had women aboard on voyages relatively routinely, usually a privilege afforded to the wives of captains. If wives didn't accompany their husbands on long whaling voyages, they risked not seeing them for at least six months at a time, so it wasn't rare for them to join the crew.

Once the women were on board on these long trips, the inevitable happened. Pregnancy might have been common, but births were unusual. Often women approaching the time of delivery would be left at a port alone to give birth while the crew carried on, instead of risking the far more life-threatening dangers of going into labour on the voyage.

When births did happen, they were recorded almost incidentally, and generally mentioned only in passing in ships' logs. Some stories are collected in maritime historian Joan Druett's book *Petticoat Whalers*. In 1862, on a voyage of the *Thomas Pope*, Charles Robbins recorded a day spent 'Looking for whales ... reduced sail to double reef topsails at 9pm. Mrs. Robbins gave birth of a Daughter and doing nicely. Latter part fresh breezes and squally. At 11am took in the mainsail.'

Captain Charles Nicholls's wife accompanied him on a trip to New Zealand on the *Sea Gull* in 1853. Knowing that she was expecting a baby, Captain Nicholls had sought advice on midwifery from a friend and fellow captain, Peter Smith, who had told him of delivering a baby, ''Tis easy.' Smith instructed his friend to ensure the first mate was there to hold the baby when it was born. When Mrs Nicholls went into labour, the ship's first mate was positioned ready and waiting outside the cabin, and was duly handed the newborn when it arrived. But a few moments after the happy presentation, Captain Nicholls came running back out again, shouting: 'My God! Get the second mate, fast!' A second baby had, to everyone's surprise, also emerged.

These sea births seem easy, funny and joyous, but the wider reality was hard. Generally births were recorded by men, who kept the logs but may not have been present for the birth itself, and their records reflect the relative importance of the birth as a trivial event compared to the greater challenges of the voyage. Women on board ship who kept diaries did not, in this age of Victorian hypersensitivity to decency and suppression of any talk of bodily functions, tend to go into details about pregnancy and birth – or, if they did, those details were delicately excised by editors in later publication of their diaries. The combined result of all this is that sea births come to sound like incidental minor miracles, and probably completely unlike the mess and pain of how they actually were.

Sea births are miraculous in myth. According to Hesiod, Aphrodite was born fully grown out of the sea foam, the *aphros*, after Ouranos's testicles were cut off by Kronos and thrown into the water off the coast of the island of Kythira. She rode to shore on a scallop shell and covered her naked body with myrtle.

Aphrodite is the goddess of love and beauty, and she is the goddess whose name is associated most often with the sea and with women. She was there before Stella Maris. The epithets that accompany her name wherever you find it in Greek and Latin – in Homer as well as in other texts and at historic worship sites – tell the story of the people who worshipped her, and hint at where in their lives they asked for her help.

They show that Aphrodite is a many-faced figure and she is many versions of a woman. In some places she is Pontia, goddess of the open ocean. In others she is Euploia, of fair sailing. She is Limenia, defender of the harbour. Aphrogenes, foam-born. Anadyomene, risen from the sea.

She has darkness too. She is Psithyristes, of whispering. Androphonos, killer of men. Tymborychos, digger of graves.

And she is Kypris, goddess of pregnancy. Mechanitis, deviser of new things. Genetyllis, our protector in birth.

THE SHALLOWS

A S STUPID AS IT SOUNDS, I have started to think the baby
will never come. The due date we were given right at the
beginning has come and gone, and the fact that a baby hasn't
arrived on schedule is making me feel almost as if I've missed the
one bus out of town, and that there won't be another. I can still
feel the baby moving in my abdomen though, that strange, deep
inward stirring punctuated by a few sharp kicks to the inside of
my solar plexus. In the weird half-light of my new shape and status
as a pregnant person, rather than my plain old self that I'd come to
know as I've grown into an adult, it is easy to convince myself this
isn't the movement of a baby waiting to be born, but just the new
arrangement of my internal organs, which have mutated and
shifted into a formation they will now assume forever.

And then early on a Saturday morning as the day dawns grey, I
wake up in the gauzy just-dawn light with an unfamiliar tightening sensation around my middle. At first I put it down as just
another of the funny twinging movements that I'd come to know,
lately, nothing to get excited about, and so I shift my limbs into a

more comfortable position and slip back into sleep almost straight away, drifting into the hyperreality of half-dreams. I am just walking down a corridor, and then looking at a butterfly in the garden that becomes a caterpillar, when that same nagging twinge tweaks me back towards consciousness again. I try to resist it and go back to sleep, but the feeling pinches into my dreams like an alarm and tugs me back from the borders of sleep.

The distant music of my body keeps playing, keeps sharpening, keeps edging me awake. At last I give in, and heave upright. I reach blearily for my phone and check the time. Six o'clock. There's nothing to get up for yet. I settle back under the duvet and tell myself it is nothing, yet again nothing, there will never be a baby. The warmth pulls me back into deep darkness until again the faint rhythm of tightening is a voice that calls me back to the surface. I check my phone again. Eleven minutes past six.

Maybe this isn't nothing. Maybe, this time, it is something. I lie very still and scroll through the apps on my phone, illuminating my face in the gloom but not really seeing or reading. Soon there is another tightening twinge. Twenty-five minutes past six. I download a contraction timer app.

Time passes surprisingly quickly as I log the tightenings. I stay in bed until nine, watching the minutes, feeling the sensations. It's nothing like pain, but more like a hug from invisible arms. I've been told that even if this is the beginning of labour, it could be hours or days before the tightenings gather into something worth listening to, so when Sean wakes up I tell him what has been happening and suggest he might just want to put the kettle on. He looks entirely relaxed.

I haul myself through the morning rituals of the pregnant human being. They involve clambering heavily into the bath and taking a slow and deliberate shower, with the door propped wide open to let in as much cool air as possible to ward off fainting. I complete my ritual of standing barefoot in the kitchen, looking out of the window at the distant hills and feeling my brain flit from one thing to the next, unable to concentrate. I notice that the tightenings have slowed right down. As I'd half-predicted, they are tailing off, like labour can often do, scared away like goldfish in the shallows. It could be days yet.

•

By lunchtime, the day already seems to have lasted for years. Sean suggests that we go for a walk with the dog, even though walks are now more frustrating than fun for the dog if I'm involved, because I have to move so slowly, and she has to keep doubling back to check that I'm all right and my lungs are still working.

I pull on the wax jacket that I haven't been able to zip up for weeks now, and Sean helps me into a pair of wellies, the only shoes that now fit over my swollen ankles. We step out into the street and I catch my breath before beginning the walk up the slight hill. The grey morning has turned into an autumn afternoon of gold. The trees in the woods at the end of the road are still covered thickly in leaves, but the leaves are all the shades of fire and sun, radiating warmth of colour against the sharp chill that's already in the air as the season opens up. With my jacket pulled around my shoulders and a large scarf around my neck and over my bump for warmth, we walk together, very slowly, Sean and the dog and I, towards our favourite woods, nestled in the hills. I can hear the drill of a woodpecker echoing.

After about fifteen minutes I have to stop and catch my breath; the tightening is stronger now, and it's getting difficult to talk through it. The feelings are accelerating, as close together as they had been before, and they colour the whole day. I feel a sharp pain any time I walk too quickly or bend forwards too far. Several times I have to ask Sean to slow down or stop and wait for me. I've been diligently entering each contraction – because that's what they are, now, I feel able to admit to myself – into the app on my phone, so I can see exactly how much closer together they've become.

'Calm down,' Sean says when I tell him this. 'You're not in labour.'

I shoot him a filthy look. 'Yes I am. Or I might be. What do you know?'

'They said at the classes that you're only in established labour once the contractions are three or four minutes apart. This isn't—' but he knows from the look in my eyes not to finish the sentence.

I don't think I'm in labour yet either, but I resent being told as much by someone who doesn't, currently, have a full-term baby pressing its head into their pelvis.

We follow the longer circuit through the woods, up to the old oak tree halfway up the hill. The oak is shaped like a huge, many-fingered hand bursting out of the earth. It's one of the most characterful trees I've ever seen; long ago its trunk has split and reformed, healed over and gnarled around itself, knotty and defiant. It feels good to visit the tree. This might be the last time that I see it as one person before I bring another into the world, my voyage gaining a passenger. I have no idea what the next few hours and days will hold, and I sense again the shiver of fear across my shoulders. I reach out my hand and press my palm into its ragged, rippled bark, and I feel the lichen alive and green to my fingertips.

THE WAVE

WHEN I WAS BORN, MY grandfather had a work meeting scheduled with some important people who had come to see him from abroad. My grandmother had little patience; she wanted to come to visit her new granddaughter in the hospital as soon as possible. And she felt that my grandpa should come along, too.

'I can't,' said my grandpa. 'These people have come all the way from Uganda to meet me.'

'This baby has come all the way from heaven,' said my granny. 'Get in the car.'

And he did. My grandmother was not a woman you could say no to. As a child, I loved hearing this story, though I was always nervous in case anybody found out that, actually, I didn't think I really had come from heaven after all, or at least that I couldn't remember it much if I had.

•

I spend Saturday evening trying to get comfortable on the sofa, sitting awkwardly and rolling my hips on the big inflatable yoga ball bought at Tesco a few days before, and timing the contractions. They are every ten minutes. Each one is lasting for a minute or more, and painful. It's difficult to talk through them when they reach their sharpest point, so I resort to heavy breathing instead.

Each contraction has its own shape and character, and I think of them as waves on a beach. They start off small, like a deep tugging, dragging me down and forcing me to stop what I'm doing and pay attention as the shingle is pulled across the sea floor. Then the tightness in my abdomen builds, becomes more and more painful, and I have to close my eyes as blotches of green and gold cloud my vision. I concentrate on breathing, and the pain reaches its most intense point, and then begins to slacken and fade, a tide on the turn.

A friend has sent me a link to download and listen to some audio breathing exercises to prepare for labour, and though I suspect they won't be much help when the real pain kicks in, for now they are helpful, and I find myself returning to their comforting meditation suggestion of imagining I am on a peaceful island far away from my troubles. I can't help but turn the beach in my own internal meditation exercise from a tropical paradise into a cold, windswept Scottish bay, scattered with gnarled driftwood and sea spray mingling with blossom on the bracing air, the sound of water and wind with the crunch of stones.

At eleven o'clock that night I decide it's time to phone the hospital and tell them what's been happening, and give them some notice that I might be coming in. I still don't fully believe that the process my body has started will lead to a baby. I am amazed by how little control I already have over the time and strength of the contractions. I feel as if my body is in open rebellion, disobeying everything I might want it to do. My conscious brain isn't in charge any more.

I know that as long as the hospital midwives on the other end of the phone can hear nothing urgent in my voice, they will do nothing more than tell me to take some paracetamol and have a bath, and to ring back when things get harder to bear. That's fine with me. Our house is only a ten-minute drive from the hospital.

Sean runs the bath, filling it as close to the brim as it can take, and helps me to get in. The relief of the warm water seems to seep into every bit of muscle, every cell. Between the contractions I can still talk normally, but now each time the tightening comes it seems to grip me so hard that the rest of my body stops functioning momentarily. The moment that the pain of each contraction – and it is pain now – begins to build towards its peak, all thoughts of breathing fall away. The only thing I am aware of is pain, and darkness, and blotching colour. Each contraction is stronger than the last, now, with the pain building steadily each time. Each lasts almost exactly a minute, and so I ask Sean to time each one and tell me when I get to thirty seconds through and the worst is over.

The light in the bathroom is dim and soothing. Sean has lit a small candle in a brown glass jar on the windowsill, and I focus on its flickering, on the light from it dancing out of the window and vanishing into the sky every time it flares in the path of my breath.

Light travelling in a straight line towards its destination, *canwyllau cyrff*. I wonder if it will meet any travellers on the road. If it will be an omen.

•

At one o'clock in the morning, the contractions are around four minutes apart. At two o'clock, they are coming so fast that the pain of them makes me cry out. Having topped up the bathwater several times to keep it hot, I can't delay leaving for the hospital any more, even though there is nothing I want more than to stay in that bath forever, the warm water soothing my back and legs, rippling around me and muffling the pain from reaching its sharpest, while Sean kneels beside me counting to sixty over and over again.

Seizing a rare moment of slackened pain I pull myself out of the bath, heavier than I've ever felt, and ring the hospital while standing at the top of the stairs, clinging to the banister for stability. As soon as the call connects, I can hardly form sentences as I try to explain what's going on. The midwife on the other end of the line remembers me from before, though I still manage through gasping breaths to tell them my name, and that the contractions are now three to four minutes apart, and then as soon as I say these words another contraction sweeps over me, waves on the shore, far stronger now that I am out of the water, and I double over the banisters as the pain rips through me.

'Yes, it sounds as if you'd better come in now,' I hear the midwife say. She sounds very far away. 'Well done for making it this long at home.' I don't feel any sense of achievement. Just a strong desire for drugs.

Somehow, in the three minutes before the next wave, I grab some clothes and pull them on with Sean's help. Sean grabs the hospital bags and shuts the dog in the living room with some food, and we head to the car. Sitting in the passenger seat feels like sitting on a porcupine that keeps rolling into a ball underneath my hips, making me squirm and my spine stretch up to the ceiling every time the car goes over a bump.

Reaching the hospital car park, I get out of the car and have to pause, lean on the door and moan through a peak of pain while Sean sorts the bags. The walk through the doors to the out-of-hours entrance is only 100 yards or so, but I have to stop every few steps to lean on Sean and moan again. The sounds I'm making are getting louder each time, and I don't seem to have any control over them at all. They echo up to the night from the hospital car park, which is a place kept too bright, an artificial daylight shining from a fairy ring of streetlamps.

CATTERLINE IN WINTER

THE SCOTTISH ARTIST JOAN EARDLEY was writing to her mother in 1954, having just moved into a new cottage. 'I'm sitting looking out at the darkness and the sea,' she said. 'I think I shall paint here. This is a strange place – it always excites me.'

Eardley painted Scotland the way it feels to me. *Catterline in Winter* shows the village of Catterline, in Aberdeenshire, where she lived and painted her most famous land and seascapes. It's not far from the sheer cliffs of the coastal nature reserve of Fowlsheugh, home to kittiwakes and guillemots looking out over waters churning with seals and dolphins. In the painting you can see the village huddled on a steep sloping hillside, the snow on the fields and the promise of another flurry to come on a crisp winter's night, and the moon clear and cold above it all. To the left of the picture is the wild, spiky brush of the field plants that survive the freeze of a Scottish winter without dying back entirely into the ground. And there are people here, living in the village, lighting their fires and drawing blankets around their children. The sea isn't in the painting, but the village of Catterline is a coastal settlement, and you can feel the sea close by in the image: the scrubbish seaside plantlife dominates the landscape, and the moon is in the centre of the sky, just as it is the centre of the movements of the sea.

Eardley is an artist who stirs me, someone that makes me feel as if art is women's work. She is an artist of wildness and wintry beaches where only the hardy can survive. She paints spiky grasses in violent ochre swipes of the brush, slicing through the grey Scottish night. Sometimes she would press the grasses and seed-heads into the paint on the canvas, too, and stick them there. Her whole project was about urgency, capturing the world and preserving it before she wouldn't be able to experience it any more.

Her short life was painful. Her father, who had been left shell-shocked after being gassed in the trenches during the First World War, killed himself. After studying at Glasgow School of Art, she took a tenement flat studio in Townhead in Glasgow, and sketched and painted the local children living in the slums. Several of her paintings can be seen in the collections of the Scottish National Gallery of Modern Art. She died young, of breast cancer at forty-two, and had only made her career as an artist for fifteen years. In the winter of her life she painted the wilds around Catterline and a series of sweeping, aggressive seascapes, some of them six feet wide. She was not a composer of pretty seaside scenes. The waves and tides in her work are self-possessed and strong, made of oil paint so thick that the impasto is almost sculpture, a wave itself stilled in time and pinned to the canvas. In *Seascape (Foam and Blue Sky)* (1962), patches and dots of white dart on the crest of waves above strong swoops of royal blue beneath. It is almost as if the sea is crackling with electricity.

My favourite of her paintings is *The Wave*, which is painted entirely outside, in stormy weather in February 1961. The sky is a long, smooth block of greyish blue with a smudge of pale cloud in the middle, above a wall of water, rushing towards the shore, ready to smash into and destroy anything in its path. The waves aren't gentle, playful, eddying things: they are one solid mass of destructive power.

Eardley couldn't escape the sea, even when she wanted to. 'And towards evening the sun appeared shrouded in heavy mist – and turned yellow and orange and red, with great swirls of mist obscuring her every now and again – I wanted so much to paint the sun but it meant turning round and leaving my sea,' she wrote.

There are photographs of her outfit and outdoor studio setup in all weathers, taken by her lover, Audrey Walker. The relationship between the two women was only publicly known when affectionate and intimate letters that they had written to one another were published after the death of Walker, who had been married. The photographs show Eardley under a mop of thick dark hair, frowning in concentration at her canvas propped up on a wooden easel, with the grasses blowing in the background beside a dry stone wall. Her left hand is so full of different paintbrushes that they spike out of it like claws. She wears large, baggy, comfortable trousers in a thick material, and what looks like an oilcloth overall, covered with paint smudges over its practical pockets. She is an artist, but she looks like a sailor, ready for all weathers.

Femininity and masculinity are both presented in the strength of the waves in the works she painted shortly before she died, her most intensely creative period. Sometimes, she mentioned in letters, if the weather was particularly cold, she would paint in a fur coat.

The north-east of Scotland, the place where the land met the sea, was the place where she was most committed and successful in art and in love. The waves that she stole from the sea are now hung in the National Galleries of Scotland. Eardley's ashes were scattered on the beach at Catterline.

HIGH TIDE

W E MAKE IT UP IN the lift and to the second floor labour ward, passing rapidly by a cheery night receptionist with Sean calling out a brisk 'We're going to the labour ward – she's in labour,' as if this isn't relatively obvious. I have time to think, briefly, that if anyone wanted to break instantly past a hospital's security system in the dead of night, pretending to be in labour would be one way to do it, before another contraction hits as we get into the lift and I try to let it pass as quietly as possible, feeling very aware of how silent the deserted corridors seem, imagining hundreds of patients in dire states of health who wouldn't appreciate being woken up by a screaming woman.

We are let into the labour ward and shown through to a room to be assessed. The midwife asks me questions and I pace incessantly, my skin very hot. I want nothing except to keep moving, moving, moving at all costs to ease the building pressure in my pelvis and the spasms of pain dancing around my spine. The contractions seem to be coming one on top of another now, with no gaps in between. I can hardly even lie still on the bed long enough for her to examine me, so strong is the need to keep moving, to be upright, to keep going forwards. I feel as if I stopped moving, the building pain would consume me. I'm a fish in a shoal, bound to the movements of a greater force.

·

Within minutes, the pain swallows me whole and spreads to every part of my body. It intensifies if I stop moving, especially if I'm lying down, and that's all this room full of people wants me to do: they want to examine me, to keep me calm, to stop me screaming. I don't understand why they want me to stop screaming. None of them understands the amount of pain that is now contorting my body, surely, or they wouldn't dare to suggest I be quiet and lie down.

They offer me codeine and I vomit everywhere. I am transformed into a different being by this pain. I don't belong in this room with these people. I am an entirely different species from them, a species of animal made of pain and contortion. I remember professional divers, their bodies spinning through the air and into the water perfectly in sync with their minds, and I imagine myself in total contrast to them, falling headlong into water punctuated by rocks, breaking the surface, my body slapped and hurt by the impact.

The only thing that helps with the pain is screaming. I tell the midwives I want pain relief, drugs, anything to make it stop, any medical concoction they can give me. I'd always wanted pain relief. In my birth plan, the largely pointless document that the midwives told me to write into my notes, I had written that I didn't want a drug-free birth. I wanted anything they could give me to make it easier. I wanted to be in water, and also I wanted the most hardcore drugs available.

But the baby is coming too fast for any of this. It's all happening too fast. 'The baby will get here before the anaesthetist does,' says a brisk midwife as she turns away from my panic-struck face.

I'm on my own, I realise. I'm in a room full of people – more midwives are coming in all the time – and yet I'm completely alone. I suck on the gas and air they've given me, which at first bought a few seconds of numbness with each inhalation, making me feel like a scuba diver surrounded by dancing coral, but even that doesn't seem to be helping any more. My body is opening up and splitting in two.

The pain might rupture my brain and pop out my eyeballs, it feels like, so I have to keep my eyes closed, wait for it to stop, beg God and the universe and anyone with any power at all to make the pain stop. Having a baby can't be worth this pain, I think. Nothing could be worth this. I would sell everything I own to make the pain stop. I'd do any deal the devil wanted. Is this what dying is like? Is it slipping into a world of pain so intense that nobody else can follow you there?

It is decided that I am allowed to sink into the birth pool, and there has never on Earth been anything like the bliss of this, the warm water lapping around me, my spasming muscles slackening a little in the movement of it. For a moment I feel I am back at home in the bath with the candle burning and Sean beside me, or in the shallows of a September sea, warmed by the end of a long summer. The midwife, who is now accompanied by a student, says that we have hours to go yet. This is my first baby, and first babies take a long time to come. I've been in hospital for an hour.

My body doesn't agree with her, though. All at once, the pain rips through me again and there is pressure in my pelvis now, too, and an overwhelming urge to push. I can feel the shape of the baby taking up a new place in my body, somewhere further down, somewhere on the way to somewhere else.

'I need to push!'

'You can't,' says the midwife. 'You're not ready to push yet. If you start pushing now you'll be pushing for ages and get exhausted. We need to examine you before you can push.'

'Do it, then, I can feel – I need to push!'

'You'll have to get out of the pool—'

'THAT'S FINE!'

Nobody else seems to realise how urgent this feels. I am helped out of the pool and up on to the bed, and the pain is rippling through me constantly, moving my legs and arms for me, and I feel as if I have been hooked up to an electric current burning my skin and acting on my nerves, spasming every one of my muscles. I am Frankenstein's creature, a plaything of this pain, a monster controlled by someone else, and I want to run away, but running is not a thing my body can do. It has utterly betrayed me. It isn't obeying a single thing my brain is telling it to do.

My eyes are mostly clamped shut, now, but I open them for long enough to register that the midwife who examines me is visibly unnerved to find that I was telling the truth, and the baby is coming now.

It's happening fast, the labour, but something is stopping it, keeping the baby from coming out. The midwife shouts to me over my screams as I lie on the bed, gripping anything close by with my hands and arching my spine against the paper-thin hospital sheets underneath, consumed by the excruciating pain of trying to keep still so she can examine me. She says the water hasn't broken yet.

'There's a bag of water just in front of the baby's head, blocking the way,' she says. 'As soon as those waters break, the baby is going to come.'

'Break them, can you break them?' I say, and my voice sounds not like my own, more like a moan, half-sob, half-scream. The effort of speaking disintegrates me.

'I can break them if you want me to,' she says.

'Please, just—'

'All right,' she says, and starts to pull a curtain around the bed.

'What are you doing? What are you doing?' I scream, and I would laugh at the absurdity of this if the pain hadn't rendered me completely incapable of humour, not understanding what she could possibly be doing that could be more important than preventing me dying of pain and my baby being stuck inside me forever.

'Well, we don't want anyone to come in and see you like this,' she says.

'I DON'T CARE!'

She abandons the curtain, half drawn, and tells me I'll feel warm liquid flow down my legs, and not to be alarmed by this, but I'm so past being alarmed by now, that as another contraction consumes me, throwing my body into spasms and arching my back, I can only scream.

The assistant student midwife keeps trying to get me to be quiet, to give me more gas and air, but screaming is much better pain relief now, and anyway I've lost any sense of the basic co-ordination you need to put the mouthpiece between your teeth and breathe. Breathing feels like something from another age. Breathing isn't a thing I can do any more without making a guttural noise from deep within me every time I try.

I feel the gush of the warm waters and there is a small pocket of rest for the pain, and then it comes on again, harder and quicker now, like someone picking me up and slamming me repeatedly into a brick wall until all of my bones shatter, and I scream some-where from deep inside me, a roar that catches ragged in my throat and reverberates through the muscles of every limb.

'Listen to me, Charlotte, don't scream, screaming is a waste of energy. You need that energy for pushing,' someone says, but the instruction not to scream feels about as relevant or possible as an instruction not to have eyes, or not to be called my own name.

The next contraction surges through me and I try not to make a noise, try to obey them, but this makes it worse.

'I have to scream,' I say. 'I have to – you don't understand,' and I don't know if I am actually saying these words in a way that anyone can hear them, or if they are just echoing around inside my own head.

Something else is wrong now. The baby's heart rate is drop-ping, the midwife says, and the bed that I'm on is being pushed fast into another room, somewhere more help is possible. There are more people here now. Another midwife has arrived and there is a trolley topped with a tray full of instruments of glinting silver, which I see only in the few seconds that I'm able to open my eyes. They start putting my feet up into stirrups, and I can hear Sean is worried now too, because we don't know what they're going to do.

'Charlotte, listen, the baby's head is stuck, and its heart rate is slowing down. It isn't coping well with the contractions,' says a new, older midwife. 'We're going to have to make a cut to get the baby out.'

There's no anaesthetic. I can't speak any more, but I can hear everything they're saying. The older midwife is directing one of the younger ones – this is a training moment, I register dimly – and then the cut is made during the next wave of pain, and I barely feel it as it stacks on top of the pain I'm already feeling, raindrops on the sea.

One of the younger midwives starts reaching for one of the shining instruments, which I realise is a set of forceps. This was the moment I'd avoided learning about in the dreaded fourth ante-natal class. To my eternal gratitude, the older midwife – whom I hadn't noticed coming into the room, but now seems to be in charge – says to her, 'No, we won't need those. We'll get Baby out in the next push.'

Aphrodite, goddess of the open ocean. Aphrodite, our protector in birth.

'One more push, Charlotte,' she says to me, shouting now. 'When the next contraction comes, push as hard as you can, and the baby will be out.'

I try to nod. I don't know if my head moves at all.

'Can you hear me, Charlotte?'

'She can hear you,' says Sean, holding my left hand tight.

•

There is an eerie silence. The contractions, which have been coming thick and fast, one on top of the other, for what seems like ages now, have stopped, and there is an unnatural lull. After so much screaming and urgency, the room feels quieter than any room has ever been, a room full of people watching and waiting for something in the air to change. I don't know how long this lull lasts. The midwives are gathered around me, ready, like a coven at a cauldron. We all wait, all concentrating in this moment. I'm panting lightly, breathing again. It feels strange, the sudden nothingness.

And then the pressure starts to build again. It starts in the top of my head and pushes down. The pain snags somewhere behind my navel and then drags itself up and through me, spreading from the middle in the pattern of a spider's web, raging and consuming, though more bearable somehow now. Now it feels as if it has a purpose. It feels as though it will end.

I hold my breath and push as hard as I can, not even really knowing what pushing means but tensing every muscle in my body, pushing into my fingers and elbows and eyelashes and everything I can, my eyes shut tight – and someone is saying 'Push push push', and someone else is saying 'No don't push!', and then someone else says 'Shallow breaths, shallow breaths and push slowly' – and the pain has lessened a little now, and maybe only two or three seconds have passed and then I hear Sean – 'Open your eyes, Char, open them' – and I do open them, and I can see something new in the room. Someone new. A small, round, dark, wet head, raised up above my belly, illuminated by an overhead spotlight.

The atmosphere is still tense, still extreme focus. And then I feel a sense of coming away, of lessening pain. The midwives are saying things I don't hear.

There are two little sounds. A crying, a snuffling.

A midwife lifts up the baby. 'Here she is,' someone says, and they put her on my chest. I hear someone sighing, relieved and relaxed. The lights are bright.

Two dark, oval eyes blink up at me. They are full of an expression as confused and exhausted as I feel.

'Hello, little one,' I say.

My baby returns my gaze. And then she sinks her body into my chest, warm and solid and real. Home.

The midwives aren't looking at us but at the clock on the wall behind my head. 'That's 5.04am,' says one.

The pain is gone now. The midwives are still working – I'm losing a lot of blood, I'll learn afterwards, and the placenta isn't coming away, and so they have a bit of work to do to keep me alive, nothing too complicated or unusual, and they catheterise my hands as I stare down at this new creature. They are working on my hands and veins and swabbing up blood, and I feel in the eye of a storm, movement all around me, and only stillness and breathing for me and this person that I have made with my body.

Aphrodite, defender of the harbour. Aphrodite, deviser of new things.

Finally the midwives seem happy that I'm not bleeding to death, and everyone looks at the baby, and two of them take her briefly to the other side of the room to weigh and measure and check her over, and someone is saying congratulations.

All sounds are muffled, as if I'm hearing underwater, in the burring silence after the roaring crescendo. I hear myself apologising for all the screaming, and I think I'm even cracking a few jokes now, and I say to the midwives that I'll just let them get on with the stitching and do whatever they want to my body, I don't care any more, I won't be needing it. The baby's hands are up around her face, tightly curled and red, little fat starfish washed in with the tide, alive and gripping on. Someone fetches a pink knitted hat, standard hospital issue for baby girls, and in it she begins to look human.

Tea and toast appear next to me by magic, and though I'm shaking with the blood loss and the reality of holding this small, real new person, it's the best meal I've ever had, breakfast with my daughter after a long night. And then eventually the midwives have cleared away their things and left the room, and so now it is just us, me and her and him, alone in the dawn.

STARFISH

MY FAVOURITE PAGE IN THE battered old secondhand Collins guide to the British coast, the book that I pored over while I was first collating my shell collection as a child, was the page about starfish. How perfect, I thought, how symmetrical and logical and sensible, that the sea would lie all over the earth reflecting the sky, and both the sea and the sky would be full of stars.

Starfish are echinoderms, a word meaning 'spiny skin', coming from the Greek word for hedgehog, and classifying a group of creatures with radial symmetry – usually five-pointed, sometimes seven or ten – and a central mouth. It's a class of creature with some poetically named members: starfish, feather stars, and the dark brittlestars that crawl in heaps over one another across the sea floor.

Feather stars aren't as common as starfish. They have ten long, delicate arms, each one with its own waving fronds clinging to it. Brittlestars are slender, too, though with only five arms, and much spinier, seemingly stealthier in their creeping movements, more like spiders of the sea. Other varieties of starfish are evocatively named too: the sun star, the sand star, the Bloody Henry. The common starfish is the kind I've seen most often, and the kind that you're most likely to find alive lurking in rockpools close to the mussels they prey on. They are pale peach in colour, and covered in tiny white spines. If you find one dead, dried out by the sun, it will be lighter still, spectral and skeletal, more like a shell of a thing than anything once alive in its own right.

Other echinoderms have less elegant names, though I was never any less eager to find them: the doughy, mud-dwelling sea potato urchin, round and honest and fat, for one. And the peculiar warty protuberance of the leathery sea squirt, a beguilingly hideous creature which attaches itself to undersea rocks and is often washed ashore after storms, lurking among the driftwood.

The distinctive five-jawed structure of an edible sea urchin's mouth is called 'Aristotle's Lantern', and the urchin uses it to scrape algae from rocks to eat. The mouth is given this name not because Aristotle ever lit a candle inside it or used it to light his night-time explorations, but because he described the edible sea urchin's mouth in his *Inquiries on Animals*, written in the fourth century BC:

In reality the mouth-apparatus of the urchin is continuous from one end to the other, but to outward appearance it is not so, but looks like a horn lantern with the panes of horn left out. The urchin uses its spines as feet; for it rests its weight on these, and then moving shifts from place to place.

In my shell collection, I have one sea potato, one edible sea urchin, and one common starfish. Looking back at my array of treasures as an adult on the bathroom windowsill – I haven't yet recruited a scallop as a soapdish, the way my grandmother did – I realise how macabre it is to collect these objects from the beach. I wonder if I am damaging the ecosystem of the shore by raiding its treasures. I see them as relics, as echoes of the living selves of the animals they came from, and I feel like a grave-robber. The shingly beaches of the British coast are littered with grave goods, with memories of lives lived in the sea. They are memento mori of the coast, and proof of life in water.

Starfish are creatures of the borders between dry land and the infinite, animals so otherworldly they might have fallen into the water from the sky. They are skeletons of the night, souvenirs of possibility scattered along the beaches, something to reach for, something we might actually be able to catch.

A PAINTED OCEAN

S HE IS WRINKLED AND CORAL-COLOURED, as if she has
spent too long in the water. When the daylight comes in the
morning after she is born, the dawn really is rosy-fingered, a
strange and unworldly shade of pink. Everything I can see from
the hospital window is blushed, full of blood. I've barely registered
the weather forecast for the last couple of days but it turns out that
in fact I'm not imagining things, my eyes haven't been rose-tinted
by the shock of labour, and the sky really is this ethereal colour.
When a midwife comes in, she tells me the bizarre weather is
because overnight there has been one of the first of the year's
winter storms, which started as a hurricane while out in the
Atlantic, and then lessened after hitting Ireland and broke apart
over Britain. It has brought with it sandy dust from the Sahara, and
is now filtering the sunlight and tinting the low clouds with the
amber-ish colours of grapefruit flesh and apricots, one last kiss
from the summer.

The baby books have told me that newborns can't yet
perceive colour in any real detail. Their eyes are blurry, with a

maximum focal distance of around twelve inches away from them, so they see the world as a series of contrasts, light and dark. They find it easier to focus on lines and shapes, the outlines of faces and shadows on walls, rather than subtle or gradual changes of hue. They have spent nine months in the dark, and are stunned by the light.

She might not be able to see it, but for me today the world seems brighter, the colours saturated, the volume on all of my emotions turned up three notches. Everything in the world seems distorted, too: birds outside the windows are bigger than they should be; my arms seem frailer and trembling; the faces of medical staff too big and close and almost aggressive, despite their expressions and gestures of warm efficiency and care. Everyone's eyes are too big. Their smiles are too wide and too full of teeth.

And my belly has shrunk magically from the size it was yesterday. Maybe it's the blood loss, making everything shift in my vision, making nothing seem certain, my eyes and ears not functioning as they should. I press my hands into my abdomen where last night there was a baby inside. It is too soft now, too yielding, too empty. My hands sink in too far. I am drained of blood and water. My organs are suspended in space, gradually making their way back down to earth and to the positions where they belong, having been crammed up into my ribs for so many months to make room for the reality of my child.

I take a moment to accept that she doesn't live there any more. She is, instead, lying in the clear perspex cot to the right of my bed. In the night, a midwife came to check on us, and offered to take her into another room and look after her for me for a few hours so I could get some sleep. I knew this would be a good idea, would make every bit of rational sense, but I said no. I wanted to be able to look at her. I wanted to look at her forever. The midwife raised her eyebrows but said nothing. I don't see her again after that. The ward staff seem to come and go and change constantly, and whenever I see a familiar face I greet them like an old friend.

The ward is quiet in the daytime, and so the same midwife who delivered the baby, back in on a new shift, has time to come to visit us both when she's in for her next shift, to pick up the baby and cuddle her. I'm amazed that she's still talking to me after seeing me in my most monstrous form, a sea-witch of a woman, all screaming rage and disobedience and muck and pain. I am so quiet now, with exhaustion numbing and shushing me. I speak more quietly and do not scream. I am different. The midwife is kind and says she likes to come and say hello when everything's calmed down.

The day is as still as a painting. The pink of the sky, the clean white of the hospital sheets, and the blue of my baby's eyes. Her dark hair. She sees everything in contrasts, and I see everything in colour. She blinks, and is human. She turns her head and observes the world changing before her again, and she is animal, and I am too, my blood returning and rising in me. We are single-minded in our new joint obsession with eating and excreting and survival. It is crucial for each of us that the other survives. Nothing else is imaginable. She is mammal, but she is also more like a plant, who must be fed and watered and given sunlight, and she will grow.

She is an alien being, new to this planet, and she is learning our ways. Maybe it's my brain playing tricks on me, but I'm half sure that the rose of her skin is so bright, so new and full of life, that she glows in the dark.

GLOW

IN TEMPERATE, TROPICAL AND SUBTROPICAL ocean waters, the sea territory of hurricanes and long summers, there are creatures called *Noctiluca scintillans*, more commonly known as sea sparkle. They are tiny, balloon-shaped jellyish cells that bob on the surface of the waves, mostly colourless except when gathered in huge numbers, generally found near estuaries and following heavy rain. They are bioluminescent. They bloom in dense concentration, in some places turning the water pink, in others blue, and always glowing vividly, lighting up the ocean brightly at night in glowing ribbons along shorelines. Aurora borealis of the water.

Though they glow a raging azure by night, by day their presence causes events that are known as red tides, when they appear crimson or orange and wash along shores, turning the water a vibrant scarlet. They feature in old sailing legends about ghost ships that turned the sea to blood. They might also be a source for some of the Ancient Greek mythology surrounding Theia, the shining Greek Titan and the mother of the sun, the moon, and the dawn. She appears as a shining light whose beauty first inspired men to prize gold as the most valuable of earthly objects. Theia is the goddess of glittering, a figure of maternal wonder and power. She is a force who, among her known powers, can be observed transforming ships at sea into sparkling, golden marvels when they are touched by her light in the morning.

Sea sparkle is made up of dinoflagellates, beings that are not strictly animals, not strictly plants, but something in between. Their name mixes Greek and Latin roots for words meaning *whirling* and *whip*. They can increase the amount of ammonia in the water, and so they can harm any fish that pass through the bloom area to feed on them. Their beauty can be poison. They sometimes occur in areas of water with low oxygen content, signifying pollution and damage to the ocean environment.

The sea is painted red and blue, and the water is still. Every stretch of sea has its own palette. I think of the colours of the shoreline at St Monans – inked and defined permanently in my mind as a sequence of blue chiffon sky, orange rocks, grey sea and black seaweed – and of the colour of water, how it changes from transparent to blocked opaque Pantone colours with the sky and weather. And I think of watercolour, a kind of art that goes all the way back to cave painting, mixing liquid with pigment for the purpose of expression alone. Watercolour can be precise or impressionistic, an exploration of the learnings of the eye in subtle dreamlike washes over paper, or dense, brilliant detail in tiny brushstrokes.

My baby is a brand new piece of paper, just tinted in the colour of life with blooms of glowing light, pink-cheeked, not animal, not plant, and with no detail in her yet. I've started a painting with a colour wash to mean the sea and sky. And the colour bleeds along the shore, the outlines still in the making.

When we get home, I wrap her in star-patterned blankets, my glittering girl, born of blue water, blood, tears and an apricot sky. The shining fabric stars reflect the light on to her face, bright light from the window dancing on her cheeks, and her eyes darting and alive. She is golder even than a fish, embroidering a black black pond.

VII

ASTEROPE

Asterope literally means 'starry-faced'. More idiomatically, it translates as 'lightning'.

MY LOVE IS A DEEP BLUE SEA

T HE BABY MOVES IN HER sleep, shifting from side to side, occasionally her whole body jerking in a startle reflex before settling back towards complete relaxation. Her hands are flexing and curling, curving at the wrists, for all the world as if she is a witch casting a spell, or a conductor leading an orchestra. On her best days she is hale and hearty, full and farty. On worse days she doesn't sleep, and cries, and I despair at not knowing how to help her, and not speaking her language.

I love her so much I might drown in it. I don't understand how anyone with a child ever gets anything done except worry relentlessly for their safety, and love them. And yet I know that the intensity of this feeling will fade with time. The mundane tasks of life will make it seem as if she has always been there. The new family that we have become is an everyday arrangement. And it changes everything.

She smells of fresh marmalade toast and my grandmother's vanilla biscuits and sugar. She is tiny and dreamy, her eyes busy and wondering. She is like a kitten, like a starfish, stretching out and finding the world and feeling for its limits.

Sean is Welsh and so we give her a Welsh name, to balance the fact that she has been born in Scotland, and Sean buys her a cuddly red dragon toy with a grumpy expression and a Welsh flag stitched on to its hip. Some of the songs we sing to her are in Welsh too. We sing 'Robin Ddiog' with its folk dance tune and its wistful words. *Agorwch dipyn o gil y drws, cewch gweld y môr a'r tonnau.* 'Open up the door a little bit, and let me see the sea and the waves.'

She hasn't learned yet that she is safe here. We bathe her in the bathroom sink, and at first she hates the idea of this, screaming and turning an alarming shade of red as I lower her towards the water. But as soon as the water is lapping at her skin, or being poured from a little jug on to her belly, her arms and legs relax, and she waves and kicks experimentally. I wash her tentatively, afraid of hurting her, ready to apologise to her for getting it wrong, to tell her that we're learning together and that we'll get there, in plain water at the exact temperature of my blood. Does she remember how that felt?

Her blue eyes look up at me in placid wonder. All babies are water babies, after all. She comes from the water and is at home in it. Lifting her out of the sink when the water begins to cool and wrapping her in a soft white towel, ready to be tucked up in clean pyjamas, is an outrage: she loves the bath now and wants to stay in it forever. She learns soon, though, that the towel is also a refuge, and that the water is still there, waiting for her to return.

MILK AND MOONLIGHT

I READ A NEWS STORY ABOUT people who want to pressure governments to make breastfeeding compulsory and enforceable by law, and to make drinking alcohol in pregnancy illegal. Women's power over themselves and their choices is ever something not to be borne, even the fluids we consume and the fluids we produce subject to observation and regulation. The law keeps looking for ways to punish women for failing to live up to imagined standards, and it never learns that there's a beauty in choice. Women's bodies don't obey laws.

Before giving birth, I had been squeamish about breastfeeding. I'd gone to the supermarket and bought a six-pack of bottles of ready-mixed baby formula to take into hospital with me in my bag, a bag which also contained painkillers, a nightie I didn't mind ruining, and lots of snacks in case of a long and boring labour. I was half-convinced that I wouldn't be able to breastfeed my baby, and that anyway in the modern age it was perverse to feed a child from fluids from the body. Why bother, when a mixture that contains all the nutrients they need – plus added vitamins – is

SALT ON YOUR TONGUE

readily available from the same place I can buy chocolate and magazines?

Three days after giving birth, the day that my breasts fill with milk, so tight and full I feel they might burst, is the closest I have ever come to feeling more animal than human. I am reduced to the most basic human function: the creation and sustenance of more humans. Whatever I do to myself, however I style my hair or whatever clothes I choose to wear, this is who I really am, this warm, soft mammal, and even if I were running naked in the woods I would be providing just the same amount of function and nutrition for my offspring. I have been a house for my child, and now I am food.

So transformed am I that it seems as though I should be hidden away from the world and not allowed to participate in polite society with other humans. This is the extent to which, I think, so many of us are ashamed of breastfeeding, of the doublethink it requires to see breasts as nourishment for a child and part of adult sexual identity, separate emotions and roles existing together in one body.

I had even expected to be faintly disgusted by the milk itself when it appeared, as if it were any other bodily fluid, something excreted which had to be mopped up and cleaned away. I had expected to try to avoid looking at it. I don't know what I expected it to look like. Somehow, I hadn't expected it to look like milk.

Milk is exactly what it does look like. When the milk comes, I realise I am not disgusted or scared of it. I'm fascinated by it. In fact I am in awe. It is immediately recognisable as food. It's white and fat and pearly and thick, infused with real cream, as if taken fresh from the most wholesome, organic, grass-fed, free-range artisanal Jersey cow on a sunny local farm. I am the Jersey cow.

'It will all fall into place soon,' says the midwife who comes to visit a few days after the birth, finding me tearful with hormones and half-naked, the pain of my swollen body too tender for clothes. I have draped myself in an assortment of muslins and am unable to focus my eyes on anything except my baby, whom I view with a mixture of astonishment, anxiety and bewildered exhaustion. 'It's just a matter of getting used to it. Everything will calm down, and you'll start to feel less tender and swollen. You won't feel quite so much like Katie Price.'

'Who will I feel like?' I ask.

'You'll feel like Charlotte, who is breastfeeding.'

She is an experienced midwife, with decades of skill behind her, and I think from the direct look, and the encouraging smile that she gives me as she says this, that she knows how radical that last sentence sounds. I am not a cow, or a patient, or a vessel, not really, though I am not yet sure what it means to be a mother. I am in-between, still. In the next few days, though, the midwife says, the strangeness and newness will start to fall away, and when I look in the mirror I'll start to recognise myself again. It becomes a private mantra beating a drum in my head. I am not this scary new creature I don't recognise. I am still myself, and still tied to something secure anchored deep within me. I am Charlotte, who is breastfeeding.

My baby drinks insatiably, all the time, food much more important to her than sleep. She swallows down the milk and it's the colour of pearls, and makes me think of the nourishment of the sea, an island's larder, full of food for us. I think of the creamy white flesh of just-caught lobster from the shack on the harbour of North Berwick, served hot with butter and lemon, in a cardboard package so you can take it down to eat by the water's edge and watch the boats come in. I think of pearls, locked inside a dark oyster, and the milky moon in the night sky above the water, feeding the sea and guiding its tides. Nutrition is power, moving the surface of the planet. Milk and sea water are liquids infused with old stories.

Pearls don't just belong to the sea. They are found in both saltwater and freshwater, in either oysters or mussels, and sometimes in clams and conches, too. The pearls of freshwater mussels are smaller, more irregular than their saltwater cousins. They feel more like gilded grit than jewels, but they are beautiful too. The multicoloured silky sheen of the milk-white saltwater pearl, and the inside of the shells where they are found, is made of a substance called nacre, mother-of-pearl. It's a tough, strong material, purest white when seen straight-on and shimmering in rainbows when seen from the side, where it catches the light. Nacre is both precious and abundant, the sea full of it, and through history it has been carved into artistic uses, ornate altarpieces, shaped into dainty pieces of jewellery, fanciful spoons and decorations inlaid in musical instruments, piano keys and violin bows, tooth and bone and ivory born in water.

A pearl is a mermaid's voice, found on the tongue of a shellfish, a crystal of salt. There is a mouth-like presence in the way that a shell opens up to reveal a pearl in its soft centre. And you can use your mouth to tell if a pearl is real or not: if you rub a pearl against your teeth, it should feel gritty and uneven and faintly unpleasant. Fake pearls feel smooth and charming. Real pearls are like truth spoken aloud. They are rough and live, creatures of mouths and lips and softness and wetness. They are sensuous. Aphrodite was a pearl, the most beautiful of the goddesses, in her scallop shell and myrtle.

THE SOUND OF THE SEA

THERE ARE TIMES WHEN MYTHS and stories and pictures fall away, and the only rhythm that governs my life is the rise and fall of her chest as she breathes in her sleep. I find it incredible that she can breathe at all. All that time she spent growing in the dark saltwater of my body without taking a single breath, and then as soon as the cold air hit her skin in the morning she knew exactly what to do.

Sound is important to her. The womb was loud and the world is quiet. There were times when she will only sleep if I play a loop of rain sounds loudly from an app downloaded on to my phone, positioned close to her ear. Running water, falling rain, and singing: these are things that make her feel safe. Sometimes the only thing that will soothe her uncertain, squawking cries is a looped tape of seashore wave sounds, occasionally punctuated by the ululating calls of gulls, and the sploshes and rattles of pebbles carried along in the breaking eddies. I feel like a parody of myself as I play her these sea sounds. *Be soothed by the sound of the sea, my child*, I might as well be saying in a grand voice, like the oracle of ages, *as the sea has soothed me also in my life.* It is improbable that she would love the sound of the sea as much as I do, at only a few weeks old, the kind of thing I would invent to tell other people, to justify my own inexplicable pull towards the seashore. And yet it's true.

I spend long hours in the winter dark holding her close to me, her head in the crook my neck makes, swaying my hips and singing to her, while the snow falls beyond the window and settles, fluffing its feathers, on the rooftops. Sea shanties are good for these long nights. They are swaying songs, with enough refrains to be sung endlessly stretching into the darkness, rhythm and shush, the melodies rising and falling.

> *O say, were you ever in Rio Grande?*
> *O, for Rio!*
> *It's there that the river runs down golden sand.*

She stirs and stares. And her eyes slowly close.

> *O once my heart was wild and free,*
> *like a flashing spar on the open sea.*
> *But now that spar has washed ashore,*
> *and come to rest at my true love's door.*

Her body succumbs, and her muscles relax into sleep. Work songs are just right for the work of finding out how to live in the world. Long before there were songs of the sea, I am sure, there were lullabies. We need to soothe our babies before we can do anything else, before any adventures can wait for us.

I work too. I write when she sleeps wrapped in a sling on my chest, or in her little grey rocker chair that was a present to her from my sister, and which I rock backwards and forth with my foot for hours in the middle of the day. I've been working as a self-employed journalist for an amount of time that means that, according to the calculator on the government's website, I'd only be entitled to about £30 of maternity pay if I took any time off. So I write every day from about two weeks after she's born, still caring for unhealed stitches, still bleeding, still unable to wear any of my old clothes over my swollen, bruised and tender body.

I write articles to order for newspapers and magazines about things that no longer feel important: TV shows, films, something a pop star has claimed or denied. I listen to the radio almost constantly and allow it to mark my days. The very early morning programmes aimed at farmers make me feel productive and useful as I feed the baby, up with the larks, milking with the cows, and as if my baby is a lamb waking in the cool dawn of the fields. I listen to the news, and become an expert on current affairs as I hear each story repeated twelve times on hourly bulletins, evolving fractionally through the day. I switch between music stations and talk, and am soothed by the sounds that drift over me. It always ends with the shipping forecast, its riddling code, and I imagine the sea and its whorls so many miles away from the shore as I cuddle the baby as close as I can while she eats, and sleeps – only ever when held – and bleats, like a lamb.

Words, sounds, and water seem connected in these shifting new hours, all moving in waves. I remember the ultrasound scans and their rippling darkness, detecting humans within water. Sound is the name for a stretch of sea inlet, larger than a bay, wider than a fjord, and the west coast of Scotland and the Hebrides are peppered with them in their geographies. I remember that sound is the best way of communicating underwater because water limits visibility so much. The sea blinds you but you can hear for miles.

Embedded in the beach in Zadar, Croatia, there is a musical instrument that's played by the sea. As the waves move into holes in the stone steps, they push air out, and it creates a strange and woozy musical effect, like the sound of mouths blowing across the tops of empty bottles. It was created by the architect Nikola Bašić. There's something similar in Blackpool, called the *High Tide Organ* and designed by artists Liam Curtin and John Gooding, which resonates in the key of B flat as the tide comes in. Instead of steps in the beach, this is a tower that rises fifty feet in steel, zinc, concrete and copper. Water swells into eight tuned pipes, keeping a rhythmic beat as the waves wash in and out, pushing the air through, sounding like a wind band warming up for a concert. And the Exploratorium arts company's *Wave Organ* in San Francisco combines the sounds of the splishes and gurgles of waves as they swirl into the gaps built into the structure with the sound of air pushed from its pipes.

These art installations are Aeolian harps, musical instruments created by humans but played naturally by the elements, and named after the Greek god of the winds, Aeolus. Modern man-made Aeolian harps are hoisted aloft in trees to be played only by the wind, but these sea organs are different; they depend on the sea to create a scattered texture of notes as the waves lap against them. The effect of the wind and water moving together through man-made objects, creating music, also happens naturally on ships, as the wind moves through the anchor lines. They sound like the songs of ghosts, wandering the earth as echoes of their former selves.

•

There is a new thing to frighten me in the night. I imagine her death. I can see it in my mind, her eyes glassy, her body limp, her arms never reaching for me again. Already I picture it so often that it makes me terrified I'll somehow invoke it, and make it happen through the force of my own fear. Please God let me die before she does.

I used to scoff at the trite maxims that I'd seen for sale in gift shops, written on little wooden notices and designed to be displayed as ornaments, or shared on social media: the people who said that their children were their whole world, and that they'd do anything for them, and that they love them to the moon and back. I rolled my eyes at those clichés. Now I drift towards them. I understand them better, somehow. She was only a few days old when I knew with a cold certainty that I would die to save her life. There's no rationality to this thought. It's just what would happen. And though she is so small, already her presence is enormous. My brain grapples uncomprehendingly with the fact that before she was not here, and now she is here. Her existence has flooded into everything.

I thought I longed for the sea because I was looking for some mystical ancient connection to nature. Now I know that the pull I felt towards the sea was really a pull towards the human. The call of the sea is the call to the absolute strength of women, telling their stories and making music of beauty and imagination, and eternal mothers and grandmothers making eternal daughters and rocking them in the night as they sing while the tide comes and goes. And the power of women is to do all of this, to follow art and the moon, and to absorb it all and go on. This is the strong magic of Athena and Aphrodite, wisdom and creation.

And all the while, death gathers herself like a waiting parent, ready to fold us into her blankets and hold us closest of all. I fell in love with the myths of the sea, and then I realised I was one. My child will always be the child I held wrapped in salt water. We sing together in the storm as the moon grows full, and spring flowers bloom where the grass meets the sand and the rocks beyond.

•

Last summer, I went to visit my grandmother's grave. Into the dark slate of her gravestone, the same gravestone that has also borne the weight of my grandfather's name for sixteen years, her name and the dates of her life and death had now been carved. But there's another word carved there, too, underneath them, where the design of the stone had left a space.

We had wondered with some trouble in deciding what should be written there, or whether we should leave the line empty, uncrowded. We had considered inscribing 'Beloved mother and grandmother', and then dismissed this as both too long and too little. Something Latin, or something Biblical, had also been discounted as not quite perfect, not quite her. In the end, my father suggested the word we should put there. It seemed just right, we all agreed.

I set down a small posy of white roses, stocks and freesias on the daisy-strewn grass. As the church bells started to ring, I read the last word written at the end of the stone:

Musician

WHEN THE LIGHT IS AT ITS WEAKEST

I KNOW I WANT TO TAKE the baby to the sea, but the winter is too cold. She is tiny, and expresses only a desire to burrow into warm blankets and arms, away from chill winds. We make plans to go to the coast in a few weeks' time, all together as a family, to see my parents, when there is more light and less snow. In the meantime, pictures and stories of the sea will have to do.

I bundle the baby up in as many layers as I can fit on to her small, wriggling body. Vest, babygro, cardigan, booties and two hats. Let the cold try to nip this cosy baby if it wants. I tuck her into the stretchy grey sling I've tied around my chest, on loan from a friend, and head outside. Her eyes, already darkening and becoming more flecked with catlike yellow and grey ferns complicating the solid blue they were born with, begin to close, and she falls asleep in the fresh air, cuddled in close to my heartbeat. I think this is perfect happiness, this moment, a precious gift snatched from darkness, as we walk briskly through town with the air cold on my face and the warmth of a child held close.

New Year's Day, a year on from my walk at Portobello, and in this part of Scotland the light reaches us for only a few hours between nine in the morning and three in the afternoon. If it's an overcast day, it doesn't seem to get light at all. This isn't the constant darkness you get further north in the winter, but it's enough darkness that it makes you want to light candles and fires, wear the brightest colours you have, and chain-drink tea and coffee and hot chocolate for long hours either side of dawn and dusk. This winter has been especially snowy and harsh, the kind of winter that nips at the face for months on end and when spring comes your cheeks are raw from it.

In Edinburgh in January, there's a cultural tradition that peeps out from the darkness like a chick from a nest, testing the fresh year before retreating again. With the earliest snowdrops and anemones, in the centre of the city there emerges the annual exhibition of J. M. W. Turner's watercolour paintings, held in their own dim oval room with green walls at the back of the Scottish National Gallery on Princes Street.

When the art collector Henry Vaughan died in 1899, he left his collection of Turner watercolours to two galleries, Dublin's National Gallery of Ireland and the National Gallery of Scotland in Edinburgh, with the stipulation that, because the colours were so vibrant and the medium so delicate and sensitive to fading under intense light, they should only be shown to the public during January, when the light is at its weakest. Thirty-eight of the paintings are in Edinburgh, where they are stored in a special cabinet designed by Vaughan for the rest of the year, and brought out for a month-long display.

The display opens today, on New Year's Day itself, and I have to pick my way towards it through the shabby remains of Edinburgh's bright and brash Christmas market, a shanty village of faux wooden huts hastily put up in an attempt at German traditional charm, erected all along the entrance to Princes Street Gardens. They blare with festive music from large speakers disguised by novelty fibre-glass sculptures of reindeer and snowmen, and rows of stalls have wooden toys and knitted scarves for sale, the air is scented with the greasy tang of fat-spitting bratwurst and the spices of hot glühwein. It's loud, and steamy against the cold, and by this side of Christmas pretty rough around the edges after a month of fairylit jollity. In a few days the markets will all be gone, and we will be able to walk through Edinburgh at its most quietly stunning: pale and watery, deserted, crisp and cool, the daylight gentle as sugared lemon.

That's the light that fits Turner's watercolours best, and lets you see his skills with shape and colour distilled into perfect painted gemstones. The thrill of the soaring scale of his seascape oils on canvas, splashed loudly up walls in famous galleries the world over, is intensified in these vivid miniatures. They are more like objets d'art than paintings; marvels in themselves, his swooshes of purple storm clouds scratching and threatening on a background of his carefully commissioned blue paper. Looking at one, even through glass, is like examining a shimmering pebble just picked up from the shore, right by the waterline so it's freshly wet, and holding it up in the sun to see the colours change in its shining surface, and then pocketing it as a reminder of the day.

Sea View of 1826 is an unassuming name for a dramatic picture; it sounds as if it should be the name of a compact little blandly decorated holiday cottage in a coastal village, replete with leaflets for local attractions. Instead it's the name of a rich and deep water-colour with a V-shaped sky in amethyst, punctured by a crackling slash of white sunlight. In the sea below are determined, solid boats with golden triangular sails, lurching on the whipped froth of waves in the foreground.

Tate Britain has another sea watercolour that's not displayed here, Turner's *Sea Monsters and Vessels at Sunset* from 1845. It's a painting from his Whalers Sketchbook, with thick red chalk rasped on to the paper along with the paint for the sunset in the sky, and the water angry beneath in black and grey. In amongst the dark sea there are the rough shapes of sea monsters squirming and recalling their presence on medieval maps, huge eyes raving and humanly pupilled, splayed fins splashing alongside their heads, breaking up the surface. Black sea spray peppers up towards the setting sun, blazing as the night grows, and gauzy sails and sketchy masts suggest the presence of ships. The edges of the sea monsters are indistinct, their forms never quite clear or easy to determine. They're like the scariest baddies in horror films, seen only partly through shadow, or like a half-remembered nightmare that haunts for days.

It's a mysterious piece, unusual for having these ghosts of a monstrous imagination flitting across it, and more unsettling than Turner's oil painting that also features mythical beasts, *Sunrise with Sea Monsters*, painted the same year. It's also generally considered to be unfinished. The colours in the oils are yellow and gold rather than the watercolour's red and black, and at first you almost don't see the ghostly grey shapes of the sea monsters at all. When you do see them, they are less malevolent in their appearance than the ones in the sketchier, murkier watercolour. They look half-drawn, their outlines unclear. I wonder if that's deliberate. They could, at a squint, just be large fish. They might not be monsters at all.

I keep walking along the gallery's curved walls. I come across my favourite of the Edinburgh watercolours, which is indistinct and suggestive in the same way, with a calmer feel to it and none of the horror. It's a picture of Loch Coruisk on the Isle of Skye rendered in dizzying blue-and-pink two-tone. The colours whisk up and down the page recalling head-spinning heights and swirling winds. I wonder how Turner got to the place in the picture, and how he made this painting of the blurred and enormous mountains surrounding the loch.

Loch Coruisk is a sharp break in the toothed landscape, a moment of serenity with an overpowering quality to it, a place with a name that means cauldron of waters. I know because I've been there too. Did Turner take a Victorian ancestor of the *Bella Jane* boat out from the jetty at Elgol to the steep landing-place at the foot of the Black Cuillin, and clamber over the great flat rocks with his drawing-set to marvel at the hidden loch too?

And then later, at home surrounded by his painting things and a warm fire beside him when the sea-spray was just a memory, maybe he let the shock of the mountain jags and the romance of its mists spill over his brain again as he wiped the paper in blue, washing away the monsters and remembering the low cloud, fixing it down to accompany the new edition of Walter Scott's poetry which he had been commissioned to illustrate.

•

In the village of Elgol, the place where I came on holiday as a child all those years ago to plunge my feet into rockpools, there is a sightseeing boat trip you can take aboard the *Bella Jane* – a sturdy Lochin 38, seating forty – and set off on a three-hour round trip to the beautiful and isolated Loch Coruisk. *Coire Uisg* in Gaelic; corrie of water. The boat deposits you beside a metal staircase reaching from the sea up the rocks and on to land, and from there you walk over the big slabs of igneous rock at the foot of the Black Cuillin and Blà Bheinn and round to the freshwater beyond, with the peaks stretching up all around you.

I have taken the *Bella Jane* boat from Elgol to Loch Coruisk lots of times as a child and a few as an adult, and it hasn't changed much in twenty years, though the numbers of people making their pilgrimage to Loch Coruisk have increased dramatically. The loch, and the Fairy Pools of bright blue and green waterfalls deep in the mountains to the north, are famous. Local restaurants have opened; a paint company has named a palette of colours after local landmarks. Robert Macfarlane has written of this place's wildness, and the mountain bike trials cyclist Danny MacAskill, who comes from Skye, has filmed impossible-seeming viral stunt videos on the ridges, capturing the views and the pink and gold sunsets in crisp high definition.

You can access Loch Coruisk in two ways, either by walking or by boat. The walk is a seven-mile coastal path that requires you to navigate the Bad Step, fifteen feet above the sea when the tide is in and a significant scramble, gripping tightly to the gabbro rock all the way along the narrow pass with grassy ledges rising above you, covered in scrubbish grass punctuated with the odd length of barbed-wire fencing, tufted with scraps of sheep's wool. The views reward you, and the physical challenge of walking has a greater attendant sense of pilgrimage.

But I prefer the water. Hardy hikers who walk to Loch Coruisk seem to look down on people who come on the boat for taking the easy option, as if the sea is a cop-out, as if you should have to earn the right to see the magic waters reveal themselves before you. I disagree: walking takes you through the island, in amongst its earth and roughness felt up close. Seeing it from the sea frames it against the water and sky that made it, and lets you stand back and feel the weight of the land and the sea stretched out under the clouds, under the abundant Hebridean weather, the 'wool-white fog', as Tennyson described the conditions in his journal of visiting Skye.

From the boat, I can see dolphins and minke whales testing the air, and sea eagles above. Rarer to see are the soft, black-and-white wings of the kind-faced Manx shearwaters, cousins of the storm petrel and albatross, far better at swimming than walking, as they sail on the wind in long glides out to sea.

There is said to be a kelpie, a shape-shifting water horse spirit, living in the volcanic bowl of the deep loch itself. Kelpies haunt Scottish waterways, and seem friendly and playful in the shallows, tempting people into climbing on to their backs for a ride. Once you've mounted a kelpie, you're in grave danger of being dragged down to the depths and drowned.

The water is very cold, and around the edges it's as clear as a shop window that you want to press your face against. Towards the middle, and the deepest parts, it fades to black. When you stand here, you stand alone, the latest link in a chain of travellers to pick their way here over inhospitable ground, a chain stretching back for thousands of years. And the mist and water swirl before you as they frame the loch, like paint on paper.

Seeing the picture in the exhibition, caught and framed and sanitised in this warm room away from the shore, has only made the sea seem wilder by comparison. It makes me feel only more keenly, again, the familiar longing for lungfuls of salt air, and the need to gaze out into the sea and feel it gazing back.

SPRING TIDE

IUSED TO LOVE JOHN MASEFIELD's poem 'Sea Fever'. I used
to think that it summed up how I feel about the sea, the in-
extricable pull that I felt towards it, to learning about it, to feeling
its constant presence even when I'm miles inland:

> I must go down to the seas again, for the call of the running
>   tide
> Is a wild call and a clear call that may not be denied;
> And all I ask is a windy day with the white clouds flying,
> And the flung spray and the blown spume, and the sea-gulls
>   crying.

I still know what he means about the mystery of the soul-lifting
experience of being by the sea, on the brink of a voyage of infinite
possibility, the moment of choosing to start out being so much
more thrilling and fulfilling than the journey itself, or the destination. Now, though, I'm more interested in the voices of people
who are not sailors. The voices of people whose lives are shaped

by the sea without them ever walking across it. The people who are only ever interested in the possibility, the taste of *maybe* on their tongues, the scent of freedom and the beginnings of things. Emily Dickinson's poem, 'I started Early – Took my Dog –', comes closer to how I'm feeling, with its description of the sea overwhelming her and shaping her steps, defining her in its beauty and power:

> I felt His Silver Heel
> Opon my Ancle – Then My Shoes
> Would overflow with Pearl –

The baby is eight weeks older and has grown. She has passed the frowny curled-up newborn stage of looking red and squished, and is now beginning to unfurl, and to open up the way that a tulip opens, or a happy morning. And the time has come to take her to the sea, to St Monans for the first time, homeward to the place where my life is shifting into a change in the weather.

Since she was born, my world has shrunk to the size of my living room, my bedroom, and her dark blinking eyes looking up at me. It has been a very cold winter.

Now she is more of a baby, and less of an alien. She feels heavy and solid in my arms when I lift her from her cot and bring her to my chest, and she relaxes there with my arms around her, and feels real and reassuring, a part of this earth. I will take her to the sea, and we will look out at it together, and I will show her the defining feature of the planet that has led to all these myths and mysteries that it will take her a lifetime to learn.

On the day we plan to leave for St Monans, to stay at my parents' house, it snows heavily. It's a new moon tonight. I think back to Oban a year ago, to the journey we took then to the sea, with the snow falling in fat flakes and the moon full and bright, the mountains and lochs just large, dark shapes, like an old legend of long-ago giants frozen and become rock, silently watching us as we drove through the heart of Scotland.

Today, the snow falls harder as we drive, mixed with rain as we hit the afternoon rush-hour traffic of Edinburgh. The journey takes us an hour longer than it should, and the baby wakes up just as we are about to drive over the Queensferry Crossing, the youngest of the three bridges over the Firth of Forth. I'm sitting in the back with her, while Sean drives. With the traffic gridlocked, I resort to a pantomime of playing the sounds of lapping waves and rain from the speakers on my phone, and singing sea shanties to her, making up new verses and singing them all through again from the beginning. Sean joins in, making up harmonies and singing in silly voices, and I have to tell him to stop because he's making me laugh, and I can't laugh and sing at the same time, and if I stop singing the baby will be upset.

Night falls as we cross over into Fife, driving up the east and following the line of the coast. The land flattens out here, and the roads narrow as you weave in and out of the fishing villages. As the day fades there is an unnerving effect as we drive through the outstretched fields, knowing that the sea is close by but invisible. It is as if, taking one wrong turn, you might at any moment drive straight into the waiting water.

These lonely roads with the smell of the sea whipped into the air are the kinds of road where unwary travellers might find themselves lost. We might encounter corpse candles, fairy folk lurking in the shallows of the incoming tide, and ghostly apparitions of pale women in gossamer gowns, leading us astray.

We arrive in the dark. The cottage is lit with golden windows, a little warm makeshift lighthouse by the shore. I haven't been back to the house since she was born, since before my body changed, and the house is different now that my parents have lived there long enough to make it theirs: it has settled into itself and become more full of home-like touches. There are ornaments and pictures on the walls from their old flat and new ones that I've never seen before.

When I step into the living room, however, there's immediately something that I recognise. Spread out on the floor is an intricate blue-and-purple rug, with sea-like swirls in its pattern and uneven and frayed white edges. I haven't seen it for a long time. It's the rug that I was sick on at my granny's house, twenty years ago.

Thankfully, you can't see the mark any more. It's just an old rug now, still beautiful, still jewel-coloured, still the witness to an ongoing family story. The worn-away texture still seems earthy, but now in this house by the sea it looks more at home than it ever has before. I grin at it like an old friend.

The baby is fractious, and we have an early night. The morning breaks with the tide coming in strong. Tonight is the night of the new moon, and there's a cold winter wind stirring up the waves.

•

In the morning light we can see the house properly. It felt like a folly, my parents moving to this house from their sensible flat. It's not a suburban bungalow with sensibly sized rooms. It's an old stone house in an unusual higgledy-piggledy shape, with white-washed walls and wooden sash windows as the only defence against the constant by-the-sea onslaught of saltwater and wind.

The house is poised on the very edge of the land. When the tide is in and its blood is up, during a winter rage or a full moon, it roars over the sea wall and into the front gardens of the row of houses closest to the beach and the harbour. The houses' foundations have been artificially shored up against ongoing erosion that is already eating its way into the ruined remains of the old salt-pans to the north-east. The sea is right on the front doorstep, and sometimes the sea wall doesn't stop it. Like Poseidon's milkman, it leaves things out for us right outside the door to pick up in the early morning – shells and rocks and driftwood – before retreating back out into the Firth. In heavy storms, it flings seaweed at the windows.

The dog is scared of the beach at night. If you let her out for a wee before bedtime, she refuses to clamber down on to the beach in the dark. She just sits up beside the sea wall, staring down at you, shocked that you would consider risking your life to tread close to the shoreline in the dark, where there are kelpies and selkies and Blue Men certainly waiting for you in the water. From inside the living room, looking out of the windows, all you can see is the sea. It is your only view, and it churns all around you. Watching the sea roll its way about, you could be on a ship, cut adrift miles from land.

In the room, beside the gas fire and the old blue-and-purple rug, there is a grey sofa where you can sit and look out of the window and watch the tide coming in. At its highest point, it comes a third of the way up the glass, so that to look at it you might be part-underwater. And you can watch the sky change the way that it does over the sea, constantly, so that the colours and shapes of the clouds are completely different from one hour to the next, even from that minute to this one, suspicions of storms and moments of bright clarity flitting across it and then spinning into nothing. There might be a storm coming soon. There might be sun.

Beyond the immediate stretch of sea that you can see from the window, on a clear day you can see the Bass Rock – the gannets are just starting to come back to nest – and even further, if the day really is as clean and transparent as cut glass, you can make out the shapes of Edinburgh and East Lothian. Today there is a brightness on the water and a creamy haze masking the distance. A gull poises on an updraught outside the window, curved wings hugging the air, and slips down the air current and out of sight. The wind is strong and the waves are devouring themselves into froth, over and into each other, foaming up the shallows with fringes of spray catching the air and rising.

I sit and look out at the sea with the baby asleep in her rocker chair on the rug beside me. The moon pulls the tide in high. Thoughts and dreams pass gently and rapidly across her face as her nose and brow wrinkle every now and then in her sleep. Now she is cross, just for a second, at some dreamed injustice, and now she smiles. Her lips pucker and suck at nothing, imagining milk. She stirs, and opens and closes her fists, and pulls the crochet blanket that I made for her, pale grey and mint green and patterned all over with daisies, up a little higher around her tummy, poking her tiny fingers through the gaps between the woollen stitches. The sea is outside, all space and possibility. We are inside, warm and protected from the anger of the waves.

HOLDFAST

U P IN THE MIDDLE OF the night, in a witchity early hour
after midnight as I'm feeding the baby, my phone lights up
with a message from my mother. If you look out of the window,
she says, towards the Isle of May, you might see the Northern
Lights tonight. I pull back the curtain, but the night is too cloudy,
and all I see is the squid-ink darkness of the moonless sky. I text
back, and ask her if she has ever seen them. In reply, she tells me a
story she has never told me before:

> Only once I saw them; when I was a wee girl and my father
> took us outside one very bitterly cold dark January night in
> Fife just before we went to bed; we were already in our dress-
> ing gowns and baffies; shivering! And he said look . . . these
> are the Northern Lights, you see them only once in your life
> and they come all the way from Greenland: and the dark
> night sky was pulsating with a green light that faded as you
> stared at it. I remember thinking . . . of course . . . a green
> light . . . from Greenland . . . I was only five . . .

In the darkness of the new moon, looking out of the window, the lights I can see are the blinking pinpricks of the lighthouses on the Isle of May and the Bass Rock. Far above them, there are no stars in the sky, but there are human lights there, lighthouses in the air, the flashing bulbs of planes coming in to land at Edinburgh airport. They are bringing people over the water and down and home.

In the *Odyssey*, *nostos* is Odysseus's painful longing for home, his returning from war to be changed utterly, and wanting to revert to how it was in the beginning, to escape from certain death, to come back to shore after a long time at sea. It's the word from which we get the English *nostalgia*, which doesn't have quite the same meaning. There isn't, really, a word in English that means the same thing. *Homesickness* isn't strong enough. *Nostalgia* is too sentimental, too tied up with the past. Sean has told me that in Welsh there is a better word: *hiraeth*. It conveys longing, loss, wistfulness, and a sense of pain, of grieving for a past and a home that can never be recaptured. Giving birth to a baby is the beginning of her childhood, and the end of my own. I'd been afraid of this, but rather than a sense of irreparable loss, it's a change that feels more like the morning becoming the afternoon. When I try to remember how the fear felt, the feeling slips away from me and dissolves.

•

The next day brings a dawn of milky mist clothing the harbour. The horizon, veiled in white, disappears before the eye, so the sea and sky are the same. I strap the baby up in the carrier and walk a little way across the village to the sandier beach on the western shore, a small inlet where the grass-covered dunes give way to smaller rocks, becoming shingle and mopheads of seaweed. There are long strands of flat and silky brown kelp, like discarded stretches of unused 35mm camera film, and knobbled bladderwrack. There's laver, too, *Porphyra umbilicalis*, thin and olivey purple. Last summer there was so much seaweed washed up on the beaches of the East Neuk that the smell hanging over the coastline was pungent with it. A few times a year the council brings in diggers to Anstruther and Cellardyke, just a little way up the coast, to scoop up the offending seaweed and take it away to landfill, to save the noses of holidaymakers. The wildlife suffers from it: the dune chafer beetles, with green heads and iridescent chestnut wing cases, that depend on the stinking weeds for food, go hungry, and elegant matt black sandgravers, which feed on sandhoppers, are deprived of shelter and hunting grounds.

There aren't many holidaymakers here in the middle of winter. The air smells fresh, with just the slightest tang of salt on the tongue. Spring isn't far now. A few people are walking here and there, some with dogs, foraging the beaches for the seaweed, all of it edible, and hoping to stumble across a juicy crab if they're lucky. The name for the structure of the roots that tie the seaweed to the mussels and rocks, anchoring them in place as the waves wash over them, is holdfast. The holdfasts are tangled claws, gripping on to the earth and dragged back and forth by the sea. Scattered along the sand here I can see several of the stems and holdfasts of kelp, like disembodied arms ending in gnarled wrists and fingers, come loose from the substrate and strewn across the beach below the high tide mark.

We walk down to the beach and the intertide as the tide comes in. I am unsteady on my feet still after pregnancy, still unable to believe that my body broadened with a baby and then contracted back down again, my muscles softer and looser and less stable than they once were, less able to keep upright. My boots slither over the rocks. I feel less confident here than I did walking pregnant over the stones to St Ninian's Cave. I am more careful now. I am on the other side of childbirth, and I know what my body can do and what it cannot, and my bones and muscles are still finding their way back into the places they belong. And still I don't fall. With each step I'm braver.

The baby, who has been awake all day and most of the night, unsettled and crying and not pleased with much of the world, is calm now, at the water's edge. Her eyes are open, watching the scene. I wonder if the sounds of the waves lapping, real waves, are acting on her in the same way that the recorded white noise of my phone did, helping her to be calm in this place. Or maybe it's the freshness of the air, the cold of it, that makes her nestle in closer to my chest, and fall into dreams. Or maybe she knows what I know, that the sound of the sea is a place to find peace. I bend down to the lapping water and cup a little of it in my hand, feel its winter iciness, and dab a wet fingerprint on her forehead. She squirms, and cries out just once at the unfamiliar sensation, then inclines her head back close to my body and falls asleep.

I head back up the beach towards the grassy dunes and the houses of the village. On the way, I see something shining on the ground a little way ahead, as the light glints off it. I stop to pick it up. It's a nugget of white sea glass, half the size of my thumb, its clarity buffed by the currents and worn opaque by a long voyage at sea. It's smooth and satisfying to run my fingertips over it and let it rest in my fist, an artefact of lost stories. Looking at the shingled sand more closely now, in the zone of the intertide, soon to be submerged by the incoming waves, I notice more shells and chunks of worn-down ceramic among the seaweed. I pick up an empty limpet shell, run my thumb into the centre of its cool, smooth inverted pyramid, and put it in my pocket, a relic of life in death. Childhood might have slipped away but I'm still drawn to this collecting. Maybe it's just nostalgia, this urge to keep curios and display them like moments from the past. I look at the sea one more time, at the boats lifting with the tide, with my right hand resting on my baby's back as she sleeps, and my left hand in my pocket in amongst the smooth clutter of sea glass and shells. I turn, and start walking, and make my way back to the land.

ATLAS AND PLEIONE

Atlas, the Titan who holds the world on his shoulders, and Pleione, the Oceanid nymph, are the parents of the Seven Sisters. They are visible as part of the same constellation of a total of nine stars in the night sky, watching over their daughters.

THE TIDE FULL IN

A N IRISH FOLK SONG WRITTEN by Francis Fahy, who died in 1935, evokes perfect happiness in its chorus:

> Oh the happy summers of the olden days
> And the brown boats stealin' through the golden haze
> And the cuckoo callin' from the woods within
> And my love beside me, and the tide full in.

It maybe veers closer to nostalgia than to *nostos*, though maybe that's just how I'm feeling, today, sitting in the living room of the house in St Monans on this sunny morning, looking out of the window at the tide as it flows in to lift the boats in the harbour. It's still winter, by any astronomical or meteorological measure, but there's a warm light reflecting up off the waves and burnishing everything, making promises of spring. When the tide is full in, from the windows it looks the exact same blue as the gown of a Renaissance Madonna. The sea is so close all around that you could be on board a ship at sea. You could almost dive in from the first floor and swim with the creatures that live there. You could walk on water.

I think of the mothers and fathers of everyone alive today, stretching back in time in an unbroken chain towards a beginning, fronds of seaweed holding fast to the rock of the forgotten start. I still don't understand why the sound of the sea can bring peace to the soul unlike any other, or why looking out at it has led to so much myth-making. The history of the sea, the history based on facts and dates and measures, has mostly been told by sailors and explorers, by people who think they have conquered it and under- stood it. There's no such thing as a comprehensive history of the sea. It was here long before us and it'll be here long after we're gone. The sea is a story that belongs to all of us, to storytellers and singers and small girls collecting shells on the beach.

The sea is quiet. It is the same water, today, that's always there, that stretches around the world and touches every country, and turns to ice at the Arctic and boils up invisible into the atmos- phere around the middle. It has its depths and its shallows, and it is surprising and ever-changing, and it is always the same sea for all of us. It's always there, the earth's skin. The tides happen every twelve hours, forever revising the shape of the islands where I have made my life, their edges erased and redrawn daily by an invisible hand.

Stan Hugill dedicated his collection, *Shanties from the Seven Seas*, to his sons, in the hope that they would share his love of the sea and keep the memory of the songs alive. I don't know if they managed to do that or not, but I find myself wanting the same for my child. I feel the presence of all of the songs of the sea when I look out at it now. I don't feel as if I've lost a part of myself, or that I 'need to get myself back', as I'd worried about before she was born. In fact all of the things I'd worried about before she was born – the sense of impending loss, of lack of control, of missing out and of growing up – feel smaller now. I am different but still whole. There is no reversion to what came before. There is only salt-forged newness, bitter and strong and true. The sea is a mirror. I looked into it and a different person looked out, though I recognise her face.

It's our last day in St Monans. I hold the baby close, and we set off for a walk with the dog into the lightness of the morning, with the sea breeze at our necks, and the harbour stretched out under a sky with no clouds in it, rosy-fingered. The baby's eyes are wide and interested, looking around at us both, squinting a little from under her soft pink hat in the bright of the day. Parenthood is something I will get over the rawness of, something that will subsume itself into my life, the way it has done for my own parents. The shock of its beginning will be smoothed over like sea glass, so I'll hardly notice its edges any more, and the reality of it will fit comfortably into my hand for the rest of my life.

It has started already. I can already feel myself forgetting the details of the birth, the minutiae of how it felt, the identity-erasing pain of it. It's necessary to forget. I lean my hip on the harbour wall. The baby stirs in my arms. Life aligns itself to a new star, and I raise the anchor, and push on.

CONSULTED WORKS

Adomnán of Iona. *Life of St Columba.* Translated by Richard Sharpe. London: Penguin, 1995.

Ainsworth, William Harrison. *Rookwood.* London: John Macrone, 1834.

Andreae, Christopher. *Joan Eardley.* London: Lund Humphries, 2013.

Anonymous. *The Complaynt of Scotlande wyth ane exortatione to the thre estaits to be vigilante in the deffens of their public weil.* Paris: 1549.

Amt, Emilie. *Women's Lives in Medieval Europe: A Sourcebook.* London: Routledge, 1993.

Aristotle. *Historia Animalium.* Translated by D'Arcy Wentworth Thompson. Oxford: Clarendon, 1967.

Baker, Sir Richard. *Chronicle of the Kings of England.* London: 1670.

Barrie, David. *Sextant: A Voyage Guided by the Stars and the Men Who Mapped the World's Oceans.* London: William Collins, 2015.

Bede's Ecclesiastical History of England: A Revised Translation with Introduction, Life, and Notes by A. M. Sellar. London: George Bell & Sons, 1907.

Beowulf: A Student Edition. Edited by George Jack. Oxford: Clarendon, 1994.

Blake, John. *Sea Charts of the British Isles: A Voyage of Discovery Around Britain and Ireland's Coastline*. London: Conway, 2008.

Boswell, James. *The Life of Samuel Johnson*. London: Penguin, 2008.

Brooke, Daphne. *Wild Men and Holy Places: St. Ninian, Whithorn and the Medieval Realm of Galloway*. Edinburgh: Canongate, 1998.

Brooke, Rupert. *Collected Poems*. London: Sidgwick & Jackson, 1929.

Campbell, Bruce. *Birds of Coast and Sea: Britain and Northern Europe*. Oxford: Oxford University Press, 1977.

Chance, Jane. *The Literary Subversions of Medieval Women*. New York: Palgrave Macmillan, 2007.

Coleridge, Samuel Taylor. *The Rime of the Ancient Mariner*. London: Vintage, 2004.

Conrad, Joseph. *The Mirror of the Sea*. Dorset: Little Toller Books, 2013.

Druett, Joan. *Petticoat Whalers: Whaling Wives at Sea*. New Hampshire: University Press of New England, 2001.

Eliot, T. S. *Collected Poems 1909–1962*. London: Faber, 2002.

Eratosthenes, Hyginus and Aratus. *Constellation Myths with Aratus's 'Phaenomena'*. Translated by Robin Hard. Oxford: Oxford University Press, 2015.

Fahy, Francis A. *The Ould Plaid Shawl, and Other Songs*. Dublin: At the Sign of the Three Candles, 1949.

First Annual Report of the Registrar General of Births, Deaths, and Marriages in England, 1839.

Gladstone, W. E. *Studies on Homer and the Homeric Age*. Oxford: Oxford University Press, 1858.

Gooley, Tristan. *How to Read Water: Clues, Signs & Patterns from Puddles to the Sea*. London: Sceptre, 2016.

Homer. *The Odyssey*. Translated by E. V. Rieu. London: Penguin, 2009.

Homer. *The Odyssey*. Translated by Emily Wilson. New York: W. W. Norton, 2018.

Hugill, Stan. *Shanties from the Seven Seas: Shipboard Work-Songs and Songs Used as Work-Songs from the Great Days of Sail*. London: Routledge, 1979.

Jackson, Hazelle. *Shell Houses and Grottoes*. Oxford: Shire Library, 2012.

Johnson, Samuel and Boswell, James. *A Journey to the Western Islands of Scotland and The Journal of a Tour to the Hebrides*. Harmondsworth: Penguin, 1984.

Kafka, Franz. *The Complete Short Stories*. London: Vintage, 1992.

Knurrhahn: Seemannslieder und Shanties. Kiel: Ehlers, 1936.

Kowaleski, Maryanne. *Living by the Sea: Women, Work and Family in Maritime Communities in Medieval England*. Lecture given at the Radcliffe Institute for Advanced Study, 18 November 2015. Accessed via Harvard University YouTube channel at <https://www.youtube.com/watch?v=Vc1zI7NDvNI>

Lambert, C. S. *Sea Glass Hunter's Handbook*. Camden, Maine: Down East Books, 2010.

Lindsay of Pitscottie, Robert. *The Historie and Cronicles of Scotland*. Edinburgh and London: 1899.

Mackenzie, Donald. *Wonder Tales from Scottish Myth and Legend*. London: Dover Publications, 1997.

Mariner's Book of Days 2017. New York: Sheridan House, 2016.

Marsden, Richard (ed.). *The Cambridge Old English Reader*. Cambridge: Cambridge University Press, 2011.

Martynoga, Fi (ed.). *A Handbook of Scotland's Coasts*. Glasgow: Saraband, 2015.

Milton, John. *Paradise Lost*. London: Longman Routledge, 2006.

Morris, Rosalind. *The Seashore*. London: Collins, 1984.

Motley, James. *Tales of the Cymry; With Notes Illustrative and Explanatory*. London: Longmans, 1848.

Murray, Francis and Tarrant, Peter. 'A social and economic impact assessment of cockle mortality in the Burry Inlet and Three Rivers cockle fisheries, South Wales UK.' Maritek Worldwide Ltd, 2015.

The North Sea: A Visual Anthology. Introduced by James Attlee. London: Thames & Hudson, 2017.

Oliver, Cordelia. *Joan Eardley, RSA: A Biography*. Edinburgh: Mainstream Publishing, 1989.

Ord, John and Fenton, Alexander. *Ord's Bothy Songs and Ballads*. Edinburgh: John Donald, 1930.

Plisson, Philip. *The Sea*. London: Thames & Hudson, 2002.

Raban, Jonathan. *The Oxford Book of the Sea*. Oxford: Oxford University Press, 2001.

Rose, Susan. *The Medieval Sea*. London: Hambledon Continuum, 2007.

Saupe, Karen (ed.). *Middle English Marian Lyrics*. Michigan: Medieval Institute Publications, 1998.

Scott, John. *The Poetical Works of John Scott*. London: J. Buckland, 1782.

Scott, Walter. *The History of Scotland*. London: Longman, 1830.

A Seaman's Pocketbook by the Lord Commissioners of the Admiralty. London: Conway, 2006.

Selmer, Carl (ed.). *Navigatio Sancti Brendani Abbatis*. Dublin: Four Courts Press, 1989.

Shakespeare, William. *William Shakespeare: The Complete Works*. Edited by Jonathan Bate and Eric Rasmussen. London: Palgrave

Macmillan, 2008.

Smout, T. C. and Stewart, Mairi. *The Firth of Forth: An Environmental History*. Edinburgh: Birlinn, 2012.

Sobecki, Sebastian I. *The Sea and Medieval English Literature*. Cambridge and New York: D. S. Brewer, 2008.

Stark, Suzanne J. *Female Tars: Women Aboard Ship in the Age of Sail*. Annapolis: Naval Institute Press, 2017.

Sterry, Paul and Cleave, Andrew. *Collins Complete Guide to British Coastal Wildlife*. London: Collins, 2012.

Stevenson, Robert Louis. *Kidnapped*. Oxford: Oxford University Press, 2014.

Stevenson, Robert Louis. *Treasure Island*. Richmond: Alma Classics, 2015.

Swinburne, Algernon Charles. *Chastelard*. New York: Hurd & Houghton, 1866.

Taylor, Marianne, and Tipling, David. *RSPB Seabirds*. London: Bloomsbury, 2014.

Tennyson, Alfred. *The Major Works*. Oxford: Oxford University Press, 2009.

The Writings of Quintus Sept. Flor. Tertullianus. Translated by the Reverend S. Thelwall. Edinburgh: T. & T. Clark, 1870.

Thomas, Dylan. *Collected Poems*. London: Everyman, 2003.

Thomas, Dylan. *The Collected Letters*, ed. Paul Ferris. London: Everyman, 1985.

Tongue, Ruth L. *The Chime Child: or Somerset Singers Being An Account of Some of Them and Their Songs Collected Over Sixty Years*. London: Routledge, 2017.

Under the Seas. Star Film Company, dir. Georges Méliès, 1907.

Van Duzer, Chet. *Sea Monsters on Medieval and Renaissance Maps*.

London: The British Library, 2014.

Verne, Jules. *Twenty Thousand Leagues Under the Sea*. Ware: Wordsworth Editions, 1992.

Wachsmann, Shelley. *Seagoing Ships & Seamanship in the Bronze Age Levant*. College Station: Texas A&M University Press, 2009.

Williamson, Duncan. *Land of the Seal People*, ed. Linda Williamson. Edinburgh: Birlinn, 2010.

Wordsworth, William. *The Collected Poems of William Wordsworth*. Ware: Wordsworth Editions, 1994.

ACKNOWLEDGEMENTS

Deep blue thanks are due to the following people for their part in wrestling the sea into a book.

Thank you firstly to my excellent agent, Kirsty McLachlan. Thanks to my editors Jo Dingley and Francis Bickmore, copy-editor Annie Lee, and to Leila Cruickshank, Vicki Rutherford, Anna Frame, Megan Reid, Jamie Norman and everyone at Canongate. Thank you to Jon Gray and Pete Adlington for the beautiful design. (And extra thanks to Jo for the wisdom and the seashells.)

I am lucky to have wonderful friends. Thank you to Caro Bridges for watery music and inspiration. When it comes to writing camaraderie, I am perennially grateful to Alice Vincent. For literary insight and sailing expertise, thank you to Robert Leadbetter. For emotional support as I was writing when the baby was tiny, and for life-changing conversations about womanhood, thanks to these warriors: Helen Beech, Esmi Freeman, Rosie Kellagher, Georgina Leadbetter, Isobel Norris, Eugenia Twomey, Grace Wright and Nancy Wu Mehmet.

Thanks to Luna the dog, best beach walking companion and early reader.

Thank you to my family. To my mother, Marilyn, who taught me about sea glass and painting with salt water; and to my father, James, who taught me about writing and faith; and to my sister, Rosie, who taught me to read. Their generosity, patience and love have been immense.

To my grandmother, whose spark I miss every day.

To my daughter, who has made the world glow in the dark.

And to Sean, who holds this book and my heart together.

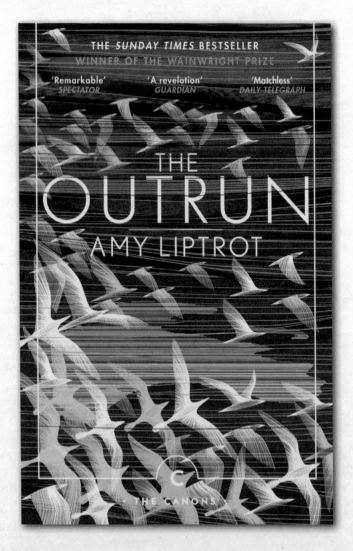

THE OUTRUN

AMY LIPTROT

THE CANONS

'A luminous, life-affirming book'
Olivia Laing

CANON||GATE

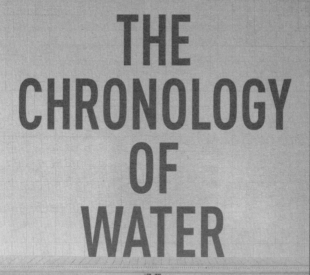

THE
CHRONOLOGY
OF
WATER

'Like water, the memoir
takes on an unpredictable
journey . . . Entrancing'
ROXANE GAY

'Rich with story,
alive with emotion'
CHERYL STRAYED

Lidia Yuknavitch

'Raw, intense and powerful'
Grazia

CANON❚❚GATE

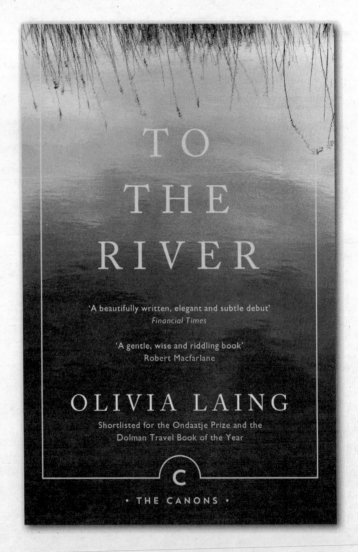

TO
THE
RIVER

'A beautifully written, elegant and subtle debut'
Financial Times

'A gentle, wise and riddling book'
Robert Macfarlane

OLIVIA LAING

Shortlisted for the Ondaatje Prize and the
Dolman Travel Book of the Year

C

• THE CANONS •

'A beautifully written meditation on landscape'
Sunday Times

CANON‖GATE